T0323095

Bella

Annabel Langbein

Bella

MY LIFE IN FOOD

ALLEN&UNWIN
SYDNEY•MELBOURNE•AUCKLAND•LONDON

N

AOTEAROA
NEW ZEALAND

TASMAN SEA

• Auckland

Te Araroa
• Ōhiwa
Ōtorohanga •
• Mātāwai
Gisborne
Hangaroa
River
Rānana,
the Whanganui River

Kāpiti Coast

Golden Bay
The Remutukas
Nelson •
• Stoke
• Wellington

Fox Glacier •
• Christchurch

Lake Benmore,
Canterbury
Wānaka •

Te Anau •

SOUTH PACIFIC OCEAN

Invercargill •

For Ted, Sean and Rose—thank you for all
your love and support; I feel so lucky.

To all the people I've rubbed up against in the world
—some have said yes, most have said no; I've learnt
from all of them and found my own road.

Contents

ONE

Growing up

A sixties kid

I would have been about seven or eight when, during a summer family holiday, the first signs of my precocious palate came to light. After piling into Dad's Plymouth, we had set off on the ferry across Cook Strait then driven south—further south than we had ever been before—to Aoraki/Mount Cook.

For a treat, Dad had booked us into the Hermitage, then run by the government-owned Tourist Hotel Corporation. Unlike my mother's dining room at home in Wellington, there was nothing intimate, welcoming or charming about the hotel's formal eating space. The carpet, patterned in giant mustard, olive-green and orange whorls, looked like someone had thrown up on it. The ornate gold wallpaper was studded with hideous orange glass lamps that emitted a stark, blazing light. It was all new and very fancy, the latest in sixties decor. The chef was Swiss—they all were in big hotels at that time. People weren't laughing and drinking and talking and having fun. You weren't supposed to do that. This was 'fine dining'.

A penguin-suited waiter who looked like he had a carrot stuck up his bottom presented the menus to each of us with great aplomb. I skirted through the offerings. Ohh, there were brains. Wow.

'How are the brains cooked?' I piped up from my corner of the table. I saw the waiter raising an eyebrow at my father. 'Please,' I quickly

OPPOSITE My first and only modelling assignment.
PREVIOUS Me and my cousin Callie as toddlers (I'm on the left).

added. I could see the waiter thinking, *There is a horrible child speaking to me in my restaurant.*

'Ahh, young lady, they are cooked in butter, with capers and lemon. You would not like the brains.'

'Yes please. Thank you.' I passed the menu back to him.

There was an aghast intake of breath from both the waiter and my parents. It felt like an Antarctic blast had come in through the door.

'You can't order anything else, you know,' my father said. 'This is dinner. There is nothing else if you don't like it.' But his attempts to browbeat me into changing my mind fell on deaf ears.

> I'd never eaten capers before. I'd certainly never
> eaten brains. As I cut into them, the crispy
> exterior gave way to a pillowy softness. In that
> first taste, the sweet flavour of caramelised
> butter filled my mouth, and carried through to
> a creamy, sweet, almost melting richness.

The brains arrived on a big white plate, looking like enormous golden walnuts sitting on a buttery golden sauce flecked with little buds of green. I'd never eaten capers before. I'd certainly never eaten brains. As I cut into them, the crispy exterior gave way to a pillowy softness. In that first taste, the sweet flavour of caramelised butter filled my mouth, and carried through to a creamy, sweet, almost melting richness. The brains tasted just like my favourite part of a lamb chop: the creamy white cord that ran in a thread inside the bone, which—did I know?—is the spinal cord. And the sauce was the cleverest thing: toasty brown butter with a fresh tang of lemon, studded with little flavour bombs of lemony, briny pickled capers. The most perfect foil to cut through the richness of the brains.

The entire dish was so deeply delicious that, if I could have licked the plate clean, I would have.

THEY SAY THE QUALITIES you least admire in a child are the ones you most appreciate in an adult. Well, I'd like to think that's the case. I was the youngest of three—a demanding, attention-seeking child, always challenging, always naughty. My sister, Prue, was four and a half years older than me, and my brother, Tim, eight years my senior. The age gap meant that, as a small child, I didn't spend a lot of time with my siblings.

My enthusiasm as a toddler for raiding my mother's baking tins and using them to transform the garden into all manner of pies and tarts was unrivalled—not that any of my creations were edible. I would proudly arrive at the kitchen door with yet another 'special pie' or 'chocolate cake for Mummy' that I had created with tiny flower buds, and the occasional herb or vegetable leaf, combined with various amounts and saturations of soil and gravel. Recipes were in the making. I can only imagine my mother's dismay at seeing her would-be posies for the house—hydrangeas, roses, anemones—dismembered by this bedraggled, muddy child and turned into an ugly brown gloop. Yet she never showed it, graciously taking my offerings and finding the means to proclaim some not-obviously-visible virtue.

Sometimes, though, I would work Mum up into such a state she'd grab the wooden spoon and chase me around the house. There was a small, secret hiding place in the back of the linen cupboard, which bizarrely had a sliding lock on the inside. I would run outside, Mum yelling and brandishing the wooden spoon in hot pursuit. After a couple of laps of the house, I'd race back inside, grabbing a can of condensed milk from the pantry on my way to the linen cupboard. I'd lock myself inside, hidden, and eat my way through the can until things had calmed down. Actually, I was a brat of a child.

I WAS BORN IN MANGAKINO, but I have no recollections of my life until the day we moved into our house in Karori in Wellington. *Parva domus magna quies*—'little house, great peace'—was inscribed on the door plate. In my mind's eye I can still recall the day we arrived, and see clearly the long line of golden poplars that ran up the street and around the corner. The front door is open, and someone is loading in a big grandfather clock and placing it in the corner of the big wide hall. I race through the house, and at the far end on the right—it's a small house—is a dark, slightly scary room with a big copper boiler in the corner. I run to the other end, and there are steps to the biggest back lawn. It dips down and then up again, surrounded by huge golden sentinel poplars. When I recall this moment it brings back a deep sense of happiness. I grew up in that house, and my parents lived there until they died.

I loved being in the garden, which is another way of saying I didn't like being inside. At any excuse, I would head out to the street on my trike, or into the garden, where I could climb trees and play in the dirt, concocting my mud tarts. I'd be happy out there for hours. But it wasn't long before Mum figured out that she needed to lure me inside and get my cooking instincts channelled into something actually edible. I can still remember the first time I watched her make meringues, never imagining that the gloopy egg whites that went into the trusty Kenwood with nothing more than a scoop of sugar would be transformed into a cloud-like puff of sweetness. Licking raw meringue from the beater for the first time, feeling a dawning breath of joy in the discovery of this melt-in-the-mouth pleasure, and a sense of awe that something so good could be created out of two such simple, everyday ingredients.

To begin with, I was happy enough to wait around for that moment

OPPOSITE Growing up in the 1960s. (Top right) With my lovely mum. (Bottom right) Posing outside our house in Karori, Wellington, with Mum and my siblings.

when the cake or cookie mixture had been dispatched to tins and trays and I got to lick the beater. I'm sure that's how it starts for many a child. Before you know it, you're in there helping—mixing dough, rolling biscuits and putting things into the oven. The house fills with comforting, lip-smacking aromas, and just like that you're cooking, and people think you're incredibly clever. I was lucky to discover this easy pleasure early in life—that the oohs and ahhs of delight from my family and my mother's friends could be achieved simply by following a recipe. My mother was always happy to have me in her tiny kitchen. She was all about making our home the place you wanted to be. It was so nourishing.

> I was lucky to discover this easy pleasure early in life—that the oohs and ahhs of delight from my family and my mother's friends could be achieved simply by following a recipe.

I adored my mother, and often marvel when I think about how she managed to do everything she did in a day. She made us all beautiful clothes, the house was always spick and span with fresh flowers and welcoming smells, and for every meal—breakfast, lunch and dinner—she set the table with candles and flowers and ironed napkins. Each night she would set the table for breakfast before she went to bed. You'd come out in the morning and think there was going to be a party. An array of beautiful serving ware, jugs, platters and bowls was laid out, along with an arsenal of cutlery. There were linen napkins and fresh flowers, and lots of pretty little bowls ready to have various home-made juices, jams and preserves put in them. Heaven forbid if a milk bottle or jam jar found its way on to the table.

Breakfast started with fresh juice, fruit and cereal, then moved on to a hot dish. When it was tomato season, we would have tomatoes and bacon on toast, but generally we ate eggs, which my mother cooked for us individually as we arrived at the table. Toast and toppings came with tea or coffee. It was like living in a five-star hotel, and it was only Monday!

Whenever we kids were sick, Mum would prepare a beautiful tray with juice, fruit, cereal, milk and yoghurt, all set out in little bowls and jugs, with a just-picked flower on the tray. A few minutes later she would return to enquire, 'What would you like next? Do you think you might need a fluffy omelette?' We could have boiled eggs with buttery toast soldiers, or scrambled eggs, or bacon and eggs, but I always went for the fluffy omelette. It was such a treat. Mum would whisk up the egg whites by hand, with a little salt and pepper, into a loose meringue, then quickly whisk in the yolks so as not to collapse the mixture too much before it went into the pan. The frying pan would be hot enough for the butter to turn to that sweet, brown nuttiness before the ripple of creamy eggs went in. The heat would go down a little so the eggs could set without burning, and then Mum would wait until just the right moment before flipping the whole thing and cooking it very briefly on the other side. The omelette would come out golden and puffy, filling the room with the most mouth-watering aroma. No matter what ailed me, this ethereal cloud of buttery egg goodness was guaranteed to make me feel better. The acquisition of a food processor took my mother's fluffy omelettes to healthy new heights, as she would whizz big handfuls of parsley in with the eggs. The result looked like something Dr. Seuss might have dished up, but it was—and still is—something I find addictively moreish. To this day I often make these green-egg fluffy omelettes for anyone who is feeling a bit off-colour, myself included.

There's a *New Yorker* cartoon by Roz Chast called 'Heimlich's Mother's Maneuvers' that always makes me think of my mother. The 'Skinned-Knee Maneuver' shows a mother sticking a plaster on a kid's knee. Underneath, the caption reads: 'Go on and on about the person's bravery. Then place the hugest Band-Aid you can find over the icky area.' The 'Anti-Nausea Maneuver' shows the mother tending to her son, who is lying in bed, and the caption reads: 'Cajole person into eating a small piece of plain chicken and sipping some warm, flat ginger ale.' The 'Splinter-Removal Maneuver' shows the mother at a desk, holding her son's hand under a lamp while he looks up at the ceiling; it reads: 'Have person look at the ceiling and think happy thoughts while you dig around with a needle.'

My mother used all of those tactics when we were kids with knee scrapes, splinters and vomiting bugs (minus the chicken—we got plain, dry biscuits with our ginger ale). She was also kind enough to hold our heads when we vomited into the toilet. I, in turn, employed these same strategies to deal with the traumas in my own children's lives. So it is with being a mother, using the passed-down rituals of nourishment and care to get one generation safely through to the next.

My dad often hosted overseas guests for his work, and my mother would look after their wives with fancy picnics up at Kaitoke, north of Upper Hutt, where there is a beautiful park in the bush by the river. Reliably on these occasions, I would have taken myself to bed with a sore throat—not quite bad enough to require the doctor to visit, but definitely bad enough to not be able to go to school. And so I would get to go on the picnic. My mother would have made her famous spinach tart, there would be biscuits and cakes, tender muffins, cheese and fruit and chutney, and thermoses of tea and coffee, all set out on pretty plates with rugs and pillows for everyone to sit on. Many, many years later when I was an adult with my own very small children, and we were talking about these splendid picnics, Mum told me she knew that I'd never really had a sore throat.

THERE WAS NO SUCH THING as a school cafeteria when I was at primary school. Our mothers all made us sensible lunches—little plastic boxes containing sandwiches (which usually got binned), some fresh and dried fruit, and a couple of pieces of home baking. One of the girl's parents owned a bakery, and each lunchtime, as we sat down to eat our dull lunchbox offerings, Jeena's mother would sail in through the door, laden with cream buns and pies for her daughter's lunch. We were in awe, as much of the lunch as the mother, who—with her stilettos, super-short miniskirt, busty tight top, Brigitte Bardot cat-eye eyeliner, and peroxide-blonde hair piled high in a bouffant—did not look like a mother, or at least not like any of the mothers we knew.

We were never going to get our hands on any of that fancy bakery food, though, so my friend Alice and I started to cook together each day after school. We enjoyed the sense of being in charge and making something we wanted to eat—and what we wanted to eat was always pancakes. The best part was the topping: a 50–50 mix of butter and golden syrup beaten together with a wooden spoon to form a fluffy, dark golden cream. We tried making biscuits and cakes as well, but it was the pancakes we kept coming back to—they were so quick and so easy. If we left out the baking powder and added more milk, we got super-thin crêpes. If we added too much milk, the mixture wouldn't hold together. Every day it was an experiment to see what we could change or how we could make them better. We never tired of those pancake afternoons in the kitchen.

WHEN I WAS LITTLE, I wanted to become a writer for *National Geographic*. We had a subscription, and the old issues got stored in stacks in the back bedroom. Eventually, they became so heavy that they collapsed the foundations. Dad had to re-pile the entire corner of the house.

Every month, I would eagerly pore over the magazine's contents. People, history, culture, nature and science were all wrapped up in fascinating stories with lots of fabulous photos. I devoured anything about the exploits of palaeoanthropologist and archaeologist Louis Leakey, or about Jane van Lawick-Goodall and her work with chimpanzees. All I wanted to do when I grew up was go to the Olduvai Gorge in Tanzania, where humankind's beginnings on this planet were being mapped out. Once I realised there would be snakes and spiders and bugs, however, my enthusiasm for such endeavours rapidly dwindled.

I've always been fascinated by history, and the stories that come with it. Among my many forebears, there are several whose lives have sparked my imagination. On my mother's father's side, there's Samuel Cave, a convicted polygamist who emigrated to New Zealand in the late 1830s after gaining his certificate of freedom in Sydney, Australia, in 1834. He became a cooper making barrels for whalers at Port Underwood at the top of the South Island. His wife, Susannah Dockrell, was also made a convict in England, and had been deported to Sydney at age 12 for stealing four pairs of stockings in Colchester.

The Cave family was very close to the local Māori community, and friendly with Ngāti Toa chief Te Rauparaha and his nephew Te Rangihaeata. With Samuel and Susannah's eldest daughter, my great-great-grandmother Ann Cave, there's the titillating possibility that she may have jumped the fence and got up the duff to a local Māori man, before being hastily married off to an English sea captain, William Boyce. To quote *Te Ara—The Encyclopedia of New Zealand*, 'The officiating minister, Samuel Ironside, reported: "She is very young—not sixteen. But reports to her discredit having prevailed, whether true or not, rendered it prudent for them to be married at once."' According to an old family story, the marriage was designed to prevent her abduction and marriage to the son of a local Māori chief.

On my mother's mother's side, there's also James Hargreaves, who is credited with inventing, in 1764 or 1765, the spinning jenny—a multi-spindle spinning frame that was one of the key developments in the

OPPOSITE (Clockwise from top) My mum is the little girl in the foreground of this family pic, with her mother standing behind her; my grandparents out boating with my mum (right) and her sister; my father before he went to war; and my mother as a young woman.

industrialisation of weaving. And, alluringly, there's a line to the Empress Eugénie via her Spanish father, the Count of Teba. As a child I would often go and look up the family tree and imagine myself prancing around as a Spanish princess.

My father's grandfather and his piano-teacher wife came to New Zealand in 1878. They must have been people of some means, these particular relations, as they purchased the famous cob house known as Broadgreen with 50 acres in Stoke, on the outskirts of Nelson. In the garden there today you can still find some of the old trees planted by my great-great-grandfather Fred Langbein—chestnuts, walnuts, holly, rhododendrons, camellias, camphor, loquat and osmanthus, some of which he brought back as specimens from his travels.

There's also that ancestor we all share, assuming that you, like me, subscribe to the theory of evolution. This one is the oldest of all, and thinking about her has always captivated me. In *Sapiens: A Brief History of Humankind*, Yuval Noah Harari tells us, 'Just 6 million years ago, a single female ape had two daughters. One became the ancestor of all chimpanzees, the other is our own grandmother.' When I consider the fact that my existence here on this planet today is connected through line after line of grandmothers—with as many greats as it takes to get back through history to that very first grandmother, 6 million years ago—it seems like a hell of a lot of luck.

MY PATERNAL GRANDMOTHER, MAUDE, was a legendary baker. She was my grandpa's second wife, having married him after my father's mother died very young, and we called her Nan. Maude had grown up in a family and an era that demanded thrift, and she was immensely resourceful.

Every Sunday we'd all hop in Dad's Plymouth and drive down from the Karori hills to my grandparents' big white house on Waterloo Road in the Hutt Valley for Sunday tea. I was always excited by the prospect. For starters, they had a TV (we didn't), which took pride of place in the very formal front room. I would sneak in to watch it, play with the three carved ebony elephants on the mantelpiece, and fiddle with the knob on the fancy 1930s ashtray stand that jettisoned the cigarette butts from the tray into a hidden container underneath. I don't think my grandparents even smoked, but smoking was very fashionable so they had this smart gadget for any guests who did.

Nan had only a coal range to cook on. There was no thermometer; she just used to put her hand in to gauge the heat. She cooked everything to perfection in that oven. Cream horns were one of her specialties—she would make puff pastry, then spiral it around these little cone-shaped metal moulds. Often when we turned up, a rack of crispy golden pastry horns would be sitting on the bench, waiting to be filled with sweetened whipped cream. Sometimes she would make waffles. These were always our favourite, and we'd have competitions to see who could eat the most. Most weekends, there was a big roast of lamb with mountains of vegetables from the vast garden out the back. Nan always made mashed potatoes as well as roast potatoes, and lots of gravy.

My grandfather was a very formal man, and prone to being a little curmudgeonly. He hated anything being bought from the shop, especially if it could have been made at home. But Nan had some tricks up her sleeve. One hot summer Sunday, when we were having barbecued sausages and chops instead of the usual roast, she was in the kitchen hunting for the tomato sauce. The big glass sauce bottle with the cork top was nearly empty. Checking that my grandpa was well out of sight, she pulled out a big container of Wattie's tomato sauce, carefully hidden in a back cupboard, and siphoned some into the glass bottle. She winked at us and laughed. 'He'll never know the difference.'

MOST OF OUR SUMMER HOLIDAYS were spent in Nelson with my mother's parents. Once a year for several years, my gorgeous cousin Callie and I would be sent to stay with Gran and Put. I would be put on a plane from Wellington, and Callie, who was about six months older than me, would come up from their farm in Otago.

My gran was an intrepid traveller. Well before most people had even explored their own neighbourhood, she was out discovering the world. Her stories of adventures in faraway places like Spain, Mexico, China and Portugal wove magical threads of scents, flavours and images, and we just couldn't get enough of them. Every morning, Callie and I would sit up in bed with Gran, me on one side, Callie on the other, eating little squares of toast slathered with butter and marmalade and sipping tiny cups of tea, while Gran regaled us with her stories.

Put, my grandfather, was a mad-keen fisherman. In summer we would take the world's worst road (guaranteed to make you vomit at least a dozen times) to Tennyson Inlet in the Marlborough Sounds, where his beautiful launch, the *Shangri La*, was moored. We would load our supplies on board and head out for days at a time to fish the groper holes near D'Urville Island on the outer west of the sounds. I remember my grandfather coming up from the galley with big platters of the most delicious hot, crispy battered cod, which he had whipped up. 'So fresh its next of kin haven't been notified,' he would say, laughing, as he handed us a plate.

Back in Wellington, there was always a weather watch for fishing. When the wind swung around to blow offshore, my uncle Tony would call and we would all head off to the beach to help put his home-made Kon-Tiki raft out. I remember he used to roll the line around a barley sugar to hold the hooks

OPPOSITE (Clockwise from top left) On a bridge in Nelson during our summer holidays; in the garden at home with the chickens; primary school days at Karori Normal; adventuring on the West Coast; and checking out the Pancake Rocks at Punakaiki.

on the raft until the water was deep enough to fish. By the time the sweet had melted in the salt water, the raft would be way out at sea, a tiny dot on the horizon, and that was when the line would drop down into the deep briny with all its baited hooks. We'd sit on the beach, meanwhile, having a bit of a picnic, and would wait a few hours before winding the whole thing in again. It was always such a thrill seeing what the little fishing raft had landed— sometimes there would be snapper, tarakihi, gurnard, even the odd shark.

During the whitebait season, we would bring out the set-net that was stored in the garage roof and head up the Kāpiti Coast, filling empty kerosene cans with our haul. The bait ran in vast shoals then, especially after a flood.

Sometimes we would go and dig for toheroa. These shellfish were Dad's favourite. Mum would turn them into soup, grinding the frills into a roux, then dicing the tender hearts and adding them to the soup right at the end so they didn't get tough.

MY DAD GOT THE ENGINEERING GENE shared by his father, who was the Commissioner of Works, and five Langbein uncles. Dad earned a Fulbright scholarship to study engineering in the States, and when he came home to New Zealand he went on to become the Director of Roading for the Ministry of Works and Development. It was when he returned from the States that my father brought back his brand-new, wing-finned Plymouth—the huge car that our family went everywhere in.

It was a four-door, right-hand-drive sedan, rich maroon colour, rego CP9241. I sometimes wonder if it's still around. Those sleek lines and red fins embodied all the glamour and sophistication of the American dream—a far cry from life in New Zealand at the time. I learnt to drive in that car. It was a huge tank of a thing, with a three-gear column change and bench seats covered with thick plastic-coated plaid. In the heat of summer, this vile seat cover would become cloyingly sticky. But put your foot down, and you could really fang it. Oh, how my dad loved that car.

Thinking back, there are so many good things I learnt from my father that I never truly appreciated at the time. As well as practical things, such as learning to drive, growing a vegetable garden and keeping bees, Dad taught me to be curious, to keep asking questions, to figure out the problem, to ask if you needed help, and to go that little bit further to be the best you could be. His enduring mantra of kindness, charm, honesty and diligence taught me the qualities you need to get you all the places you might want to be in life.

> Dad taught me to be curious, to keep asking questions, to figure out the problem, to ask if you needed help, and to go that little bit further to be the best you could be. His enduring mantra of kindness, charm, honesty and diligence taught me the qualities you need to get you all the places you might want to be in life.

Even as a senior civil servant who earnt much less than private engineers, my dad still had to pay tax in the top bracket. For many years during the sixties and seventies, he paid nearly 70 per cent of his income in tax. We didn't have a lot of money, but the intelligence, resourcefulness and care with which my parents approached life and bringing up a family meant that I for one never felt we were going without.

My mother had a university education and was also a talented artist, but she made the decision (as did many mothers of her era) to put her energy into being a stay-at-home mum. Once I'd entered high school I couldn't understand why she didn't want to earn her own money (though she did sell some of her beautiful paintings) and feel the independence and freedom that I had come to consider our birthright as women. Now,

I think how lucky we were. We were spoilt—not with stuff, but with love, books, experiences and always lots of time around the table, talking and discussing ideas over my mother's delicious meals.

My mother's menu rotation was based around the weather and the harvests from Dad's bountiful vegie garden. During the week, Dad would come home from work, take off his suit, put on his gardening clothes and head out to tend the garden. His carefully washed and trimmed offerings were then placed at the back door by the kitchen. Combined with the weekly meat pack from the butcher, they formed the basis of my mother's meals. Stewy, slow-cooked things featured heavily in winter, with chops, schnitzel and cold meats in summer. Once the new potatoes from Dad's garden came on-stream we went from mash to boiled new potatoes, and if there was lettuce we would have salad.

> We were spoilt—not with stuff, but with love,
> books, experiences and always lots of time
> around the table, talking and discussing ideas
> over my mother's delicious meals.

Every week, Mum cashed her weekly housekeeping cheque down at her favourite butcher in Cuba Street. Her carefully cultivated friendship with the smiling, red-cheeked Cyril ensured that we always got the best meat. My mother's cross-cut blade-steak casserole was one dish that made it through all but the hottest months of the year, probably because we all liked it. It was one of those 1970s casseroles that used a packet of soup mix as the flavour booster. You threw in a couple of thinly sliced onions and a can of tomatoes, set individual steaks on top, and then mixed a packet of

OPPOSITE My mum always filled our house
with fresh flowers from the garden.

cream-of-mushroom soup with a cup of water and poured it over. Tightly covered, it took about an hour and a half to bake in a moderate oven. I probably haven't made it for more than 30 years, but I can still remember the formula,

My mother was an incredible cook, and had brought masses of cookbooks back from the States. She was always delving into *The Joy of Cooking* by Irma S. Rombauer (still a bible), *The Hostess Cookbook* (lots of gelatine moulds and elaborate piping) and a range of books by Julia Child, whose TV shows Mum later became a fan of. She loved hearing Julia's long, low, syrupy voice oozing encouragement, and seeing the way she so effortlessly produced these glamorous French dishes.

My parents were always entertaining at home. I would sneak out from my bedroom when I was supposed to be asleep and hide behind the sofa, listening to everyone chatting and laughing and having a good time. There would be candles and music and always amazing food—elaborate dinners for 20 or more laid out on a buffet, each dish stuck with a little flag that had its name on it. I'm sure that it was those nights, eavesdropping on everyone having so much fun, that instilled in me an understanding of just how much enjoyment there was to be had when you invited people over for a meal.

WHILE OUR MOTHER LOVED HAVING people over, she didn't care for eating out at restaurants. Their prices and the inadequacy of the culinary offerings offended her sensibilities, and she always said she would rather cook at home. My dad, sensing my budding culinary curiosity following the brains episode at Mount Cook, would sometimes take me downtown in Wellington to a slightly grungy hole-in-the-wall Chinese restaurant on

OPPOSITE (Clockwise from top left) Starting to fall in love with fashion thanks to Mum's superb dressmaking skills; summer fun at Kaitoke, the scene of many picnics; with Mum at Tāhuna Beach in Nelson.

Vivian Street. Plastic Chinese lanterns adorned with dragons hung from the ceilings. More dragons painted that particular garish green you always find in hospitals and ferries glared from the walls. There were green and white Formica tables, and chrome chairs with green seat covers and backs.

As soon as you sat down, a plate of thinly sliced, buttered white bread would arrive. It seemed completely out of place, but there it was: a great pile of soft white bread. We always ate some of it. The menu ran the gamut of what we now consider classic Canto-Kiwi favourites—in other words, bastardised versions of sweet-and-sour pork, lemon chicken, chow mein, chop suey, fried rice, chicken and cashew nuts, egg foo young, and wontons. There were so many new flavours and ingredients to discover. Best of all, there were canned lychees with vanilla ice cream for dessert. It may not have been authentic, but I loved it all.

I would have been 13 when Dad took me to a snazzy new restaurant around the waterfront on Oriental Bay. I remember ordering the sautéed scallops, then as soon as I tasted them insisting to the waiter that something was wrong with them. My father was so embarrassed about his teenage daughter making such a fuss, but there was no stopping me. I wrangled my way into the kitchen and asked to see how the scallops were cooked. As soon as I saw white wine going into the steel pan after the scallops had been browned in butter, I knew what was giving them that nasty metallic taste. I informed the chef that the wine had oxidised in the pan and he needed to use a different pan—not a steel one—if he was cooking scallops like this. The chef stood staring, open-mouthed, in angry disbelief as I went through the chemistry. Dad was furious. It was the last time he took me out anywhere to eat.

My culinary lexicon had expanded to places that made me a complete pain in the neck as a dining companion. In fact, by this stage, I was becoming a complete pain in the neck in general.

APART FROM MY PRE-BUG-PHOBIA PERIOD of wanting to follow in Jane Goodall and Dr Leakey's footsteps and go digging for the remains of early humans in Africa, I really didn't have any idea what I wanted to do when I grew up. I certainly never considered cooking. Classes at school were streamed in those days, and when I arrived at Wellington Girls' College I was put in the top stream. We had to study Latin, French, Maths, English, History and Geography. I pretty much hated it all. I was elected class captain every year I was at high school, but I was a rebel, always being sent out of class for talking or being disruptive.

I was already way past being told what to do by anyone.

IT'S BEEN SAID THAT, after a tragedy, you may not see the trajectory of an individual or a family for about five years, but the path will always be different from 'before'. Everything changed when my brother took his life at the age of 22.

I was 14. Looking back, I can see that my brother's death catapulted me into a kind of reckless grief. This beautiful young man, the idol of my life, was gone forever. Was I to blame? It's a question I'm sure every sibling, parent and friend asks themselves when this horrific thing happens. Now, nothing could touch me. There was nothing to risk, nothing to lose. The rest of my family each struggled in their own terrible sorrow. My parents, my lovely older sister and I, drowning in an abyss of loss, each trying to survive the wildest storm of our lives.

CLASSIC PISSALADIÈRE WITH CARAMELISED ONIONS, ANCHOVIES AND OLIVES

READY IN 1½ HOURS · SERVES 6–8

OLIVE OIL PASTRY

2 cups plain flour, plus
  extra to dust
1 tsp baking powder
1 tsp salt
⅓ cup extra virgin olive oil
⅔ cup water

CARAMELISED ONIONS

5 medium–large brown or
  white onions, halved and
  very thinly sliced
½ cup water
3 tbsp extra virgin olive
  oil or butter
1 tsp finely chopped fresh
  rosemary leaves or
  ½ tsp dried rosemary,
  plus extra to garnish
2 tsp fresh thyme leaves
  or 1 tsp dried thyme
1 tsp salt
ground black pepper, to
  taste

TOPPING

14–16 anchovy fillets,
  drained and halved
  lengthwise
about 20 kalamata olives
1 egg, whisked with
  2 tbsp water or milk to
  make an egg wash
fresh thyme sprigs, to
  serve (optional)

A savoury tart is such a useful go-to for a picnic or a potluck. You can use commercial pastry, but once you've tried my easy Olive Oil Pastry you won't look back—it's just so simple to make.

To make Olive Oil Pastry, place flour, baking powder and salt in a large bowl and make a well in the middle. Mix oil and water then add to the flour and stir with a knife until dough comes together. It should be soft and supple, so add a little more oil if it is too firm to easily press out. Form into a log shape and allow to rest for at least 20 minutes before use. (If not using within an hour, wrap in baking paper and chill or freeze until needed.)

To make Caramelised Onions, combine onions, water, oil or butter, herbs, salt and pepper in a large pot, cover and cook over a medium heat for 35 minutes, stirring occasionally. Remove lid and cook, stirring now and then, until water has evaporated and onions are just starting to stick on the bottom (20–40 minutes, depending on age and variety of onions). Allow to cool.

Preheat oven to 180°C (350°F) fanbake.

Roll out pastry into a large rectangle about 40 cm x 30 cm (16 in x 12 in) on a piece of lightly floured baking paper. Spread with Caramelised Onions, leaving a 2.5 cm (1 in) border around the edge. Arrange anchovies in rows diagonally across the top, then arrange olives between the rows of anchovies. Fold in pastry edges to create a rim, pinching the corners together. Brush pastry with egg wash. Slide tart (still on its baking paper) onto an oven tray and bake until golden and crisp (35–40 minutes). Garnish with thyme sprigs (if using). Serve hot or at room temperature.

THE WHOLE SHEBANG ROAST CHICKEN WITH STUFFING AND GRAVY

READY IN ABOUT 2¼ HOURS · SERVES 6

1 whole chicken

salt and ground black
  pepper, to taste

1 onion, skin on

juice from zested lemon
  below

1 tbsp butter, melted

HERB STUFFING

60 g (2¼ oz) butter

1 large onion, finely
  chopped

about ⅓ loaf of sliced
  bread (can be stale)

½ cup walnut pieces
  or toasted pine nuts
  (optional)

finely grated zest of
  1 lemon

½ cup finely chopped
  parsley leaves

2 tbsp chopped fresh
  thyme leaves or
  2 tsp dried thyme

1 egg

salt and ground black
  pepper, to taste

The enticing aroma of roasting chicken always takes me back to my childhood. Roast chicken was a treat: something we only got to eat on birthdays and special occasions. To this day, whenever I roast a chicken it feels like a celebration.

To make Herb Stuffing, melt butter in a frying pan and cook onion over a medium-low heat until softened but not browned (about 8 minutes). Whizz bread in a food processor until crumbed (don't let it get pasty). You should have about 4 cups. Place in a large bowl with softened onion and all remaining ingredients and stir to combine evenly. (The stuffing can be prepared ahead and chilled for up to 48 hours until needed.)

Preheat oven to 180°C (350°F) fanbake. Season inside of chicken with salt and pepper, then fill with half the stuffing. Tie chicken drumsticks together with heatproof string. Form remaining stuffing into a 20 cm (8 in) log on a piece of tinfoil or baking paper. Roll up and twist the ends, then set aside.

Place chicken breast-side up in a roasting dish and season with salt and pepper. Halve onion lengthwise and place cut-side down in roasting dish. Halve the lemon you zested for the stuffing and squeeze the juice into the melted butter, mix to combine and brush butter mixture all over the top of the chicken. Place lemon halves in roasting dish.

Roast until chicken is golden, the juices run clear when it is skewered in the thickest part of the thigh, or a cooking thermometer inserted into the thigh shows at least 78°C (170°F) (about 1¼–1½ hours). Halfway

INGREDIENTS AND RECIPE CONTINUED OVERLEAF

LEMON GRAVY

3 cups chicken stock

3 tbsp cornflour
  (cornstarch)

¼ cup water

juice of ½ lemon, or more
  to taste

salt and ground black
  pepper, to taste

through cooking, place stuffing roll on an oven tray and add to oven. If the chicken starts to brown too quickly, cover those parts loosely with tinfoil.

Transfer chicken to a serving platter, cover with tinfoil and a tea towel, and allow to rest for 10 minutes while making the gravy.

To make Lemon Gravy, discard onion and lemon shells and place roasting dish over a low heat on the stovetop. Add stock (or use the cooking water from any green vegetables you're cooking as a side dish) and stir over the heat, scraping to loosen pan brownings. Combine cornflour and water and add to the pan, stirring constantly until gravy starts to thicken. Simmer for 5 minutes. Add lemon juice and adjust seasonings to taste. Strain into a hot serving jug and serve hot with chicken and stuffing. The gravy reheats well and can be frozen.

MERINGUES WITH LEMON CREAM

READY IN 1¼ HOURS + COOLING · MAKES 12 LARGE MERINGUES · GF · V

4 medium egg whites, at
  room temperature
a pinch of salt
¾ cup caster (superfine)
  sugar
½ cup icing
  (confectioners') sugar
1 tsp vanilla extract
fresh raspberries,
  blueberries or
  passionfruit, to garnish
  (optional)

LEMON CREAM
1 cup cream, chilled
1 cup home-made or
  store-bought lemon
  curd (see overleaf),
  fully cooled

The transformation of clear gloopy egg whites and sugar into an ethereal sweet cloud of meringue is a magical alchemy. Don't attempt these without an electric mixer—you'll get RSI—and don't make them on a humid day, as the meringue collapses if the air is damp. Be sure to check that the beater and bowl are clean and free of grease, and that there's no broken egg yolk in the whites.

Preheat oven to 120°C (235°F) fanbake. Line 2 oven trays with baking paper for easy clean-up.

Place egg whites and salt in a very clean bowl and whisk with an electric mixer or beater until fluffy. Gradually add caster sugar and beat on high speed for 10 minutes. Check the sugar is fully dissolved by rubbing a little of the mixture between your fingers—it should not be grainy. Beat in icing sugar a little at a time, then mix in vanilla until just combined (don't over-mix at this point).

Scoop large spoonfuls of meringue onto prepared trays (you should get about 12). Use the back of a spoon to make a small hollow in the top of each meringue. Bake for 1¼ hours. Turn off oven and allow meringues to cool for 1 hour without opening oven. If not using at once, they will keep for months in an airtight container.

To make Lemon Cream, whip cream to soft peaks, thick enough to hold on the whisk. Swirl in curd so it marbles through the cream.

Pile about 2 tablespoons of lemon cream into the hollow of each meringue, and scatter with berries or passionfruit (if using). Serve leftover cream in a bowl on the side.

PICTURED OVERLEAF

LEMON CURD

READY IN 30 MINUTES · MAKES ABOUT 2¼ CUPS · GF · V

120 g (4 ¼ oz) butter

1½ cups caster (superfine) sugar

1 cup lemon juice, strained

5 eggs

This is such a useful fridge fixing—slather it on toast, or spoon it into small cooked sweet pastry cases to make individual lemon curd tarts. You can also swirl it through whipped cream to make a fabulous filling for meringues or a topping for pavlova.

Combine butter, sugar and lemon juice in a heavy-based pot or double boiler and heat, without boiling, until sugar is dissolved and butter is melted. Remove from heat.

Whisk eggs in a bowl. Whisk a little of the hot butter mixture into the eggs, then return all the eggs and mixture to the pot and cook over a gentle heat, stirring constantly, until it thickens enough to hold a line when you run your finger across the back of a coated spoon (about 5 minutes). Don't let it boil or it will split.

Remove from heat and strain through a sieve immediately (don't worry if it seems a little runny; it will thicken as it cools). If not using at once, transfer to a sterilised jar and seal. Once opened it will keep for several weeks in the fridge. Bring to room temperature before using.

TWO

From the river to the Riviera

Ideology rules

By the age of 14, in a state of anger and rebellion about everything in life, the first notions of left-wing feminist ideology had begun to creep into my psyche. I railed at my mother for not having a 'proper' paid job. What kind of feminist role model was she? I yelled at my father for just existing. Everything became a challenge.

At home I started my own organic vegie plot, competing with my dad to see who could grow the best vegetables. At the start of spring we staged a bet to see who could grow the biggest red onions from seed. Consulting my newly purchased copy of *Grow It! The beginner's complete in-harmony-with-nature small farm guide* by Richard W. Langer, I tilled my soil and mounded my rows with organic compost and horse poo. Dad, meanwhile, went to the garage to raid the arsenal of chemicals he had stashed there. On the strength of my win—a giant orb of a red onion that weighed in at well over a kilo—my father went out and bought a compost bin. For all his conservatism, Dad was actually always open to new ideas.

Around this time, I acquired a gorgeous boyfriend. Billy lived at the other end of Karori with his family. We met at Bible class (my friend Lucy and I had worked out that this was a great place to meet boys), and he was a year older than me. Billy was wise and funny and kind and good-looking. My heart fluttered every time I saw him. We went to judo classes together and

OPPOSITE Enjoying Dad's bountiful garden in Karori.

PREVIOUS A budding hippie.

used to practise throwing each other around in Mum and Dad's living room.

Billy and his mates were into tramping, and most weekends we would all head out for hours or days over the hills to Mākara or Pariwhero/Red Rocks, or for weekend trips up into the Remutakas. We'd drive up to Kaitoke Regional Park, often starting the day with a swim in the river and ending it high on a ridge, tramping through the snow, and staying at one of the small Department of Conservation huts.

> We became 'les hippies'. Not just regular 'peace and love' hippies, but righteous hippies with a mission to change the world. Billy had become an ardent Maoist. Soon, I too could feel the flame of the revolution starting to burn inside me.

Billy was in charge of cooking on these trips. He knew I didn't like sausages so he would always bring along a nice piece of steak for me. We would wrap up big slabs of his mother's famous wholemeal fruit cake, and make bags of scroggin, with peanuts and raisins and chocolate, that we'd pack into our parka pockets to snack on as we hiked in the wilderness.

Like me, Billy was sprouting ideological horns, but his were sharper and pointed further left. He was always reading books on ideology, and was feisty about the need for change. I hung on every pronouncement he made. We became 'les hippies'. Not just regular 'peace and love' hippies, but righteous hippies with a mission to change the world. Billy had become an ardent Maoist. Soon, I too could feel the flame of the revolution starting to burn inside me. I didn't really have a clue what it was all about, but there was this sense of belonging to something big and important that could change the world for the better. Chairman Mao—father of the Chinese revolution, patriot, combative revolutionary, Marxist theorist and devoted Leninist, soldier, statesman and poet—was our hero. To many millions in China, Mao was the embodiment of a living god. Billy and I joined his legion with fervent zeal.

To put all this in some context, New Zealand was operating under a Labour government with Prime Minister Norman Kirk at the helm. Kirk's government had become well known for its strong social conscience—stopping conscription for the Vietnam War, postponing the Springbok tour of 1973 on the grounds of apartheid, and putting up strong opposition to nuclear testing in the Pacific.

In the mid-seventies, the Labour government set up the ohu scheme, an alternative land-settlement scheme which allowed communities to settle on Crown-owned land. In Māori, the word 'ohu' means to work together as a voluntary group, and the aims behind the scheme included reconnecting people to the land, assisting them to become self-sufficient, and providing a communal environment. (Someone also said they thought it was a good way to remove radicals from urban settings.) A 1975 government brochure about the scheme suggested that it may be of interest to people keen on organic farming, alternative energy and recycling, and referred to the kibbutz (a type of communal settlement founded in Israel in the early 1900s) as an inspiration, although ohu communities were not expected to be a copy of this.

An ohu was established up the remote Ahu Ahu Valley, one of the tributaries of the Whanganui River. Further north up the valley, James K. Baxter had set up a commune at Jerusalem (Hiruhārama), drawing a swathe of young hippies, most of whom were interested in taking drugs and zoning out and not doing a lot. We didn't want to be drug-taking hippies, and we didn't want to live on an ohu. We wanted to change the world. Billy and his equally zealous anti-establishment friend Jake moved up the Whanganui River when they left school, the year before I did, and based themselves in Koroniti.

During my school holidays, I would head up to stay with them, camping on a rough platform the boys had built next to the pigsty outside. To the horror of my poor parents, the day that school was finally over, with my University Entrance thankfully accredited (thus nullifying any requirement to sit final exams), I was ready to eschew the trappings of the capitalist Western world. I upped sticks and went to live with Billy and Jake, trading miniskirts and heels for gumboots, jandals, shorts and T-shirts. Out went the bra. Out went the make-up. I was an equal here. I could do anything the boys could do. Well, I thought I could.

The three of us moved to the tiny, remote settlement of Rānana on the Whanganui River, and offered ourselves up for work in the local community. Down on the river flats, below the big pink hall at Rānana, there was a derelict turn-of-the-century cottage. The chimney had collapsed into the roof, the outer wall of the kitchen had rotted away, and all the windows were smashed. George, the local kaumātua, let us live in the cottage rent-free in exchange for helping to clear the flats and fix up the wharepuni (sleeping house) on the old marae.

Everything was overgrown with blackberry and bracken. The boys set to work to clear the site and make repairs, tacking clear plastic into the window cavities, building a new kitchen wall with second-hand timber, and repairing the roof so it was *almost* waterproof. There was no electricity or running water, and all our meals (as well as all my preserving and baking) were cooked over a big open fire. At night we would sit up and read under the hissing light of an old Coleman lamp.

One of the first things we did at Rānana was to build a huge organic vegetable garden down on the flat between the cottage and the wharepuni. It was a great source of pride that we could feed so many people from our garden. Billy built some big compost bins out of split willow, and we

OPPOSITE Life up the river at Rānana.
George is putting in a hāngī at centre right.

collected cow pats from the cattle grazing the flats for fertiliser.

After a few months, the boys had rigged up an alkathene pipe from the top of the hill so we had running water for the garden and for cooking. They then set about building a lean-to outdoor kitchen, where I could cook over the fire under cover. Like most places that are verdantly green, it rained a lot. When it rained, the lazy olive-green river transformed into an angry torrent. Once, when the water was on the rise and we had left the dinghy on the other side, I (being the best swimmer among us) had to swim across to get it. By the time I was rowing the dinghy back, the river had risen another half-metre and it became challenging to navigate in the current. Through the day, the water rose and rose before our eyes. By nightfall, it had risen nearly 10 metres and become a savage flood of wild, foaming rapids and huge, coffin-like logs, which had washed out from tributaries further up in the watershed.

When we had been at Rānana some time, a first-time farmer's gathering was organised—someone said it was basically an excuse for a whole lot of wannabe hippies to get together, sit around and talk, play volleyball, and eat. George taught us how to put in a beautiful hāngī. It was cooked to perfection.

For centuries Māori have followed the ancient tradition of cooking food over hot rocks buried in a pit oven, and there is a lot of skill to getting a hāngī right. It's not something you can just whip up. The process of making a hāngī starts with digging a hole deep enough to hold the hot rocks at the base and the baskets of food on top; the hole should be slightly narrower at the bottom than at the top. There also needs to be enough room down the sides to easily drape the sides of the baskets of food with wet cloths. About three to five hours before you want to start cooking, you need to light a fire to allow enough time for the stones, which provide the heat to cook the food, to reach around 700 degrees Celsius. The stones need to be volcanic, as non-volcanic stones will crack and explode. The rocks

George used would have most likely been in his family for generations and fed hundreds if not thousands of people.

The way I remember it, big pieces of seasoned meat and chicken were placed in a steel basket on top of a deep bed of fern leaves (the greenery provides a buffer between the food and the hot stones, as well as infusing the food with flavour and providing additional moisture to build steam). Chunks of root vegetables—kūmara, potatoes, pumpkin, carrots—were packed into wet muslin bags and put in another basket. The hot stones were placed side by side in the hole, and then slapped repetitively with wet sacks to create steam. The food baskets were then placed on top of the hot stones, with the meats on the bottom and the vegetables above. A layer of clean, wet tea towels and piles of wet sacks went over the top and sides, to create more steam and to prevent any dirt getting on the food. More earth was shovelled back over the top and any little vents of steam were packed with dirt, sealing the heat in.

> We were stridently idealistic. There were no
> drugs or booze in this slice of paradise . . .
> I carried Mao's *Little Red Book* around in my
> pocket as if it was some kind of talisman
> with invincible magic properties.

After about three hours, the hāngī was ready. The earth was carefully shovelled off, the sacks removed, and then finally the baskets of food were lifted out—cooked to steamy, smoky tenderness.

Occasionally for long weekends, groups from teachers college in Wellington would come up, and we'd sit up late around the campfire, someone playing the guitar while we all sang along. We were stridently idealistic. There were no drugs or booze in this slice of paradise. Billy had hung a huge poster of Mao on the scrim wall of our rat-infested old cottage and regularly consulted his stack of *China Today* magazines. I carried Mao's *Little Red Book* around in my pocket as if it was some kind of talisman with invincible magic properties. I called my kitten Ms Mao. She used to hitchhike in my pocket with me up the river.

Did we have any idea that Mao's regime was responsible for many tens of millions of deaths, as a result of starvation, persecution, prison labour and mass executions? Ahh no, we did not. We were living the dream.

OF THE FEW STAPLES WE PURCHASED—tea, rice, grains, oil, soy sauce, Vegemite—it was the fresh stoneground wholemeal flour that I couldn't manage without. With the *Tassajara Cookbook* as my guide, I gradually perfected a yeasted potato bread cooked in the camp oven, using a natural yeast bug known as rēwana, which my local Māori friends taught me how to make. You take a medium-sized potato, chop it into small pieces and boil it with water and a small spoonful of sugar. (It is important that the water used to cook the potato isn't salted, because salt inhibits the bug from growing.) Once the potato is cooked, you mash it with one and a half cups of the cooking water, then mix it to a paste with one cup of flour. This paste is left to ferment, usually over several days, and forms a natural leavener for bread. You can also keep the bug going by adding a teaspoon of sugar and a cup of potato cooking water every few days. The locals would mix the fermented rēwana with four cups of flour, one teaspoon of baking soda and some salt to make their bread.

I made my loaf with the rēwana starter and a little of the dough from the previous day's bread. Each day I would light the fire and, once it had burned down to a bed of deep embers, I was ready to cook my loaf. It was a magical dough—light yet dense, with enough grunt to lift the heavy cast-iron lid off the camp oven by a full finger's width as it baked to golden, crusty perfection.

It took me a while to master the quantity of hot coals needed. Four shovels under and around the camp oven, and a big shovel over the top, replenished about 30 minutes into cooking with another shovel over the top resulted in a glorious round loaf that gave a good drum roll when you tapped the top. The most thrilling part was when the loaf started to lift up the lid. Ahh, the power of yeast. A generous, enticing aroma wafted out. This was my cue that the loaf was ready, or nearly ready. I'd carefully remove the lid and shake off the embers, then inspect the top of the loaf and give it a tap. If it sounded hollow and the crust was golden and firm, I knew my bread was ready. If it wasn't, I'd put the lid back on, add another shovel of coals underneath the camp oven and a small shovel on top, and leave it to cook for another 15 to 20 minutes. Once the loaf was fully cooked, I'd wait for about 40 minutes before tipping it out onto a clean tea towel.

To some extent, with its impressive good looks and equally impressive taste—a chewy crust and fine, moist texture that sliced beautifully—my daily loaf, coupled with our impressive garden, established among the local community the fact that, while we might have been hippies, we actually did seem to know what we were doing.

I cooked everything over the fire, even transforming our summer harvests of peaches, tomatoes, cucumbers, pears and apples into a line-up of smoky bottled preserves that would see us through the colder months. I was always cooking—baking scones in the camp oven, making pancakes or hotcakes, slow-cooking stews, stir-frying cooked rice with carrots, spring onions, egg and soy sauce. (This is still a dish I whip up from time to time when I'm away from home without a well-stocked pantry. There's something about that combination that makes it very satisfying to eat.)

Every now and then we would be offered work up the road at Morikau Station, either helping in the yards or working out the back of the farm, and I'd always bake scones to take with us. For our efforts we each got given half a sheep a week. The boys also shot lots of wild goats across the river, so there was always plenty of meat. Depending on the cut, I would roast or slow-cook it in the camp oven over the fire, and serve it up with whatever vegetables we had to hand from the garden.

As well as working on the local farms, cutting scrub and clearing blackberry, we got involved with helping to clear out old cemeteries and painting the kōwhaiwhai patterns in the old wharenui buildings up and down the river. Many of the wharenui were rundown, and local kuia and kaumātua were thrilled to have willing helpers to repair them. The wharenui, the most important of the buildings within a marae, resembles the human body in structure and usually represents a particular ancestor of the iwi. But in many rural communities at that time (and even still today) there were not enough hands to keep the wharenui warm. Arriving at an old wharenui, we would be given big cans of red, black and white paint to go over the old kōwhaiwhai patterns—black for te pō (the darkness), red to represent the sacred realm, and white for te ao mārama (the world of light).

There was so much protocol to learn. Even though I had spent a lot of time at my friend Te Ara's house down the road in Karori when I was growing up, I had never lived in a traditional Māori community. I quickly learnt not to leave my hat or anything related to my head on the table, that it was very bad to sit on any kind of table, and that you needed to take off your shoes before entering the meeting house. Whenever we finished work clearing at an urupā (cemetery or burial ground), the kuia would always take us to the river to wash our hands so that we didn't break tapu.

I also learnt that manaakitanga—the welcoming and care of guests, and the surrounding kindness and generosity—was the single most important thing to think about whenever anybody arrived. On the marae, once the welcoming pōwhiri was completed and you had been officially received, you became whānau. Along with manaakitanga, whanaungatanga—that sense of a family connection—is a key aspect of tikanga Māori.

IT DIDN'T TAKE LONG TO make friends in this tiny community.

Mary and Mike lived at the top of the hill with a tribe of kids. Mike was Pakeha, he had a bung eye, and worked full-time as an agricultural labourer earning $60 a week. They had six kids of their own, plus a bunch of foster kids Mary had taken in. This wonderful woman had a magic way of knitting everyone tightly and safely together. I'd never met anyone with such a big heart. With so many mouths to feed, you might think that she would have been strung-out, but the only time I ever saw her get anxious was when her two-year-old daughter brought out a packet of contraceptive pills while we were all having a meeting with the neighbours in Mary's living room. This was a 100 per cent Catholic community.

Mary either knew, or was related to, everyone up and down the river. Whenever anybody died, she would always be there to help with the tangihanga. Once she realised, after a few months, how practical I was, she'd get me to come along to help. The car horn would toot several times at the top of the hill and I'd hear Ma yelling down the valley, 'Annaaaabel! Taaaangiiii! I need your help.'

I'd drop whatever I was doing, grab a bag, and stuff in my toothbrush and a change of clothes, then race up the hill and slide onto the front bench seat of her old white station wagon. Our first stop was Whanganui, a drive of nearly 60 kilometres, to buy tiny bottles of coloured fizzy drink, sweets, and big rolls of paper to use as tablecloths for the trestle tables. Once we had all our goodies stashed in the car, we'd head back up the river to the marae where the tangi was getting under way.

There was so much important etiquette here, with each iwi having their own particular tikanga. We would be welcomed on to the marae with a karakia, then head to the tent to pay our respects with a gentle hōngi to each person. The immediate family of the deceased would be sitting cross-legged in a tight circle round the open coffin in the middle of the tent. The act of a hōngi requires pressing your nose and forehead against someone else's nose and forehead. Through the exchange of hā (the breath of life) one is no longer considered a stranger, but rather an honoured visitor.

And then it was time to get to work. Everyone came laden with food. Freshly slaughtered sheep or wild pigs would be hung in the trees nearby, waiting to be butchered by the men for the hāngī. Mary would send me to the kitchen to help peel sacks of potatoes and prepare pumpkin and kūmara with the other women. Meanwhile, she went to set up housie (or bingo, as it was sometimes called), a major form of fundraising for the tangi. The entire community chipped in to assist in whatever way they could, both to honour the person who had died and to support their grieving family. 'Nāu te rourou, nāku te rourou, ka ora te manuhiri.' *With your food basket and my food basket, the people will thrive.*

The keening, weeping, speeches and songs went on for days, while we cooked and washed and cleaned. All the time someone stayed with the body, until it was ready to be buried. The whole process seemed to me a much better way to grieve than our tight 'keep a stiff upper lip' Western approach to death and dying. I felt so privileged to be accepted as one of the locals in this small, tight-knit community.

GEORGE LIVED A FEW KILOMETRES up the road with his wife, Shirley, and their children. He was thrilled to have three keen, strong young kids in town, wanting to restore old buildings and help out in the community.

For all her kindness, Shirley was no great shakes as a cook. Her repertoire seemed to run solely to a big pot of boil-up simmering on the stove. When it's well made, a boil-up is a very delicious thing—like a French pot-au-feu. To make it well, you simmer pork bones until the meat

OPPOSITE (Clockwise from top) A picnic with my parents and friends beside the wharepuni at Rānana; some local kids on horseback outside the old cottage we lived in; volleyball games on the river flats; and another local youngster beside our fledgling vegie gardens.

falls off. Next, watercress or pūhā is added to the rich pork stock, and this simmers for about 15 minutes, until the greens are very tender. Meanwhile, in another pot, you steam potatoes, pumpkin and kūmara. The tender root vegetables get divided between bowls, and everything from the other pot meat, bones, greens and stock—gets poured over the top.

Shirley wasn't going to go to any of this fuss however, apart from scrubbing the pūhā under the cold tap to release its bitter, milky sap. Into the pot it went with a few potatoes, some kūmara, a shoulder of mutton and a big chunk of cabbage. The whole thing would simmer away for hours, until the meat had reached a state of fall-apart tenderness, and the kitchen was filled with that doubly offensive smell of overcooked sulphurous brassicas and fatty boiled mutton. Sometimes for a special treat, if she'd been to town, Shirley would make a boil-up with saveloys—yes, those dyed bright-pink sausages. The broth from this particular brew came out a dirty pink blush. It was greasy and even more disgusting than the mutton version.

When it came to offensive-smelling food, nothing was worse than kānga pirau, aka rotten corn. Up and down the valley, the locals considered kānga pirau an absolute delicacy, even though it smelt like vomit. In the autumn, cobs of maize would be placed in a sack in the running water of a stream, weighted down and left for about three months to ferment. Once the kernels were soft enough, they were scraped off the cob and cooked up into this revoltingly stinky porridge that was often served—as regular oat porridge might be—with cream and brown sugar. I have no idea how anyone figured out that rotten corn was a delicacy rather than something that might kill you. But, if you could get it past your nose, the taste was actually surprisingly good—creamy, sweet and nutty, not unlike a washed-rind cheese.

IN THE MIDDLE OF ALL THIS, my mother suggested we go to Europe together. She could see her 17-year-old daughter disappearing into the wilderness forever. So she proposed a trip around Europe, an educational 'rite of passage', to look at art and culture and the roots of Western civilisation.

By now you may perhaps have gathered that I was the world's most difficult teenager. My mother packed a jar of Vegemite, a bottle of whisky and a container of Valium to help her survive our trip.

Arthur Frommer's *Europe on $10 a Day* was our steer, providing us with a terrific selection of wonderful little pensioni, places of historic interest and ancient art, and suggestions of where to eat. We would snack through the day on an assortment of breads, cheeses, olives and fruit from the local markets, and each night treat ourselves to a new restaurant from Mr Frommer's list of recommendations.

One night in Naples, after one of our el cheapo Frommer dinners, we were walking back to our pensione. As we were waiting at the traffic lights, we stood alongside an attractive man who was probably a good ten years older than me. He turned to me and said, 'Excuse me, *signorina*, do you know Naples is the most famous place in the whole world to eat pizza?' His accent was charming—that lilting Italianesque English. I nodded, thinking, yes, I had heard Naples had the best pizza in the world.

'Do you like pizza?'

I nodded again.

'I know where there is the best pizza in all of Naples. Let us go. I can take you there now.'

I turned to my mother. 'Mum, I'm going to get some pizza.' And, just like that, I was off, leaving my poor mother standing at the crossing with her jaw on the pavement.

It took me under five minutes to realise that this elegant man's intentions had not really involved pizza. Now I had to figure out how to safely extricate myself from the situation. It was going to take a lie. I looked down at the pavement, fluttering my eyelashes. 'My father, he's a famous judge from England, and he's working on an important case here. I've just started high school and my mother brought me over to be here with them. I think I should go home now.'

My would-be paramour's hand, which had been slowly angling from my shoulder down towards my breasts, snapped to his side as if he'd touched a hot coal. He stepped back. '*Ah, signorina, dobbiamo portarti a casa dalla tua famiglia.*'

I looked at him blankly.

'I ahh must ahh take ahh you back ahh to your family.'

Whew. Safely home. My poor mother.

IN GREECE WE ATE TINY lamb skewers cooked over the coals from roadside vendors, the meat marinated with rosemary, lemon and garlic. In Florence there was *bistecca alla fiorentina*, a vast steak grilled over a woodfire, succulent and so tender. I ate my first gelato in St Mark's Square among eddying flurries of pigeons. In Switzerland, there was cultured butter, home-made apricot jam, crusty bread, frogs' legs and fondue.

In Corfu, I rented a moped with a girl I had met on the ferry from Brindisi. Sylvia and I scooted up into the hills of the Greek island with not a worry in the world, full of the sheer adventure of life. We stopped at a small café among the olive trees on the side of the road—if you could call it a road—and drank retsina and ate wrinkled black olives with crumbly, salty feta. It all tasted so new, so different and exotic. On the way back to our pensione, weaving down through terrace upon terrace of ancient olive trees, Sylvia flipped off her moped on a tight, gravelly corner and gave her leg a nasty scrape. A band of olive pickers materialised to our rescue— short old women made even shorter by their deeply stooped physiques, dressed head to toe in black. They made us herb tea, found bandages and then called, 'Angelo, Angelo! *Éla, éla!*' *Come, come.* A young, bronzed Greek god with flowing golden hair and green almond eyes appeared through the olive trees. In halting English, he explained he could escort us safely back to town.

And so we were three, with Angelo leading the way on his noisy old bike, turning at every corner to flash me the most brilliant smile. I was highly flattered, but Sylvia's confidence was shattered, and she was frightened and angry—even more so for the fact that this gorgeous man's attentions were not being directed in any way towards her.

It took us hours to get back to the moped hire, and after that I never saw Sylvia again. Angelo, on the other hand, became an outrageously persistent suitor, waiting in the lobby at the pensione at all hours, offering to take me to new, exotic places afar on his bicycle . . . to walk, to drink, to dine. But I had left my heart on a marae up the Whanganui River.

SO IT WAS THAT, when my mother and I finally returned to New Zealand several months later, I went straight back up the river to the arms of my beloved communist boyfriend. I had missed the life we had built down on the terrace at Rānana—growing vegetables, working on the local marae, helping out at tangihanga, and generally going about saving the world.

Spring rolled around, and Billy's brother-in-law Simon called to tell us that he needed some help with a big catamaran he was building. And so we started to commute back and forth between Rānana and Wellington in order to work on the boat. Eventually, we made the move back to the city to work on it full-time.

A new dream was emerging, one that would take us even further away from mainstream society—or so we imagined.

GREEN GOODNESS LEMON AND PARMESAN RISOTTO

READY IN 45 MINUTES · SERVES 4 · GF, IF STOCK IS GLUTEN-FREE · V

3 tbsp butter or
  neutral oil
2 onions, finely chopped
2 cloves garlic, crushed
1½ cups risotto rice
½ cup white wine
6 cups hot vegetable
  stock, plus a little extra
  if needed
1 tsp salt
ground black pepper,
  to taste
4 handfuls baby spinach
  leaves
2 cups frozen peas,
  thawed
1 cup grated parmesan
finely grated zest and
  juice of 1 lemon
pea tendrils or rocket
  (arugula), to garnish
  (optional)

HERB OIL
½ packed cup fresh
  parsley, watercress or
  rocket (arugula) leaves
2 tbsp extra virgin
  olive oil
a pinch of salt

Puréeing frozen peas and adding them to a risotto just before it's ready provides this wonderful zing of freshness. You can also purée lightly cooked broccoli, zucchini or spinach and use them in place of the peas.

Heat butter or oil in a large, heavy-based pot, add onions and garlic and cook over a medium heat until softened but not browned (8 minutes).

Add rice and stir for 1–2 minutes to lightly toast. Add wine and allow to evaporate fully, then add hot stock, salt and pepper, and stir to combine. Simmer gently, stirring now and then, until rice is creamy and just tender (about 18 minutes). If the mixture dries out during cooking, add a little more stock or water—it should be wet enough to fall from the spoon.

While rice is cooking, make Herb Oil by puréeing herbs with oil and salt, adding a little water if needed to thin to a pouring consistency.

Boil a jug of water. Place spinach and peas in a bowl, cover with boiling water and allow to stand for 2 minutes. Drain, then purée with a hand wand blender or in a food processor. Add to risotto with parmesan, lemon zest and juice, and stir to combine. Adjust seasonings to taste and warm through.

To serve, divide risotto between heated serving bowls and top with a drizzle of Herb Oil and pea tendrils or rocket (if using).

BRAISED SHORT RIBS
WITH GINGER AND STAR ANISE

READY IN 4¼ HOURS + CHILLING + REHEATING · SERVES 8–10
DF · GF, IF GLUTEN-FREE SOY SAUCE AND CORNFLOUR ARE USED

about 3 kg (6 lb 12 oz)
  beef short ribs
salt and ground black
  pepper, to taste
2 cups tomato juice
2 cups water
¼ cup soy sauce
2 tbsp rice wine vinegar
1 tbsp soft brown sugar
2–3 heads garlic, halved
  crosswise
about 18 thin slices fresh
  ginger
4 star anise
4 dried chillies
zest of ½ an orange, cut
  with a vegetable peeler
2 tbsp cornflour
  (cornstarch)
¼ cup water
fresh coriander (cilantro)
  leaves or sprigs,
  to garnish
Gingery Asian Greens
  (see overleaf), to serve
  (optional)

When it comes to slow cooking my preference is for meat on the bone, as it's so much sweeter. If you can, make this recipe a day or two in advance to allow the flavours to mingle and to make it easier to remove the fat that rises to the top when the meat is chilled.

Preheat oven to 220°C (425°F) fanbake. Arrange beef ribs in a large, deep roasting dish and season well. Roast until the ribs are well browned and the fat has rendered off (about 45 minutes).

Remove from oven and reduce oven temperature to 150°C (300°F) fanbake. Lift out ribs and transfer to a deep-sided Dutch oven or casserole dish that can be heated on the stovetop. Combine all remaining ingredients except cornflour, water and coriander in a jug. Pour mixture over ribs. Cut a piece of baking paper to fit over the top, then cover the dish tightly with a lid or a double layer of tinfoil. Bake until the ribs are very tender (about 3½ hours).

If possible, chill ribs in the casserole dish overnight.

When ready to serve, skim fat from the top and discard. Cover and return casserole dish to a 180°C (350°F) oven for 30–40 minutes to fully heat through.

Remove from oven, lift out ribs and place them in a bowl while you thicken the sauce. Place casserole dish on the stovetop and bring to a simmer. Combine cornflour and water and add to casserole dish, stirring mixture over the stovetop until lightly thickened. Adjust seasonings to taste. Add ribs and simmer for 5 minutes to fully heat through. Garnish with coriander and serve with Gingery Asian Greens.

GINGERY ASIAN GREENS

READY IN 15 MINUTES · SERVES 6 AS A SIDE · DF · GF · V · VE

6 heads bok choy,
  quartered lengthwise,
  or a big bunch choi
  sum leaves
2 tsp sesame oil
2 tsp finely grated
  fresh ginger
¼ tsp salt
¼ cup water
1 tbsp black sesame
  seeds, to garnish
  (optional)

Cook this just before serving—because bok choy has such a high water content, it doesn't reheat well. You can also cook other Asian greens in this way.

Place bok choy or choi sum in a pot with sesame oil, ginger, salt and water. Cover and cook over a high heat until wilted and just tender but still vibrantly green (3–4 minutes).

To serve, transfer to a platter and garnish with sesame seeds (if using).

HEAVENLY HOTCAKES WITH MAPLE-ROASTED PEARS AND CRISPY BACON

READY IN 30 MINUTES + STANDING · MAKES 16–18
GF, IF GLUTEN-FREE FLOUR IS USED · V

2 eggs, separated
2 cups milk
¼ cup sugar
1 tsp vanilla extract
2 cups plain flour or
  gluten-free flour
4 tsp baking powder
½ tsp salt
50 g (1¾ oz) butter, plus
  extra for frying

TO SERVE
crispy bacon
Maple-Roasted Pears
  (see overleaf)

A big stack of hotcakes on the table makes such a welcome start to the weekend. You can also prepare the batter the night before and store it in the fridge—add the melted butter and whisked egg whites just before cooking.

If the batter starts sticking to the frying pan, try this simple trick: heat a thin layer of plain dry salt in the pan for 3–4 minutes, then wipe out without washing. The salt resurfaces the pan so that food won't stick anymore.

To make the hotcake batter, beat together egg yolks, milk, sugar and vanilla. Add flour, baking powder and salt and beat until smooth. Allow to stand for at least 15 minutes. (The batter can be prepared ahead and chilled for up to 12 hours until needed.)

When ready to cook, melt butter and stir into batter. Whisk egg whites to soft peaks and gently fold into batter.

Melt a little butter in a frying pan over a medium heat. Spoon ladlefuls (about ¼ cup) of batter into pan, allowing plenty of space in between. As bubbles form, turn to cook the other side until golden brown and fully cooked through. Add a little butter between batches as needed.

Serve the hotcakes as they are cooked or place on a baking tray, cover with tinfoil and, when they are all cooked, reheat in an oven preheated to 180°C (350°F) fanbake until warmed through (4–5 minutes).

Serve with crispy bacon and Maple-Roasted Pears.

PICTURED OVERLEAF

MAPLE-ROASTED PEARS

READY IN 30 MINUTES · SERVES 6–8 · GF · V

3–4 pears, such as
  beurre bosc
2 tbsp butter
3 tbsp maple syrup or
  runny honey
2 tbsp sugar
¼ cup water

I like to use beurre bosc pears or other firm varieties for this dessert as they hold their shape well, but any pear will work. Softer-fleshed pear varieties release more liquid and cook to tenderness in a shorter time. Allow half a pear per person.

Preheat oven to 180°C (350°F) fanbake. Peel, halve and core pears.

Melt butter in an ovenproof frying pan over a medium heat. Add pears cut-side down and brown for 2–3 minutes without turning. Add maple syrup, sugar and water. Bring to a fast boil, then transfer to preheated oven.

Bake until fruit is lightly golden (15–20 minutes, depending on firmness of pears). If caramel reduces too much and is no longer runny, add 2–3 tablespoons of water and mix to loosen. Serve the pears with caramel sauce on the side.

THREE

Crossing the tracks

Life on the wild side

A feast of crispy potatoes, tender roast lamb, broccoli and carrots, with a big jug of steaming gravy, sat on the table ready to serve. I was at my cousin's flat in Kelburn, behind the Botanic Gardens, and I hadn't eaten a roast meal in months. It all smelt so good.

After living salubriously at home with my parents for a few months, Billy and I had moved into a flat on Adams Terrace, off Aro Street, in Wellington. Since all our savings were squirrelled away and put towards the boat, there were slim pickings in our flat life. We ploughed our way through sacks of rice and beans, and the delicious food of my mother's kitchen was soon a distant memory.

Just as I was about to sit down to eat at my cousin's table, the phone rang. I'd been expecting a call from Simon, so I headed out to the hall to answer it.

'You need to be at the dock by 7.30 p.m. at the latest. The boat's leaving then, regardless.' Our skipper spoke abruptly and hung up before I could say anything.

This wasn't the message I'd been expecting. According to the weather forecast a big storm was meant to come through, with gale force winds reaching 50 knots. And yet Simon had decided we'd leave port that night.

OPPOSITE Preparing to leave the harbour.

PREVIOUS Always ready for a good time.

I went back to the table to gobble down my dinner, then said my goodbyes and headed to the wharf.

IT HAD TAKEN OVER THREE YEARS and around $20,000 to build the dream: a beautifully designed catamaran that would take us around the world, far from the trappings of capitalism and consumerism.

When Billy, Jake and I had moved back to Wellington, I got a job in the cafeteria of the Westpac bank down on Lambton Quay. My day there started with 20 loaves of sliced white-death bread, which had to be transformed into sandwiches: four loaves of ham, four of ham and mustard, three of egg (no curry), one of tomato (why, when we all knew they would go soggy?) and two of cheese and pineapple (disgusting). The remaining loaves were used to make fiddly club sammies. The pay was lousy, but the hours meant I was free in the afternoons, so I could get out to the boat and my sander in the workshop at Tawa. (I built the cockpit and did a *lot* of sanding.)

Simon was married to Billy's elder sister, Antonia, and was more idealistic than the rest of us put together. He had bought a copy of the boat plans and, without any professional help, set about building it, engaging our help and funds as it started to take shape. *Eternity*, as Simon named the boat, weighed about four and a half tons, with a draught of just two feet eight inches. It was known to reach speeds of more than 15 knots. Its design included many of the features of the resilient catamarans used by early Polynesian navigators.

Billy's other sister, Jacquie, and her boyfriend also joined us out at the workshop, and Jacquie's friend Michele turned up a bit later in the piece. That took our working crew to eight—not including Simon and Antonia's new baby, who was nonetheless often in attendance in her pram. With so many hands manning sanders and saws and paintbrushes, the boat started to take shape quickly. Layers and layers of laminated ply went into the boat's construction, and the two hulls were held together with thick laminated beams set on fat rubber washers. Once the last coat of paint was dry, the boat was finally finished.

It was time to head away before the cyclone season kicked in.

AND SO IT WAS THAT four teachers, a computer programmer, three hippies, a baby and a cat (Antonia and Simon's) embarked on the adventure of a lifetime. My parents waved goodbye from the wharf, while Billy's mother stood alongside. My sweetheart's father had drowned on a boating trip some years earlier, and now his mother watched as three of her children sailed off into a storm. I wondered how she felt. I thought about the awful weather forecast, and felt a little thread of anxiety twist in my stomach.

The plan was to sail to Gisborne for the first leg of our journey, where we'd moor up for the winter and head into the bush to trap possums. Fur prices were high, and the East Coast region produced some of the best possum fur in the North Island. According to our great leader Simon, possum trapping was going to be the smartest way to raise the money we needed to all sail off into the blue horizon.

> The plan was to sail to Gisborne for the first leg of our journey, where we'd moor up for the winter and head into the bush to trap possums. Fur prices were high, and the East Coast region produced some of the best possum fur in the North Island.

In preparation for the trip, I had gone to the Wellington markets and purchased crates full of vegetables and fruit—cabbages, onions, pears, apples, a few pumpkins and a sack of potatoes. These were lashed firmly to the foredecks, while other perishable supplies like eggs, bread, milk and cheese had been put in the small fridge under the bench. Condiments and snacks were packed into the galley cupboards, and a stash of containers of fresh water went into the bilge. The trip to Gisborne was expected to take two or three days, but we had enough food and water for a couple of weeks—just in case.

None of us were experienced sailors—least of all me. Did I have any idea of the true risks of this idealistic endeavour? Did I have any idea I would soon be so sick I wouldn't actually *want* to eat any of that food?

Billy was rostered on first watch, and I went below deck to our tiny cabin, which consisted of a not-quite-double mattress with shelving on either side and a small storage cupboard up at the pillow end. I was unpacking my belongings onto the mattress when the storm hit, slapping a huge, juddering wave into the side of the boat. I had failed to check that the portholes were secure, and a gush of water poured through and pooled on the mattress. I quickly secured the windows and started grabbing the things that had begun floating around me. Another wave whacked into the side. The giant laminated beams that held the two hulls together groaned on their rubber washers. Up came the roast dinner. Now everything wasn't just wet; it was wet and vomit-covered. I sat there in a swill of puke and sea water, holding on for dear life, as the boat lurched on.

It was all hands on deck. Great white-capped waves steamed shoreward, their long overhanging crests whipped up into a heavy, foamy mist. The wind howled a high-pitched hum of fury in the rigging. We reefed the mainsail, then brought it down entirely and put up a storm jib. Each time a wave caught us broadside, the boat would surf sideways closer to the shore. Until the gale abated, all we could do was beat into the wind to prevent ourselves from getting dashed onto the rocky coastline. It was like riding a bucking bronco.

OPPOSITE Building the dream,
and finally on the water ready to sail.

There was no going back. Simon had that resolute look on his face that made it impossible to question anything. Even if the boat had gone down, I doubt his expression would have changed. It seemed to me that he was a 'my way or the highway' kind of guy, fixed in his views, and an absolute master of the art of the intellectual argument.

Everyone, except the baby and the cat, was horribly seasick.

The wind swung round to the southwest, and now we had to ride downwind in the rising swell. This was almost more terrifying—hanging on to the tiller for dear life, reaching the bottom of the swell and looking behind into the dark, deep green water at the stern, always the risk the boat might broach as it hurtled down a wave. If it flipped us, there would be no recovery.

Finally, the seas started to flatten out, and everyone stopped being sick. Except me. I continued to retch on the clock, every 15 minutes, 24 hours a day. If I could have swum to shore, I would have. I went from feeling like I would die to feeling like I wanted to die. Near the end I felt like I was almost dead.

NEARLY A WEEK LATER, after what felt like a lifetime at sea, we sailed past Young Nicks Head (Te Kuri) at the southern end of Poverty Bay, past the breakwater, and into the safe harbour of the little East Coast port town of Gisborne. We could have moored in Antarctica and I would have been happy. All I wanted was to get off that boat. I was exhausted, incredibly weak and dehydrated. During the trip I had lost over 10 kilos in weight. Whatever dream I'd had about sailing around the world with these people was gone. The trip we had undertaken had tested every inch of me. Somewhere, something felt broken.

At the dock, a tall, skinny guy with straggly shoulder-length blond hair and a big walrus moustache ambled over. He was wearing a black cable-knit fisherman's jersey, dirty jeans and stubby Red Band gumboots. 'That's quite a boat you've got there,' he said. 'She must be . . . what? Over fifty-odd feet?' (Our arrival into the harbour subsequently made front-page headlines in the local newspaper.) He introduced himself as Luke, and chatted with my crewmates. He'd been helping a mate with his cray pots, he said. It had been a good summer for crays.

I wasn't saying anything. I still felt like death warmed up. Luke looked about 30. *Louche*, I thought. There was something dangerously attractive about this man.

Someone invited him aboard for a look around. He peeked into Michele's tiny cabin up the front. 'Well, that's a good coffin,' he said. 'Wouldn't want to get stuck in there in a storm.' He stared at us all standing there, bedraggled and tired. 'Looks like you could all do with a bit of a shower. How about I take you over to my place? There's lots of towels, and I can make you a cuppa.'

He stubbed his cigarette out on the wharf, pulled his keys out of his jeans pocket and dangled them at us with a wide, crinkly smile.

WE ALL PILED INTO LUKE'S blue Thames Trader van, and he drove us over to what looked like the rough side of town. We pulled up against a hill into a narrow driveway, and stopped outside a cowshed. A shiny new 650cc Yamaha motorbike was parked on the lawn.

It turned out that the cowshed was actually Luke's house. Inside, the concrete floors had been painted a vile pea green and the walls a bilious violet. The combination could not have been more revolting. I thought I might puke again. On the wall in the dining room hung one of those giant black-velvet 'paintings' depicting a Tahitian maiden twirling her arms and her hips. Not a book in sight. But the place was clean and amazingly tidy, there was loads of hot water, and Luke was funny and charming. We all had showers and a cup of tea, and then he took us back to the boat.

'What a great guy,' we all agreed.

We'd discovered that, when he wasn't fishing, Luke was a possum trapper—and he knew a hell of a lot about it. So, for the next few days, he would pick us up, take us back to his place for a shower and coach us on how to trap possums. When the rest of the crew headed inland to Lake Waikaremoana to reccie our campsite for the winter season of possum trapping, Billy and I stayed on board to look after the boat. One afternoon, Billy fell off the wharf and had to go to hospital. Luke was the only other person I knew in this small seaside town. I phoned him, distraught, from the red phone box on the wharf.

'I'll be right there,' he said.

He arrived a few minutes later, and took me to the cowshed-house in Kaitī with the hideous green floor, the puke-violet walls and the awful velvet painting on the wall.

I never went back to the boat, except to collect all my stuff.

My departure from the group caused a huge drama. Abandoning my long-term boyfriend like this was not a kind way to exit our relationship, but when Luke opened the door for me I saw an escape route to a different life—somewhere I could be free of all the head trips and intellectualising that had been part and parcel of life with the group. Michele was the only person who came to visit me to say goodbye before the gang left for Waikaremoana.

THE WORLD I HAD SUDDENLY stepped into could not have been further from anything I knew. There were no mind games, no lofty ideals, and there was definitely nothing academic about this new life I now found myself living. I rode on the back of a fast motorbike, I drank at the pub, I played pool, and I went shooting and hunting. I had never felt so liberated.

Just before we had met, Luke had come out of the Gisborne hospital. He'd had tuberculosis—he'd caught it from the possums—and he was always going back in to the hospital for check-ups. I had no idea that people still got TB in this country.

About six weeks into our relationship, we were at the gun club shooting skeet. Since Luke wanted to get his eye in for duck shooting, we would go out to the club every Sunday, and I was actually getting to be quite a shot with the old over-and-under shotgun Luke had lent me. Pull, *boom*. Pull, *boom*. All the little clay discs would blow to shreds. By the time the opening day of duck-shooting season came around, I could drop two ducks on a double barrel.

It had been a long afternoon, and Luke had been doing a lot of drinking. I was driving us home when he waved his hand across the steering wheel, gesturing for me to stop. I pulled over, and Luke flung the door open and threw up on the side of the road. And—*woooah*—his teeth came out. I had never met anyone with false teeth before. These ones had certainly never come out before in my presence. We drove home in silence, Luke nursing the vomit-covered falsies in his lap. He didn't look great without his pearly whites but, as the saying goes, love is blind. I was 19 and crazy about the guy. I had no idea just how far I had crossed the tracks.

WINTER WAS THE TIME WHEN fur prices were the highest, so Luke and I would head into the bush just out of Mātāwai for two or three weeks at a time, coming out only to replenish our supplies and get our skins tacked and dried.

I had a 185cc Yamaha trail bike that got me an hour up the track, and from there it was another hour's tramp on a poorly marked path to our 'home'—a miserable, cold shack in the middle of the bush that Luke and I shared with a brainless red setter called Heidi. At the start of the season we lugged all our supplies and gear into this hovel, fording thigh-high rivers while toting camp ovens and cast-iron toastie-pie makers, sacks of rice, pumpkins and onions, bread and spices, cheese and butter, toilet paper and toothpaste, bedding and clothing. We never had to worry about anything going off, because the whole place was one giant fridge. My sole reading material was a small dictionary that I stashed in my pack, along with a pen and a squirrelled roll of loo paper to write on.

Now and then, we would come out of the bush and stay in a nearby farmer's shearers' quarters. We would dry our skins there, sleep in a rough bunk and play music on Luke's small boom box. To this day, I can't stand the sound of Neil Diamond or Dire Straits—all I can think of is that shitty, cold shearers' quarters.

> Back in the bush, my daily routine involved checking and laying traplines or cyanide poison over a radius of about 24 kilometres. It would be close to dusk before I'd traipse back to the hut, tired, hungry and cold.

My saviour was the farmer's wife, Kirsty, who I struck up a wonderful friendship with. I would come out of the bush filthy and freezing, and she would run me a huge hot bath. I would disappear for hours with a pile of books, and Kirsty would appear through the steam, like some kind of angel, with glasses of Scotch on the rocks and nibbles of cheese and crackers. After a lengthy soaking, I would be ready to emerge and face the world again, several shades lighter.

Back in the bush, my daily routine involved checking and laying traplines or cyanide poison over a radius of about 24 kilometres. It would be close to dusk before I'd traipse back to the hut, tired, hungry and cold. Luke would usually turn up after dark. We didn't have a Primus, so I'd light a fire to cook our dinner.

Sometimes Luke would shoot a deer and, after gutting and skinning it, he would hang it on a high branch near the hut. We would always pull out the backstraps and fry them up. Occasionally, we would go through the laborious process of breaking the leg meat down into its various muscle groups, peeling off the tough silverskin around each muscle to reveal the tenderest steak meat inside. Deer are the only animal I know that have their muscles contained in this way, and beneath the protective suture-strong silverskin the meat is fillet tender.

I would make tea with the heart-shaped leaves of kawakawa (*Piper excelsum*) or boil up pūhā (*Sonchus kirkii*) for a soup in late winter and spring, when other greens were scarce. In the spring, there would also be watercress (*Nasturtium officinale*) in the creeks to gather for soup and stews. Bracken fronds were everywhere, and although they looked like they would be tender and good to eat we knew better—these fronds are very carcinogenic.

Most nights everything would go in the camp oven—some bacon or salami, a packet of barley soup mix, lentils or rice, onions, carrots and potatoes, a stock cube, and lots of water. At the end, maybe some wild greens to finish it off. Sometimes, I'd fire in a spoonful of curry powder, garlic salt or cumin, but usually I was so tired I didn't really care what anything tasted like. Eating at this point had become purely about sustenance.

We would huddle over the fire and gulp down our meal as quickly as we could, before retiring, usually fully clothed, to bed. In the mornings it would be so cold that the eggs would be totally frozen.

THIS PROBABLY SOUNDS LIKE SOME kind of nightmare, but I loved the bush, with its infinite greens, browns and greys, and the way the landscape morphed from valley to valley and ridge to ridge. There was such a raw sense of freedom and connection to nature out there. Even though it was bone-chillingly cold and we lived on the smell of an oily rag, I had never felt so alive.

Luke taught me to mark the back of the trees along my path with a fluoro spray can, so I could easily find my way back to the hut. Once I knew I wouldn't get lost, I got much more confident about exploring the terrain. Scrambling through supplejack and bog, fern and cutty grass, I might chance on a glorious ridge of tawa forest. The ground here was free of undergrowth, the brownish-black tawa trunks rising up in majestic lines from a carpet of golden leaf-fall. Walking between these trees felt like being in a cathedral. In early summer the kererū would arrive in droves to gorge on the berries.

Each day before I set out, I'd take some leftovers for lunch, along with my can of fluoro spray. In my pack went my traps, a hammer, a pocket of U-shaped fence staples, a small axe, a knife and a container of lure. (The 'lure' consisted of a few drops of oil of cloves shaken into a talcum-powder container filled with flour.) I learnt to look for 'sign'—well-worn animal tracks, bark with urine stains, the little pellets of dung that possums produce. Luke taught me to angle a small log off the ground to make a run, setting it onto a tree trunk at a 45-degree angle from the ground, then hammering on the trap and sprinkling a little lure above it. I caught over 2000 possums that first season, and averaged $10 a skin. By the end of the winter, I could skin a possum in under two minutes and tack out the skin in 40 seconds.

In the summer we headed up the East Coast to trap and poison the big grass-fed possums. It was all farmland up the coast back then, and forestry was only just beginning. We would call in to ask the farmers' permission to trap or poison, and they were always happy to see us, as possums were such a pest. It was big country, open grassland broken with stands of kōuka, or cabbage trees (*Cordyline australis*), and mānuka (*Leptospermum scoparium*), with the occasional kōtukutuku (*Fuchsia excorticata*) and giant pūriri (*Vitex lucens*)—the latter two being trees that possums love to browse on.

Occasionally, I'd come up against a herd of wild cattle and have to make a run for a pūriri tree, then spend the next few hours up there with an irate wild cow butting at the trunk below.

When the weather packed in, we would head back to town and make cray pots for the commercial fishers. Luke had a jig set up in his garage, and I soon became proficient at weaving a giant roll of number-eight wire into neat beehive baskets.

When autumn rolled around, Luke did a deal with a guy at the pub for 50 Dutch fyke nets, so we went eeling for a season. We sold most of our catch to a local export business that sent eels to Holland, but Luke always smoked a few to sell at the pub in Gisborne. Fortunately, his parents didn't seem to mind him digging up the lawn behind their house for his cold-smoker. It was quite a set-up: a big pit lined with fire bricks, with a steel pipe running out of the base and under the ground for about two metres, into the bottom of the drying shed. The drying shed had a rack at the top to hook the eels onto. Before they went into the smoker, Luke would salt them so their slime could be easily rubbed off, then he split them and rubbed them with a mix of salt and brown sugar. A meat hook would go in behind the gills, and he'd leave them to hang in the smoker for a few hours before lighting the fire out in the pit. Once the fire had built up a decent bed of embers, he would throw on a pile of mānuka sawdust, then cover the fire tightly and leave it to slowly smoke. The smoke cooled as it travelled down the pipe into the drying shed, and after somewhere between 18 and 24 hours the eels would emerge firm, oily and sweetly unctuous. Something about the complex flavours of the smoke and the oiliness of the eels really amped up the flavour. They were meltingly delicious.

Catching the eels in the first place, however, was another matter. Eels wriggle and thrash a lot. They produce a lot of sticky slime, and they are really difficult to kill. Long after they are dead, they continue to twitch and judder. It is really unnerving.

One day, when I had a boatload of full nets, all the ties came loose. The eels started to spill out, slithering angrily around my feet and legs. I had to climb up and balance on top of the rowlocks, rowing the oars forward like a Venetian gondolier to get safely to shore, while a hundred-odd kilos of eels writhed in the boat below me. It was the stuff of nightmares. I refused to go eeling again.

Now and then, I would join a local helicopter crew on live-deer recovery expeditions. It was the beginning of the deer-farming industry in New Zealand, and a number of helicopter operators were bringing deer in from the wild to sell to farmers. Live deer were worth a couple of grand each in those days, and we all got a divvy. The shooter would fire a tranquilliser dart, the chopper would whirlybird round, following the deer until it passed out, and then it was my job to jump out of the buzzing machine with a net and a hook. The size of the jump depended on just where the animal finally came to rest. Usually it was only a metre or two to the ground, but sometimes you would really have to leap. It would take me a few minutes to roll the drugged animal into the net and hook it on to the chopper, then I'd have to swing myself back up onto the machine again and we'd be off, tracking down the next animal. To say it was hair-raising is an understatement.

I SQUIRRELLED AWAY MY SAVINGS until I had enough for the deposit on a small house in Gisborne. Then I went to the bank with Luke, and we got a loan and a joint bank account. At the age of 20 I was a proud home-owner. But I soon began to realise how different this life was from my past life, in which I'd had all this time to think—about life, ideas and ideals. Here in this world, it was all about survival and hanging on.

OPPOSITE My hunting, shooting and fishing days.
(Clockwise from top) In the wilderness, with my motorbike parked in the background; making craypots; duck shooting from my hiding place in the maimai (shelter); and making toastie pies. I'm wearing the ultimate in fashion: a Swanndri and pink long johns.

I tried to keep a handle on the cheque book, but Luke and money were like water in a sieve. If he had any cash, he would blow it at the pub with round after round for his mates, who were, for the most part, a dodgy lot. One couple, Heidi and Pete Buckle, were legendary for disappearing into the bush to go possum trapping for months at a time, leaving their tribe of Dickensian children with an old alcoholic called Stumpy. Before each trip, they would head down to the local Wattie's factory and fill their pickup with cases of damaged cans, which the factory sold for next to nothing. Back home again, they'd line the walls of the kitchen with their loot, hand Stumpy a can opener, and off they would go. No money. No nothing. Not even a phone call or a message as to when they might return.

The main problem (there was no limit to the strife in this particular household) lay in the fact that the damaged cans were unlabelled, so it was luck of the draw as to what they might contain. One year the entire hoard—all 40 cases that had been purchased—was canned beetroot. Not a single can of anything else. Apparently Stumpy and the kids spent the first week opening can after can, in the hope there might actually be something to eat, like baked beans or spaghetti or even corn, but no. It was all beetroot. Miraculously everyone lived to tell the tale.

The family lived in a derelict two-storey state house. A lady further up the road was known to have called the housing department once, to report that she was standing in her living room and could see a horse looking out of the top-floor window of the Buckles' house.

When the couple eventually came out of the bush and sold their skins, they would head to the local booze merchant, Williams & Kettle. Every cent earnt from that season's trapping would be spent on beer. This would get delivered to the house, and a chain gang would pass the crates of beer inside. Where there had been cans of food before the couple went bush, there were now crates of beer stacked high up the walls. Once everyone was inside, the door would be locked, and no one came out until the booze was finished. It was another world.

NOW THAT WE WERE LIVING in town, Luke made the pub his home. I hardly ever saw him. If he wasn't at the pub, who knew where he was? I didn't really know anyone other than Luke's suspect friends, and so as well as being exhausted I was lonely. Cooking became my refuge.

My mother, knowing my love of Julia Child's cooking, had given me the beautiful tome *Mastering the Art of French Cooking* for my birthday when I was 16. It had come on the boat with me, made the move to the cowshed, and was now by my bedside in the new house. I would go home laden with my bounty—a haunch of venison, a brace of squab, maybe a haul of crays—and escape into this masterly volume for hours, planning what to do with my loot. Julia recommended that newcomers to cooking approach it 'with courage and daring'. I was up for that.

Wild pigeons—the non-native kind—were my favourite. After the maize had been harvested in the autumn, kits of pigeons would fly into the cut paddocks to feed on the grain left behind. Most people have this image of pigeons as 'rats of the sky'—noisy birds that descend in parks, congregate around public statues and crap everywhere. Few would ever think of eating a pigeon. In the countryside, pigeons feed on grain and seeds, and their big breasts are fat and sweet, with a fine texture and a truly delicious flavour. In France, squab—young pigeons that have not yet flown—are considered the ultimate in game delicacies, and you'll pay more for them than any other bird.

Luke had taught me to stuff black socks with newspaper and set them out in the golden stubble of stalks as decoys. I'd hide in the long grass and wait for the pigeons to come zooming in around dusk to feed. Pull, *boom*. Pull, *boom*. Birds aplenty would fall out of the air. I'd take them home, and pluck and gut them. I'd learnt there wasn't much to the rest of the bird, and you only wanted the breasts. I checked to see what Julia had to say about them, but she didn't say anything, unfortunately. So I worked out that marinating the breasts, then barbecuing them to medium-rare rendered them unbelievably juicy, sweet and tender.

With all the crayfish we were catching, I quickly became a master of Julia's lobster thermidor. The recipe ran to four pages of instructions, and took several hours to prepare. First you had to simmer the lobsters— or, in my case, crayfish—with white wine, water, vegetables, herbs and seasonings. While that was happening, mushrooms would be sliced and gently cooked in butter with some lemon juice and salt. The cooking liquid from the mushrooms was added to the lobster stock. In another pot, you made a roux, thinned it with a little cream, mixed up egg yolks, more cream, mustard powder and a little cayenne, and added it to the roux sauce. You split the crayfish, took out the tail meat and chopped it up, then sizzled it in butter, added cognac and let it flame. Then it was time to mix the lobster meat with the sauce and the mushrooms, pile it back into the shells, sprinkle it with parmesan and bake until golden and bubbling. By the end, I always felt like I'd run a marathon and the kitchen was a bomb site, but cooking with Julia was a world I could happily get lost in for days.

I used to make a delicious cassoulet using wild ducks by adapting Julia's recipe for *cassoulet de porc et de mouton*. Sometimes I would roast the ducks with an orange sauce, adding an hour or two of cooking time in an attempt to coax some tenderness from their skinny, muscular frames.

There were no recipes for venison in Julia's book, but I liked to make Julia's *daube de boeuf à la provençal*, swapping the beef out for venison, and larding the meat with strips of ham instead of prosciutto, which was impossible to find. I'd then marinate it for a couple of days in red wine, olive oil and red wine vinegar, with onions, carrots, garlic and herbs, before simmering it for about four hours with the marinade liquid and some beef stock, tomatoes, orange peel and anchovies, and a roux thickening. Again, this was a dish that took forever to prepare, but it was sensational—heady, rich and meltingly tender.

My neighbours over the back fence became the enthusiastic recipients of my cooking endeavours. Peter and Veronica owned the local bakery, and I had worked there occasionally, helping to make meat pies and serve out the front. They loved my food, and their company was more than welcome. It was so good to have people appreciate and enjoy my cooking. Luke wasn't interested in any of my culinary creations, preferring his calories in the liquid form of a bottle of beer.

ONE DAY WHEN WE'D BEEN together for about a year, Luke said he needed to go and see his kids.

'Kids?' My eyes bugged. Like a guppy in a fishbowl, my mouth opened and closed, but no words would come out. This was the first I had heard about any kids.

'Yeah,' he said, looking out the window.

'Pardon?' It was all I could say. I must have misheard him.

'Four,' he said. 'All boys.' He shook his head and looked at the floor.

A million thoughts were rushing through my head, none of them joined up. It didn't make sense. He had four children? The idea beggared belief.

'So, um . . . Ah, what?' I said.

'I came home from fishing one day and found my wife in bed with my best mate,' Luke said. 'I jumped out the window and never went back. Then she put the kids in a children's home and did a runner.'

He had a wife? He had four small children? They were in a children's home, and had been for the entire time we had been together?

How could I not have known any of this?

I WENT WITH LUKE TO the children's home, and my heart nearly broke. It was beyond depressing. I brought the eldest boy home to live with us full-time. In the weekends, I'd pick up the three little ones to come and stay for the weekend. To try to make ends meet, I'd spend the mornings tacking skins to frames so they'd dry in a neat rectangular shape, then I'd scrub my hands and plait my hair, put on my red uniform and head downtown to front the till at KFC. ('Would you like the mash or the fries with that, sir?') Any spare time saw me running my traplines and doing the occasional stint as a jumper for the deer recovery guys.

One day, when I was collecting empty milk bottles so I could get the refund and have enough money to make Luke's four small children lunch, I had what you might call a lightbulb moment. *Bang.* The light went out. A physical sensation, as if something had cracked inside my heart. The love was gone, snuffed out forever.

With total clarity it came to me that, actually, these weren't my children, and this wasn't the life I wanted or had envisaged for myself. I had fallen for the wrong person. I needed to leave. It had taken me two and a half years.

I moved out, got a job at a vineyard out in the countryside, and continued to run a few traplines on my days off.

ONE DAY, I HEADED UP into the hills to work a stretch of bush that ran alongside the Hangaroa River. I'd been eyeing it up for a few months, as it looked like a nice, easy place to run a few traps.

I was busy laying out my traps when I heard the *clip-clop* of a horse's hooves, a man's voice and some dogs yapping. Maybe this wasn't a reserve, as I'd assumed. Maybe this was someone's farm. In which case, given that I hadn't asked anyone's permission, I would be poaching.

I scarpered up a big pūriri tree and hid, out of sight. I could hear some guy muttering about 'bloody possum trappers', as he threw my traps into the bushes. Horse and rider came to a stop right under my tree. My heart was pounding so loudly I was sure that whoever was below could hear it. *Kerthump, kerthump, kerthump.* In my head, it sounded like the wheels of a locomotive train as it winds up to leave the station. I peeked down through the branches, and the guy sitting on the horse was so good-looking I nearly fell out of the tree. But he never even glanced up, so he never saw me.

When he finally left, I waited for about an hour, then quietly climbed down out of the tree, gathered my traps and headed back to town.

It was the last time I ever went trapping.

IT WAS TIME FOR A fresh start. Back in Gisborne, I went in search of a flat with people who were from my side of the tracks. I found one on Hospital Road with two girls who were cousins, and moved in. There were farm maps all over the walls, places that looked very familiar from my trapping days, but that was an old life I wasn't going to talk about.

Susie was about five-foot-six, and Debbie was six-foot-three. She was by far the tallest girl I'd ever met. On my first night at that flat, I laughed so much that in the morning I thought I'd broken my ribs. These gals were so much fun.

One day, this really skinny, good-looking guy with the longest legs I'd ever seen turned up. He sat with us in the living room, and chatted with my tall flatmate.

I know you, I thought, *but you don't know me.*

He was the man I had spotted when I was hiding up that pūriri tree. Unbelievably, he was also Debbie's brother. I smiled, and said nothing.

PORK RILLETTES

READY IN 3½ HOURS + COOLING + CHILLING
MAKES FIVE 1-CUP-CAPACITY DISHES · DF · GF

800 g (1 lb 12 oz) skinless pork slices or pork belly, cut into finger-wide strips

3 cloves garlic, crushed to a paste with 1 tsp salt

2 bay leaves

1 small bunch fresh thyme or tarragon

2 star anise

½ tsp ground black pepper

½ cup white wine

¼ cup brandy

Rillettes are a kind of chunky pâté, and despite the fancy French name they're incredibly simple to make. I love to keep a stash of rillettes in the fridge or freezer, ready to serve to impromptu visitors or use for an easy lunch or a picnic. You can also make them with rabbit: use 500 g (1 lb 2 oz) rabbit meat and 300 g (10½ oz) pork fat.

Serve rillettes on open sandwiches with grain mustard, cress or rocket (arugula), radishes and Tangy Dijon Vinaigrette (see overleaf).

Preheat oven to 150°C (300°F) fanbake. Arrange pork in a single layer in a shallow roasting dish. Rub garlic paste over pork. Scatter with the herbs and star anise and season with pepper. Pour wine and brandy over pork. Cut a piece of baking paper to fit over the top, then cover the dish tightly with a lid or a double layer of tinfoil. Bake for 3 hours.

Discard herbs and star anise. Allow pork to cool, then chop coarsely and transfer to a food processor with 3–4 tablespoons of the cooking liquid. Pulse to form a coarse purée (don't blend to a smooth paste) or shred with two forks.

Divide pork rillettes into five 1-cup-capacity serving dishes. Cover and chill for at least 24 hours before serving. Rillettes will keep for up to 10 days in the fridge and can also be frozen.

TANGY DIJON VINAIGRETTE

READY IN 5 MINUTES · MAKES ½ CUP · DF · GF · V · VE

2 tbsp red wine vinegar

6 tbsp extra virgin
 olive oil

1 tsp dijon mustard

1 tsp honey or sugar

½ tsp salt

ground black pepper,
 to taste

½ clove garlic, crushed, or
 1 tbsp very finely diced
 shallot (optional)

Vinaigrette is such a signature dressing—I like to have a jar on hand in the fridge to liven up salads in a flash. If you prefer it less tangy, add a tablespoon or two of water.

Place all ingredients in a small jar, and stir or shake to dissolve honey or sugar. Adjust seasonings to taste.

The dressing will keep in a jar in the fridge for up to a week if it has garlic or shallot in it, or for weeks if it is made without. Shake before using.

BOUILLABAISSE WITH ROUILLE AND CROUTONS

READY IN 1½ HOURS · SERVES 8 · DF · GF, EXCEPT CROUTONS

½ cup extra virgin olive oil
2 small leeks, thinly sliced
1 onion, finely chopped
1 fennel bulb, thinly sliced
2 tbsp tomato paste
2 x 400 g (14 oz) cans chopped tomatoes
½ cup vermouth or dry white wine
4 cloves garlic, crushed
2–3 bay leaves
1–2 red chillies, to taste
a big pinch of saffron threads
1 tsp honey
8 cups fish stock
5 waxy potatoes, peeled and cut into bite-size chunks (optional)
salt and ground black pepper, to taste
24 cockles, clams or small mussels
8–16 large raw prawns (shrimp)
8 scampi (optional)
1 kg (2 lb 4 oz) boneless, skinless white fish fillets, cut into bite-size chunks

TO SERVE
Rouille (see overleaf)
Croutons (see overleaf)

This is my go-to recipe for weekend lunches and fishing holidays, and it always makes people feel as if they're being treated to something special. You can use as many different kinds of fish or seafood as you want, and it's a good way to enjoy lesser-known fish species. I always serve my bouillabaisse with rouille-topped croutons floating on top, and I put bowls of extra rouille and croutons on the table so guests can refill.

Heat oil in a large pot and cook leeks, onion and fennel over a low heat until they are soft but not brown (about 15 minutes).

Add tomato paste and sizzle for a couple of minutes. Stir in tomatoes, vermouth or wine, garlic, bay leaves, chillies, saffron and honey, and cook over a low heat for 20 minutes.

Add fish stock and potatoes (if using), bring back to a simmer and cook until potatoes are nearly cooked through (10–15 minutes). Season to taste with salt and pepper. (The soup can be prepared ahead to this stage, chilled for up to 2 days until needed, then brought back to a simmer to finish at the last minute.)

Five minutes before serving, add cockles, clams or mussels, cover and simmer for 3–4 minutes. Then add prawns, scampi (if using) and fish, and simmer for another 2–3 minutes until seafood is cooked and cockles, clams or mussels are open (discard any that don't open). Lift out and discard bay leaves and chillies.

To serve, divide soup between heated soup bowls. Spread rouille on a few croutons, float some in the bowls of soup, and serve the remaining rouille on the side with a bowl of croutons.

PICTURED OVERLEAF

ROUILLE

READY IN 15 MINUTES · MAKES ABOUT 1½ CUPS · DF · GF · V

1 large potato, boiled then mashed or put through a ricer
4 cloves garlic, crushed to a paste with a little salt
1 tsp minced chillies, or more to taste (it should be quite fiery)
1 tsp dried espelette pepper (optional)
1 tsp paprika
¼ tsp sweet smoked paprika
1 egg yolk
½ cup extra virgin olive oil

My wonderful cooking friend Danièle Mazet-Delpeuch showed me how to make this classic French rouille, which uses mashed potato as the base. It's so much nicer than a mayonnaise one.

Mix all ingredients except oil. Stir in oil to form a smoothish, spreadable paste.

Rouille will keep for 4–5 days in a jar in the fridge.

CROUTONS

READY IN 30 MINUTES · MAKES ABOUT 24 · DF · V · VE

1 loaf French bread, cut into slices
½ cup extra virgin olive oil
a little flaky salt

Preheat oven to 180°C (350°F) fanbake. Line an oven tray with baking paper for easy clean-up.

Brush or spray bread slices on both sides with a little oil and arrange in a single layer on prepared oven tray. Sprinkle with a little flaky salt. Bake until lightly golden and crisp (about 15 minutes). Allow to cool.

Croutons will keep fresh for up to 2 weeks in an airtight container. If they become a little stale, refresh for 5 minutes in an oven preheated to 180°C (350°F) fanbake.

RHUBARB TARTE TATIN

READY IN 1 HOUR + STANDING · SERVES 8–10 · V

60 g (2¼ oz) butter, soft but not melted
12 thin stalks rhubarb
1 tsp vanilla extract
finely grated zest of 1 orange
¾ cup sugar
⅓ recipe Sweet Sour Cream Pastry (see overleaf) or 200–250 g (7–9 oz) store-bought puff pastry
whipped cream or vanilla ice cream, to serve

The first time I ever ate tarte Tatin was in a little roadside trucker cafe on the outskirts of Paris. The tart was sitting on a raised cake stand on the counter looking very rustic—nothing like the fancy French pastries you usually see—but I just knew it would be good, and I was right.

Spread butter over the base of a 26–28 cm (10½–11¼ in) diameter ovenproof frying pan. Trim base from rhubarb and peel stalks with a small, sharp knife, stripping off the fibrous outer layer in long strands and discarding. Cut lengths of rhubarb so you have a row of tightly packed stalks covering the entire base of the pan. Stack any extra pieces on top here and there. Sprinkle with vanilla and orange zest, then sprinkle sugar evenly over the top to fully coat. Allow to stand for 30 minutes—the sugar will draw out excess juice from the rhubarb and stop it from falling apart when cooked.

Place pan over a medium-high heat and cook, shaking now and then, until the pan liquids are reduced and starting to caramelise around the edges (8–10 minutes). Remove from heat and allow to cool. (If not baking at once, it will hold at room temperature for up to 8 hours.)

Preheat oven to 180°C (350°F) fanbake.

Roll out pastry on a lightly floured board to a circle just a little bigger than the top of the pan. Arrange on top of fruit, tucking excess pastry inside the pan. Bake until syrup is caramelised around the edges and pastry is golden (45–50 minutes).

Remove from oven and allow to stand for 5–10 minutes. To turn out, place a plate on top of the pan then carefully flip the pan over to invert the tart onto the plate. Spoon any caramel from the pan over the top. Serve warm or at room temperature with whipped cream or vanilla ice cream.

SWEET SOUR CREAM PASTRY

READY IN 15 MINUTES + CHILLING · MAKES ABOUT 800 G (1 LB 12 OZ) · V

2¼ cups high-grade (bread) flour
2 tbsp sugar
240 g (8½ oz) butter, chilled
1 cup sour cream

This light, flaky pastry is excellent for any kind of sweet fruit tart. It makes enough for 3 tartes Tatin, 2 large, shallow tarts, 24 individual tarts or about 50 mini tarts. It will keep in the fridge for about a week or can be frozen. Leave out the sugar for a savoury version.

Place flour, sugar and butter in a food processor and whizz until the mixture resembles fine breadcrumbs. (If making by hand, cut butter into small cubes and use your fingertips to work into combined flour and sugar.)

Add sour cream and pulse or mix until the dough starts to come together into a ball. If it is still crumbly and does not bind, add a little cold water.

Form into a log shape, wrap in baking paper and chill for at least 20 minutes before using. It also freezes well.

FOUR

From paddock to plate

Growing grapes and restaurant rules

'Annabel! Annnnnabelll!' I looked up from the pavement to see someone waving furiously at me out of a car window as they drove past on the other side of the road. The car did a quick U-turn in the bustling Gisborne traffic, and pulled up with a screech beside me. A man jumped out and rushed up to me. 'Annabel! At last. I've been trying to find you for months.'

'Hey, Peter.' It was my old neighbour, the one who owned the bakery. 'Good to see you.'

'Where have you been?' he said.

'At uni down in Christchurch,' I replied. I'd just completed Lincoln University's Diploma in Horticulture, which was designed as a year-long intensive for people working in the industry. I'd had a vague idea that maybe I'd like to have my own vineyard, without really considering the fact that I didn't have the wherewithal to set up such an enterprise. Even so, the course enabled me to pirouette into a different life. During the year, I had polished up my Latin, thanks to the plant nomenclature system developed by Swedish naturalist Carl Linnaeus, studied economics and plant science, grown cells in Petri dishes in a lab, and learnt how to weld and how to fix tractors. I had arrived in Christchurch at the start of the year skinny and fit,

OPPOSITE Pruning in the vines at Patutahi,
near Gisborne, with one of my fellow workers.
PREVIOUS Working on the land always makes me happy.

but by the end of the year, as a result of a steady diet of beer and pies, I had gained a great many kilos and knew that I didn't want to own a vineyard.

The night before my final exam, I had received a telegram from the bank threatening to foreclose on the house in Gisborne, which Luke was still living in. I'd come back to sort it out, and ended up having to buy him out of the house.

'You,' Peter said. '*You*. Cooking at my new restaurant. It's going to be Italian.'

'What are you talking about?'

'I've built a new restaurant. I want you to be the chef.'

Peter and his wife, Veronica, might have shown great enthusiasm for the culinary creations I used to deliver over the fence to them, but I found it hard to believe that my cooking might have inspired the couple to start a restaurant with me as the chef.

'I don't actually know how to cook, Peter,' I said. 'I'm not a trained chef. I've never cooked professionally in my life.'

But Peter was not to be deterred. There on the side of the road, he coaxed and cajoled. 'You are an incredible cook, Annabel. Just amazing. This could be the start of your career.'

'But I'm saving up to go to South America.'

His face dropped. 'When?'

'In May.'

He perked up. 'Well, that gives us more than six months.'

And so it was done. In late November 1980, after finishing my Diploma in Horticulture (in which I gained, to my father's happiness, a distinction grade), I found myself at the helm of a small Italian restaurant just off the main street in Gisborne. It was called Morelli's. (Number 96 Derby Street is now occupied by the Gisborne Denture Clinic. Times change.)

I wrote a letter to my uni friend Glenys:

Right now I'm working in the vineyard. D. and M. are away, so I'm running the place in their absence. But some great news!!! I have been offered a job running and cooking at a new Italian restaurant which opens here in a few weeks. I've pretty well decided to take it, as it's something I've always wanted to do. It should be really good. It seats about 40 and there will be a kitchenhand and waitresses etc. so I won't have to work too hard.

Well, I sure as hell got that last bit wrong.

The restaurant seated maybe 36 people in a long, narrow room. Out the back, in the kitchen, Peter had installed the old Hobart mixer from the bakery. There was a commercial eight-burner gas oven, a big stainless-steel bench down the middle, a huge freezer and not such a big fridge. I decided I would have a daily blackboard menu that I'd put out on the street, next to the lunette window at the restaurant entrance. I thought about the gelato I had eaten with my mother in Venice, the markets in Rome, the pizza in Naples, the vegetable gardens in Capri, the wild spring flowers and almond blossom, and the way Italians lived so well and seemed happy, no matter what their circumstances were. I loved the ethos of Italian food, and the way Italian cooking was all about instinct and memory, not written recipes. Each week the same weight of cheese, so many bunches of spinach, so many onions, a hand-measure of flour or rice or parsley . . .

The wonderful Italian proverb 'at the table no one grows old' seems to sum up the way that Italian life is built around the pleasures of the table. Every day, old and young sit together, sharing delicious food and conversation. Everyone belongs and is welcome. The idea of eating close to the earth and the seasons, of being resourceful and wasting little, of respecting nature and sharing friendship—these were the things I wanted to bring to the new restaurant.

Elizabeth David was my muse, and I carried my dog-eared Penguin paperback edition of *Italian Food* wherever I went. I liked her advice that 'apart from the normal equipment of a good kitchen, Italian cooking demands few special pans or out of the way equipment', and her suggestion that 'as far as quantities, times of cooking and oven temperature are concerned I find it misleading to give exact details. So much depends upon appetite, mood and habit . . .' While Julia's recipes were written with exacting precision, down to the last eighth of a teaspoon, Elizabeth offered mostly broad-brush strokes of ideas. She conveyed how a certain dish might go together with the rough-and-ready amounts by which Italian cooks tend to measure their ingredients, where and why you might eat the dish, and, most importantly, the bits that actually mattered in the recipe.

> This was my kind of cooking. It required
> me to engage my senses and be present, not
> just follow the road map of an exact recipe,
> which might or might not work depending
> on the size and heat of my pan.

Her tasty little appetiser *crostini di fegatini*, or chicken liver crostini, quickly became a mainstay on my menu. The ingredients are listed for two people as: '6–8oz chicken livers, a slice of ham, butter, 4 slices of French bread, lemon juice, a little flour, a few tablespoons of stock'. Elizabeth tells us to: 'Clean the chicken livers, taking care that the little greenish piece which is the bile is removed. If any is left you ruin the flavour of the livers.' After the livers are cleaned, you chop them up and dredge them in flour. In a frying pan, you heat some butter, chop the ham and brown it, then add the chicken livers. The instructions are to cook the livers gently, and that they must not be fried. Once they have started to colour, you add a little stock and lemon juice, salt and very little pepper, then cover the pan. 'The livers will be perfectly cooked in 10 minutes.' What else do you need from a recipe?

This was my kind of cooking. It required me to engage my senses and be present, not just follow the road map of an exact recipe, which might or might not work depending on the size and heat of my pan. Yes, a basic understanding of cooking was required, but then you had to use your own taste and judgement. It made sense to say you needed enough oil to cover the bottom of the pan when cooking aromatic vegetables for a stew, rather than specifying an amount. As Elizabeth so wisely says: 'What, in fact, you need is enough oil to cover the bottom surface of your pan; enough for your onions and other vegetables to be evenly spread out in it, neither swimming in oil because there's too much nor rapidly drying out, catching, and burning because there is not enough.' The amount will depend on the size of your pan, how wide and heavy it is, and the nature of the heat source you are using to cook on.

While Julia Child had taught me how to follow a recipe to a successful outcome, it was Elizabeth David who taught me how to become a good cook.

I NEEDED TO WORK OUT a menu with lots of things that I could just assemble or heat up, and a couple of last-minute things that could be cooked quickly on the stovetop. There were no sous-chefs here, just Sue, my able, helpful kitchenhand-cum-dishwasher.

It was coming in to summer when the restaurant opened, so too hot for stalwart Italian dishes like minestrone or osso bucco, but baked pasta dishes like lasagne and cannelloni were always popular, and could be made in advance and heated to order. I also had a stash of home-made ravioli that I stored in the freezer. Dishes which required the pasta to be cooked precisely to order, such as carbonara or marinara, were off the menu—I just couldn't manage the timing, and nor did I have the stove space. Risotto was out too, since I didn't know then, as I do now, how to par-cook it so that it takes a mere 10 minutes to finish cooking. (Start by using only half the stock and cooking the rice until it has just absorbed the liquid, then set aside for later. About 10 minutes before serving, add the rest of the stock and finish cooking.)

I decided that a small board of pizza bread topped with nothing more than rosemary, salt and olive oil would be served to guests as they arrived and sat down—just a little wedge to pique their appetites. And, at the end, a home-made amaretti cookie or a tiny piece of panforte would be sent out with the coffee.

Antipasti were a great starter offering—grilled and marinated vegetables, seasoned olives, marinated cheeses, stuffed mushrooms, and cold cuts that could be mixed and matched. They were easy to construct as platters, and people liked them.

Elizabeth's recipe for saltimbocca caught my eye. Literally meaning 'jump into the mouth', it required thin slices of veal, an equal number of sage leaves, salt, pepper and Marsala. You flattened out the veal with a mallet, rolled a sage leaf inside, secured it with a toothpick, pan-fried it in lots of butter until golden, then finished by simmering it in the Marsala. It didn't take me long to work out that this sweet Sicilian dessert wine wasn't appealing to most New Zealanders' palates, so I riffed on Elizabeth's version—I sautéed sliced button mushrooms in butter, added the sage-filled rolls to brown, then sizzled them in some garlic and lemon zest, followed by white wine, cream, a small grating of parmesan, and lots of black pepper. The sauce would boil down to a rich, creamy coating, and in less than 10 minutes this thing of glory would be ready for the table. Soon, people were calling ahead to ask if I had 'the creamy meat rolls' on the menu that night. They really were delicious. If you boiled the sauce down too far, though, it would annoyingly split, but I discovered that you

OPPOSITE (Clockwise from top) Cooling down after a day's work in the vines; Lincoln Uni days; and making a cuppa in my new house in Gisborne.

could rescue it by adding a splash more cream—with a stir, it would come back together like magic. Adding cream became my default for so many sauces, whether spinach and garlic, mushrooms, tomatoes or peppers. It was a reliably easy shortcut to rich, satisfying flavours.

By far the most popular dish on my menu was based on Elizabeth's *maiale al latte*, or pork cooked in milk. Her method used a pork loin or boneless, skinless pork leg, but this was tricky for me, as the whole thing had to be cooked on the stovetop and required careful watching to make sure it didn't catch. But there was something in the milk that rendered the pork unctuously, meltingly tender. (I now know it's the enzymes in the milk, which act on proteins to break them down and soften the muscle fibres.) I decided to make the dish using pork belly and cook it in the oven instead. I'd get the skin puffed and crackling first in a hot oven, then turn the temperature down to low and pour milk all around the meat, then leave it to slow-cook for a couple of hours. The result was sensational. Even better, I could get quite a few portions out of each roast and, if needed, reheat it to serve the following day. In my first series of *The Free Range Cook* on TV, I featured this recipe. Apparently when that particular episode aired, the whole country sold out of pork belly.

Dessert was probably my greatest strength. Each night there would be a fruit tart and some kind of dense cake, usually made with almond flour. My mother's recipe for ice cream was the starting point for many of the frozen desserts I served at the restaurant. I scaled up her recipe for the base 20 times, first whipping up 10 litres of cream in the old Hobart, then taking that out and beating 60 egg yolks and 10 cups of sugar until pale and ribbony. The egg-and-sugar mixture then got added to the cream. Next, I had to wash the bowl *really* well before beating the 60 egg whites with another two cups of sugar, until they formed a smooth meringue— if you got even a drop of egg yolk in the mixture, it wouldn't pillow up. Finally, the three mixtures got folded together, and could be flavoured in multiple incarnations—chocolate and nuts, berries and white chocolate, marmalade and macadamia, as well as fruit purées. Apricot, feijoa, plum ... The great thing was, you didn't need an ice-cream machine to achieve a smooth, creamy texture.

For my Italian cassata, I would soak currants in amaretto then fold them through the ice-cream base with chopped glacé fruits, pistachios and berries, and freeze the mixture in loaf pans so I could easily portion it into slices.

Sometimes I learnt the hard way. Overwhip 10 litres of cream too far, and you can't get it back. You just have to keep going until you have butter. But, if you catch it just as it starts to clod, you can gently fold in more cream and bring it back. *Whew.*

IT WAS, IN SO MANY WAYS, a different time. Many of the ingredients that Elizabeth called for simply didn't exist in New Zealand at the time. Olive oil was more likely to be found in a chemist than a supermarket. You'd never see vegetables like fennel or fresh artichokes anywhere. And, when it came to cheese, you could forget about fresh mozzarella or good-quality parmesan. If an ingredient wasn't available here, you had to either find an alternative or find another recipe.

Then there was the mindset New Zealanders had about food and eating. People weren't coming to Morelli's to show off their sophistication and status. They didn't want to be challenged when they sat down to eat, or to be served anything they couldn't actually recognise as food. They weren't interested in exotic, technique-driven dishes that demonstrated the technical prowess of the savvy person at the stove.

The celebrity chef, the celebrity farmer, the celebrity vegetable— all that was yet to come. There was no notion of food as a 'new religion', with restaurants as temples of status and chefs as super-celebrities. The politicisation of food, the ideas of environmental stewardship and ethical purchasing, the dietary trends of removing whole categories of food, the concept of culinary appropriation—none of it existed. People ate for sustenance, and sometimes to be sociable.

Back then we were, to put it bluntly, a nation of neophobes. Steak was a firm favourite with the customers at Morelli's, and, even though I offered it served with a tangy sweet-sour eggplant caponata, it was the garlicky herb butter that remained the number-one favourite. And so, for all the adrenaline and energy of nightly cooking, it wasn't long before I realised that working at a restaurant stove was not my long-term vocation. People basically wanted to eat things they liked and were familiar with. 'Make it like my mother made, please. Not different, please. I don't like it different.' If I put anything new or slightly challenging on the daily menu, it was ignored, and I'd be asked, 'When can we have the veal rolls again?' or, 'Why isn't the pork belly on the menu?'

COOKING THE SAME THINGS OVER and over was actually really boring. The antidote? Party hard after work. Gisborne was a fun place to be in your early twenties. The town was already a surfing mecca, the wine industry was getting established, and the well-heeled young farming crowd were always up for a shindig.

When I came back from Christchurch, I had moved back in to my old flat on Hospital Road with the two cousins. At the end of December, a new friend, Mary—who coined my nickname, Bella—called to say that one of her rellies was having a New Year's celebration out at their farm. Did we want to go? We arrived to a huge, spectacular scene—marquees, bars, bands, and stacks and stacks of hay bales laid out for people to sit on. As midnight approached, a flying fox dispatched a blazing hay bale about

OPPOSITE (Clockwise from top left) Sun, sea and happy times on the East Coast; at the Lincoln Uni ball; and with a Gizzy friend at Secret Bay.

50 metres down into an old wreck of a car that had been filled with petrol. *BOOM*. Welcome to the New Year. Those Gisborne people really knew how to party.

Sometimes after work, when nothing else was happening in town, my coworker Sue and I would drive to the carpark at the back of the Royal Hotel and get really stoned. If someone had asked us to open the door, they would have thought the car was on fire. We laughed until we cried. When the munchies set in, we would sneak back to the restaurant and raid the freezer for ice cream.

AFTER I LEFT LUKE, I had sold my motorbike and bought an old green Vauxhall for a couple of hundred bucks. It didn't have reverse—which was a challenge for Gisborne's angle parking, so I rode my pushbike into work at the restaurant—and you couldn't get the key out of the lock, so it wasn't secure. I was always worried that someone (like Luke) might steal the car, so I'd take the rotor out and carry it around in my handbag.

I liked fixings things, and was always pottering with cars—changing brake pads, checking fuel filters, changing the oil and spark plugs. The annoying beep when you reversed in one of my friend's new Toyotas was easily eliminated by disconnecting the fuse—you just had to remember to reconnect it, as it also controlled the indicator!

For all my time up the river and in the bush, however, I knew next to nothing about horses. My flatmate Debbie, on the other hand: there wasn't anything she didn't know about them. In the weekends, she would often invite me up to her family's homestead property, where there were over 160 horses. The entire family was horse-mad. As well as running the family farms on horseback, Debbie's dad had a business contract packing for other farms—loading horses with fencing materials and scrub-cutting gear, and taking them out to the back country.

Debbie taught me to ride on Bonanza, one of the family's trusty ponies.

She was a clever, greedy little horse. If the grass looked to be even slightly greener on the other side of the fence, Bonanza wanted to be there, but at heart she was profoundly lazy. To get herself into those greener pastures, Bonanza would trot up to the fence, stop abruptly, snort, then turn around and bite herself on the bum. It took about half an hour of repeating this— up to the fence, turn and bite—to work herself up to actually jumping the fence. Bonanza always cleaned up at the local sports, but for all her speed on the flat events she was a 100 per cent safe steer for any new rider. Debbie and Bonanza guided me safely up and down the razorback hills on the farm. Before long I was happy to saddle up my own horse and ride out the back. There was nothing I loved more than that wonderful feeling of freedom, cantering over the hills with the wind in my hair.

Debbie's handsome brother Ted wasn't often around, but occasionally he would pop in to see us at the flat. There was just something about this guy. I could feel the spark. I can even remember contemplating the idea of asking him if he might like to go to South America with me—but of course I didn't. I didn't want him asking about what I did, and I certainly didn't want him to know that it was me who had been poaching on his farm.

I needed to save as much money as I could for my upcoming trip. When I wasn't at the restaurant, I was either working at the vineyard or painting houses. By the time May rolled around, I had managed to save $5000. My Spanish-language book lay on the floor of the farm loo. I had only made it to page seven: 'The verb'. I had no idea that, where I was headed, almost no one spoke English. There was one thing I was sure of, though: cooking in a restaurant was not for me. It would remain a hobby.

My friends Julio and Sylvie had travelled ahead, and were waiting for me in Buenos Aires. It was time to leave for new horizons.

MELT-IN-THE-MOUTH PORK BELLY

READY IN 3¼ HOURS + RESTING · SERVES 6 · GF

about 1.3 kg (3 lb) pork
  belly, skin scored
ground black pepper,
  to taste
1 tsp salt
2–3 sage leaves
2–2½ cups milk
Smoky Red Pepper Sauce
  (see overleaf), to serve

This is a very traditional Italian way to cook pork belly—one I learnt from Elizabeth David's book. You blast the pork in a hot oven to get the skin crunchy, then slow-cook it in a bath of milk, which makes it really moist and tender. I used to serve this dish when I was cooking in a little Italianesque restaurant in Gisborne.

Serve with Smoky Red Pepper Sauce, lightly cooked green beans and crispy potatoes.

Preheat oven to 240°C (475°F) fanbake.

Pat the skin of the pork belly dry and season the flesh side with pepper and half the salt. Place sage leaves in the base of a metal roasting dish (do not use a glass dish as it might shatter when you add the milk) and place pork on top, skin-side up. Season top with remaining salt. Roast until skin is starting to blister and crackle (20–30 minutes), watching closely for burning.

Remove from oven and pour milk around pork (not on the skin) to come a little more than halfway up the sides of the pork. Reduce oven temperature to 160°C (315°F) and return pork to oven. Roast until pork is meltingly tender (a further 2½ hours). Check liquid during cooking and if it has evaporated add a little more milk.

Lift pork out of dish and allow to cool. Discard the cooking liquids (they will break into curds, which are delicious but look very unappealing). For easy cutting, place pork flesh-side up on a chopping board and use a heavy, sharp knife to cut it into slices about 3 cm (1¼ in) thick. Serve warm or at room temperature with Smoky Red Pepper Sauce.

SMOKY RED PEPPER SAUCE

READY IN 45 MINUTES · MAKES 2 CUPS · DF · GF · V · VE

6 red peppers
¼ cup extra virgin olive oil
2 cloves garlic, crushed
1 tsp paprika (plain)
1 tsp sweet smoked
  paprika
½ cup almonds, roasted
salt and ground black
  pepper, to taste

Preheat oven to 240°C (175°F) fanbake. Line an oven tray with baking paper for easy clean-up.

Place peppers on tray and roast until skin is blistered and blackened (15–20 minutes).

Remove from oven, cover with a tea towel or transfer to a plastic bag (this will make it much easier to remove the skins). Set aside to cool for about 20 minutes.

While peppers cool, heat oil in a small frying pan and sizzle garlic and paprika for a few seconds to bring out their flavour.

Once peppers have cooled, remove and discard skins and seeds, saving the juices if you can. Place the flesh and any reserved juices in a food processor or blender with garlic mixture. Add almonds, salt and pepper, and purée until smooth. If mixture is too thick, add a little more oil to create a spoonable consistency. Smoky Red Pepper Sauce will keep for a week in a sealed container in the fridge and freezes well.

BEST-EVER LASAGNE

READY IN 2½ HOURS · SERVES 10–12

400 g (14 oz) dried instant lasagne sheets, preferably an Italian brand

1 cup grated mozzarella (not fresh mozzarella)

½ cup grated parmesan

BOLOGNESE SAUCE

2 stalks celery, coarsely chopped

1 large onion, coarsely chopped

1 large carrot, coarsely chopped

3 cloves garlic, coarsely chopped

¼ cup extra virgin olive oil or 60 g (2¼ oz) butter

100 g (3½ oz) tomato paste

5 canned anchovies, drained (optional)

1 kg (2 lb 4 oz) beef mince (ground beef)

2 tsp salt

1 tsp ground black pepper

3 x 400 g (14 oz) cans chopped tomatoes

1 cup red wine

½ tsp freshly grated nutmeg

a pinch of ground cloves

I can't think of another dish in the world that better represents comfort food. Making lasagne is always a bit of a production, but you end up with a big dish that feeds a crowd. If I'm not serving lots of people, I portion the lasagne up and freeze it—it's such a great meal to pull out on a cold night after a long day. You can make a vegetarian version if you prefer: replace the meat sauce with 10 cups of vegetable filling (such as spinach and ricotta or ratatouille). Serve with a crisp green salad dressed with Tangy Dijon Vinaigrette (see page 96).

To make Bolognese Sauce, place celery, onion, carrot and garlic in a food processor and whizz until very finely chopped (almost a purée), or chop very finely by hand.

Heat oil or butter in a medium heavy-based pot or deep frying pan. Add chopped vegetables and cook over a medium heat until soft but not brown (about 8 minutes).

Make a space in the bottom of the pan and drop in tomato paste and anchovies (if using). Cook, stirring, until aromatic (about 1 minute). Add beef, salt and pepper and stir over heat, breaking up beef with the back of a spoon, until no longer pink.

Stir in tomatoes, wine, nutmeg and ground cloves and bring to a simmer. Reduce heat to lowest level and cook, uncovered, stirring now and then, for 40 minutes. Adjust seasonings to taste. (Bolognese Sauce can be prepared ahead and chilled for up to 4 days or frozen until needed.)

While Bolognese Sauce is cooking, prepare White Sauce.

INGREDIENTS AND RECIPE CONTINUED OVERLEAF

WHITE SAUCE
4½ cups milk
3 bay leaves
100 g (3½ oz) butter
¾ cup plain flour
½ tsp freshly grated
  nutmeg
salt and fine white
  pepper, to taste

Place milk and bay leaves in a pot or microwave-proof bowl and heat gently. Melt butter in a medium pot. Add flour and stir over a medium heat for 1 minute, until flour is lightly toasted. Discard bay leaves from hot milk. Add about half the milk to the butter and flour mixture, stirring continuously. As sauce starts to thicken, add remaining milk and continue stirring hard until sauce is smooth and thick. (If it goes lumpy, whizz it with a hand wand blender or electric beater.) Stir in nutmeg. Season to taste with salt and pepper. Simmer gently for 5 minutes, stirring now and then so it doesn't catch on the bottom. (If not using at once, transfer to a bowl and cut a piece of baking paper to sit directly in contact with the top of the sauce so it doesn't form a skin. It will keep for 2–3 days in the fridge. Reheat with a little extra milk to loosen.)

When ready to cook the lasagne, preheat oven to 180°C (350°F) fanbake.

Spread 1 cup of White Sauce thinly over the base of a deep 20-cup-capacity oven dish measuring about 32 cm x 22 cm (12½ in x 8½ in) or two deep-sided 10-cup-capacity oven dishes. Cover with a layer of lasagne sheets, breaking them to fit as needed to fully cover sauce. Spread a fifth (about 2 cups) of the Bolognese Sauce thinly over the pasta (it's just a thin layer and this gives the lasagne the right balance).

Repeat layers of pasta and Bolognese Sauce, finishing with a layer of pasta. You should have 5 layers of sauce and 6 layers of pasta. Spread a thick layer of White Sauce evenly over the top. Combine mozzarella and parmesan cheeses and sprinkle over the top. (Lasagne can be prepared to this point, covered and chilled for up to 24 hours. Bring back to room temperature for an hour before final cooking.)

Loosely cover lasagne with tinfoil and bake for 45 minutes, then uncover and bake until golden and cooked through (a further 15–20 minutes). Cooked lasagne will keep in the fridge for up to 4 days. It can also be frozen; thaw before reheating.

PERFECT PANFORTE

READY IN 1¼ HOURS · SERVES 20 · DF, IF DARK CHOCOLATE IS DAIRY-FREE · GF, IF GLUTEN-FREE FLOUR IS USED · V

1 cup skin-on almonds

1 cup hazelnuts

2½ cups dried fruit, such as mixed peel, raisins, chopped dried figs, dried cranberries or dried cherries

⅔ cup plain flour or gluten-free flour

2 tbsp cocoa

1 tsp cinnamon

½ cup honey

½ cup sugar

60 g (2¼ oz) dark chocolate, chopped

icing (confectioners') sugar, to dust

I always don a clean pair of dishwashing gloves to mix this dense festive Italian fruit cake, as it's very heavy to mix with a spoon and you need to work fast so the toffee mixture doesn't set before it's mixed through the fruit and nuts. The recipe scales up easily and you can play around with different types of fruit and nuts as long as you keep the ratios consistent.

Preheat oven to 180°C (350°F) fanbake. Thoroughly grease a 20 cm (8 in) diameter springform cake tin or line it with baking paper. Line a shallow roasting dish with baking paper for easy clean-up.

Spread almonds and hazelnuts out at either end of prepared roasting dish and roast until nuts are fragrant and skins are splitting on hazelnuts (12–15 minutes). Cool. Place hazelnuts in a clean tea towel and rub between your hands to remove most of the loose skins (don't worry if they don't all come off). Transfer nuts to a large bowl, add dried fruit, flour, cocoa and cinnamon, and stir to combine.

Boil honey and sugar in a pot until mixture reaches 'soft ball' stage. You'll know it's ready when it reaches 112–116°C (234–241°F) on a candy thermometer, or when a small drop of mixture dropped into a glass of cold water forms a soft ball when rolled between your fingers.

Remove from heat, add chocolate and stir until it is melted and the mixture is smooth. Pour into dry ingredients and, working quickly, mix with gloved hands or a very strong wooden spoon until combined. Press evenly into prepared cake tin and bake until set (about 35 minutes).

Remove from tin while still warm. When cool, dust liberally with icing sugar. Panforte will keep for weeks in an airtight container.

FIVE

South America

A gift in disguise

It was a bizarre series of events—the likes of which could only ever happen when solo backpacking around South America in the eighties—and a bout of near-lethal food poisoning that landed me in Búzios, on the coast of Brazil, in the summer of 1981.

At the very start of my journey, I had spent a few days there with some friends of my parents who lived in Rio de Janeiro. We had relaxed on the glorious white-sand beach, eaten the freshest grilled-prawn skewers from a beach vendor, swum for hours in the clearest azure waters, and windsurfed out round the tiny green knuckle of Ilha do Caboclo, just a few hundred yards out to sea. In the early eighties, Búzios was already the place to party. The moneyed élite from Argentina, Uruguay and Brazil had been coming there to play since the sixties, when Brigitte Bardot first hid in the town with her Brazilian boyfriend, Bob Zagury. The city's full name, Armação dos Búzios, told of its fishing past, with *armação* denoting a fishing method, and the town retained the rustic charm of a fishing village, with cobbled streets and tiny colourful fishing boats pegging the curve of the bay.

Seven months of solo travelling later, I was lonely and homesick. It had been months since I'd come across anyone who spoke English, so when I met up with three young gringo guys near the border of Ecuador and Peru, I tagged along with them. It was a relief to spend time in the company

OPPOSITE Travelling in Peru, before I got hit by Montezuma's revenge.
PREVIOUS Hanging out in Búzios on the Brazilian coast.

of these friendly and easy-going Americans, and I could see myself continuing to travel with them for a while. We headed south together, to cross into Peru, and stopped en route at a tiny beach shack selling ceviche. I hadn't ever eaten ceviche before. It was delicious—tangy with lemon, and fragrant with coriander, with a light chilli kick. However, when we reached the border, my new friends informed me delicately that it wouldn't be a good idea to cross into Peru with them. It seemed they'd been involved in running drugs, and didn't want me getting roped into it. And so I found myself on my own once again.

> I longed for home, for books and for conversations around the table. I missed the scent of my father's sweetpeas, raiding the home baking in my mother's pantry, the landscape, the light, the bush, the scents and earth and hills of home.

I got on yet another bus, this time heading south towards Lima. As the bus rumbled along, I felt more homesick than ever. I also started to feel queasy. Thinking it was a product of the travel and the fishy smell in the seaside air, I hopped off the bus six hours into the journey, in Pisco, home of the pisco sour. And it was there, sitting in a bar, that, *bang*—as if it had been hit by a train—my normally cast-iron digestive system turned itself into a fire hydrant of unhappiness. I made a sprint to the bar's dark, filthy bathroom as my body attempted to eradicate every vestige of that innocent-looking ceviche. The wrath of Montezuma knew no bounds. Never in my life had I been so sick.

I ended up holing up with a friend of my sister who worked at the embassy in Lima, but it took weeks for me to slowly regain my strength. I called home several times, and cried a lot. Illness, exhaustion and loneliness had triggered an intense homesickness. I longed for home, for books and for conversations around the table. I missed the scent of my father's sweetpeas, raiding the home baking in my mother's pantry, the landscape, the light, the bush, the scents and earth and hills of home. My parents, aware of a great many of my hair-raising travel experiences, were anxious to see me back in one piece. 'Come home,' they said. 'We can lend you the money for your flight. Please, come home.'

But, homesick as I was, I wasn't ready to go home. 'I'm going back to Brazil,' I announced. I needed to keep going, to find out who I was and what made me tick, away from the framework of my own culture. 'I'm going back to Búzios, that beautiful place by the sea. I think I can stay there a while.'

Once I made it to Brazil, the first leg of my journey back to Búzios was a relaxing, air-conditioned trip of under three hours from Rio to Cabo Frio. *Things are looking up*, I remember thinking. Then it was time to jump off and find the local Salineira bus B150. For the next 45 minutes, the bus bumped and shuddered along an unsealed road out to the peninsula, finally reaching Búzios in the early dusk. I stepped off into a throng of locals, all gabbering in Portuguese, not another tourist in sight. On my back was my faithful red pack, containing all my worldly belongings, and clutched in my hand was a crumpled piece of paper bearing the name and phone number of a friend of a friend who might have a room that maybe, just maybe, I could rent.

BEFORE MY TRIP, back in Gisborne, I had been living off the radar. I'd had no idea of the genocide that had been going on in Argentina. Between 1976 and 1983, military and security forces and right-wing death squads hunted down, tortured and killed thousands of people in an attempt to silence social and political opposition. Their efforts were targeted at anyone they even vaguely considered might pose a political or ideological threat to the right-wing regime. Night raids were a common feature of this time, and people would be dragged from their beds, their families sobbing and pleading, never to be seen again. The number of people who were killed or who disappeared during these years is put at between 9,000 and 30,000. In 2005, a conviction was made against a former Argentine naval officer for his part in a regular exercise that saw groups of up to 20 prisoners held at the infamous Escuela Superior de Mecánica de la Armada, a naval mechanics school in Buenos Aires. The prisoners were held temporarily, then drugged and taken to the airport, put on board a plane, flown out to sea and pushed out. This took place every week for about two years.

> One day we were chased and shot at by police
> in a car. We got away, and no one was hurt, but
> it was truly terrifying . . . after that incident I
> made the call to head off and travel on my own.

I had briefly come up against this oppressive regime when I had first arrived in Buenos Aires in the autumn and, through friends of a friend, found myself joining up with a group of young left-wing idealists. For a couple of months, I had squatted with them in a building site in San Isidro and worked as a painter (not the artistic kind) in the city. Then one day we were chased and shot at by police in a car. We got away, and no one was hurt, but it was truly terrifying. I had absolutely no idea of the potentially life-ending consequences of being caught, but after that incident I made the call to head off and travel on my own. I hadn't come all this way to get killed in anyone's Dirty War.

MY SCRUFFY PIECE OF PAPER led me to a small house at the far end of Búzios, near the sea. When I arrived, I explained who I was and who had sent me. 'Ahh . . .' The woman who had answered the door smiled kindly at me. She would've loved to have had me stay, she said, but the problem was her mother had come to live with her, and now there was no space in her house. She took my arm and led me across the road to a white wooden cottage. One of her friends lived there, and might have a room I could rent.

Margara, my new landlady, was a very chic, well-heeled Argentinian. She lived with her boyfriend and their rangy dog, and she designed and made clothes that she took up to New York to sell. Petite and dark-haired, she was always stylishly dressed, with a wide, laughing smile framed in dark cherry-red lipstick. She welcomed me into her home, including me in her circle of friends, a privileged crowd of ex-pats. Most of them were from Buenos Aires, and had moved to Búzios to escape the horrors of the Dirty War.

It was easy to see why they had come to this enchanting place. The beauty of Búzios was one long, rolling cliché—the sun shining with a sultry benevolence in the bluest of blue skies, lush swathes of creamy jasmine flowers, purple passionfruit and scarlet bougainvillea spilling down walls and fences, filling the air with giddy tropical aromas, dreamy white sands and a glittering cobalt sea. With Rio just 160 kilometres away, the city's wealthy Cariocas would descend upon Búzios every weekend to party, filling the beaches with beautiful bronzed bodies, playing frescobol on the white sand, and jiving away the nights in the clubs. The friends I made in Búzios were all residents, building their own businesses—hotels and restaurants and tourism ventures. When the tourists ran away, they would stay.

My room was small with a little window framed in blue. The walls were freshly painted a bright, clean white, and there was a single bed. With a price tag of NZ$130 a month, it was expensive at the time. I couldn't quite see the ocean, but it was right there, about 50 steps away: the Praia dos Ossos. The cottage was tiny—just two bedrooms and a small living area—but, best of all, there was a kitchen, with a stove with a gas-burner top.

I had a visceral need to cook. It was all I wanted to do. The past months had been a continual film reel of new faces and new places, and deep inside

I knew that cooking could anchor me and make me feel whole again. In Búzios, I felt that I'd finally found a place I could put down roots and make friends. Here, I could cook, and the world would be right again. Every morning I would get up and bake chocolate cake with dulce de leche, choux pastry puffs, panettone, genoise sponge, churros, cashew-nut ice cream, sweet-potato cake, and fudge. Lots and lots of fudge.

Once my sweet-tooth cravings had been satisfied, I would move on to savoury imaginations, whipping up empanadas filled with a tasty mixture of minced beef, onions, potato, raisins, hard-boiled eggs, sherry and spices. I prepared braised tongue, chilled and thinly sliced with chilli and coriander-spiked vinaigrette that I had learnt to make in Buenos Aires. I baked fish with oranges and limes and chillies, the way they did on the coast in Colombia. I made lobster thermidor à la Julia Child and even, dare I say it, ceviche.

> I had a visceral need to cook. It was all I wanted to do. The past months had been a continual film reel of new faces and new places, and deep inside I knew that cooking could anchor me and make me feel whole again.

There was so much fresh seafood to be had, and a good butcher right in town. It was hard to find all the pantry ingredients I wanted—spices, soy sauce, Dijon mustard, even honey—but luckily I knew enough to improvise. At night I would cook dinner for the house. The table only seated six, but people would turn up and we would squeeze them in—the

OPPOSITE (Clockwise from top left) Boating in Brazil; the pack of dogs that always joined me on my daily beach walk; backgammon in the bar with Golero and Mario-José; having a laugh with Margara, my fabulous landlady; and wild times in Búzios on a steady diet of caipirinhas and croissants.

more the merrier. Seldom was I out of the kitchen. I think my newfound friends thought I was barmy. We were having dinner one night when Manolo, a tall morose man enquired, '*¿Puedes hacer medialunas? ¿Cómo se dice? Croissants . . . croissants.*'

By this stage, I was dreaming in Spanish, so understanding him wasn't an issue—but *could* I make croissants?

'*Sí, puede ser,*' I replied. 'Yes' tends to be the customary answer when you are young. You figure it out afterwards.

I had eaten ethereal croissants in Paris with my mother, and also gorged myself on the little crisp ones served for afternoon tea every day in Buenos Aires, so I knew the finished product needed to be flaky and light, not cloddy and doughy. It needed to just disappear like a cloud in your mouth.

I also knew that making them was a complex process involving layers of butter and a yeasted dough that had to be warm enough to rise but not so hot that the butter would melt. It was time to call my mother. She was the expert, with her fabulous collection of recipe books and understanding of the chemistry of cooking. Over the phone, she explained the whole process to me, and promised to send me some drawings. A few weeks later a pile of detailed, beautiful step-by-step sketches outlining the process of making croissants arrived.

There was just one problem. Butter, a key ingredient in the recipe, was hard to find and also very expensive. As luck would have it, I discovered that in Argentina croissants, or *medialunas*, are often made with lard instead of butter, which makes them shorter and crisper. Lard's fine texture and delicate flavour make it perfect for pastries and pie crusts, and it was in fact this kind of croissant—the croissant of their homeland—that my newfound friends were hankering for. And so I went to the butcher in search of the soft white fat found around a pig's kidneys, which produces the finest lard. Next, I had to render it. You can't just whizz up the fat—you need to heat it so that it is creamy and smooth and spoonable. Rendered fat is also shelf-stable, like olive oil or clarified butter, because the process removes all the impurities that might cause it to spoil.

After a bit of trial and error, I found the best way to make lard was to finely chop the raw fat, then put it in a pot over a very low heat with a cup of water and the lid on. Over the next few hours the fat slowly melted, while the water stopped it from browning. By the time all the fat was completely melted, the water would be fully evaporated. Along the way, little bits of crackling would rise to the surface. I'd lift them out with a slotted spoon and sprinkle them with salt, and they were the crispiest, most moreish nuggets of crackling imaginable. As far as my weight was concerned, it was the beginning of the end. My new diet consisted of croissants, crackling and cocktails.

I still have the croissant recipe I used in my old travel diary, but it is so vague and lacking in detail that I don't know if I could make it work now. It reads:

9 cups H_2O

5 tbsp salt

5 tbsp sugar

¾ cup oil

2½ kg flour (½ kg for kneading)

Yeast 1 cup water

Larding—10 cups lard, i.e. divide into 10, each turn ¼ cup

400°C 10 minutes

350°C 10 minutes

Whatever it was, it worked. Soon people were knocking on the door, wanting to buy my croissants. I decided to charge 12 cents each for them, and before long I was making money—real money.

It was a moment of realisation. I could do something I actually liked *and* earn a living. There was no one to tell me what to do or where to be. If I wanted a day off, I could take a day off.

BEFORE LONG, MY LITTLE KITCHEN at Margara's had become too small. I managed to do a deal with the owner of a nearby pousada: in exchange for managing his little hotel from 2 p.m. to 6 p.m. each day, I got free rent and after-hours use of the kitchen. What a good deal that was.

The owner's name was Golero. Well, that's what we called him, but he was no goalkeeper. An enormous man with thick, curly grey hair and a dense beard, Golero was given to wearing nothing more than a long sarong. Vast folds of flesh would roll over the top of the fabric at his waist. A small gold crucifix on a gold chain adorned his hairy grey chest. It wasn't in any way an attractive sight, but he was kind and funny and wanted to help me. Golero was from Uruguay, but he was friends with the Argentine community here. He knew everyone.

I quickly became known as 'the croissant girl', and wherever I went I was always hailed and greeted warmly. Of the resident population of around 10,000, roughly a third were from Argentina, so I had no shortage of customers. I found a woman with skin like polished mahogany to come and help me in the kitchen in the early mornings. She moved slowly, but she knew the dough like a mother knows her baby. Did it need a little more warmth, or a tiny pat to let the gas out? Was it hungry for water or salt or flour? Anita's massive girth made her look much older than she was, but she was probably only a few years older than me.

She would arrive at around 5 a.m., usually just as I was coming home from a nightclub, and help me to roll out and cook the dough. Then we would make a new batch for the coming day. I would always save a small portion of dough for my late-afternoon bake, and also to help the next day's dough, like a biga. By 7 a.m. my little crescent moons were ready for the oven, by 8 a.m. I was on my bicycle doing deliveries, and by 10 a.m. I was on the beach revelling in the sun and the sea, or playing backgammon with my neighbour Gato—who everyone called El Gato—another exiled Argentine and frequent customer at Golero's.

El Gato was a lot older than me. He and I became very good friends. I knew he would have liked to embark on a romantic relationship, but my heartstrings were still tethered to a sweetheart I'd left behind in the north of Brazil. There was no number or name on El Gato's gate, just a painted wooden cut-out of a black cat (*gato* means 'cat' in Spanish). You had to put your hand through a hole in the gate and feel around for the latch inside, then a winding brick path took you to a pretty white house by the sea. I still fantasise about this beach house. The whole front opened out to the ocean. Thick white shelves were filled with collections of tropical shells, books and pretty ornaments. Crisp-white walls displayed a jumble of fabulous art. You had to clamber over piles of books on art and design and gardens in order to plonk yourself on one of the many comfortable sofas. Before we got to the backgammon board, El Gato would disappear into his white-tiled kitchen for a late-morning snack, and return with platters of sweet, fragrant melon and paper-thin slices of prosciutto or, as the season rolled into autumn, big plates of chilled, jellied persimmons—the astringent kind need to be eaten when they are so soft they almost fall apart.

Around two in the afternoon, I would head back to the pousada to take over from Golero. My little stash of the morning's reserved dough would get rolled into tiny croissants, which I would fill with a fillet of anchovy. Then I would get behind the bar and start making caipirinhas. Into the muddler went a handful of sugar and two or three diced limes. I'd smash these up to dissolve the sugar. Next, a big slug of cachaça, with another muddle to mix everything together before it was all poured into a glass filled with ice cubes. With a quick swirl, it was ready to serve. Caipirinhas were—and probably still are—the signature drink of Búzios, seductively delicious with the kick of an angry mule.

My friends would arrive, the backgammon boards would come out again, and we would all settle in for a few hours of sipping cocktails and snacking on my crispy anchovy croissants. Now and then, a new customer would want to check in or get a drink. It was hardly strenuous. Around 7 p.m. Golero would return from his afternoon's sailing. I would drift off to bed to sleep for a few hours before heading out to party.

> When youth is on your side, you think nothing
> of squeezing those 92 kilos into the world's
> smallest bikinis. I don't think I was oblivious
> to looking the way I did, but there was nothing
> I really wanted to do to change it.

After six months of this, I had put on about 20 kilos. And my new nickname (which was at least said with affection) was La Gordita, the chubby one. When youth is on your side, you think nothing of squeezing those 92 kilos into the world's smallest bikinis. I don't think I was oblivious to looking the way I did, but there was nothing I really wanted to do to change it. I was just having too much fun. I had made so many great friends through Margara's fabulous introductions. Fofi, with the glittery eyes and wicked smile. Raúl, the swarthy son of a famous industrialist. Margara's boyfriend, Javier—not the guy to take home to meet your parents, but kind and helpful nonetheless. José, the builder who was building a new pousada with Manolo, his business partner with those gloomy eyes that had probably seen things I couldn't imagine. Alicia with the pet toucan. Mario-José, the property developer who held his eyebrows high so he always looked amazed. Cherub-faced Gabriel, straight out of a Michelangelo painting. Patricia, who on the twenty-ninth day of every month threw the best *ñoquis de papas* feasts. Fernando, my teenage snorkelling companion. And, of course, El Gato and Golero. I had made so many wonderful friends.

AND THEN THE FALKLANDS WAR arrived. Like the weather, which had become cooler and often rainy, the mood in the town changed. Suddenly, even though I wasn't from England, people weren't so welcoming or friendly. My friends treated me just the same, but we were a tribe of 20, maybe up to 50 on the outer rim. The other 3000 Argentinians living in the town were a wall of animosity. One day they staged a parade through the town, burning the English flag and chanting words of hate.

It was time to leave.

I went to Rio, bought 300 bikinis and a ticket to Barcelona. I figured I'd sell the bikinis in Ibiza and pay my way forward for a few months. When I arrived on the jet-set island, however, I discovered that the rich and famous no longer bothered with bikinis—or, indeed, any form of attire when they went bathing—and all the package tourists who came in droves from the cold climes of England and Germany were way too big to fit into my itsy-bitsy beachwear.

But, even if this idea didn't work, I knew there would be another. The seed of enterprise had been sown. And, finally, I understood that food was part of my DNA. When I cooked, I was happy and I made other people happy.

Montezuma's revenge had turned out to be a gift in disguise. The horrendous experience of food poisoning on the Peruvian border had sent me back to Búzios, where I had cooked myself back to happiness and health. As to where it would take me, I had no idea.

RICOTTA GNUDI WITH TANGY ROASTED TOMATO SAUCE

READY IN 25 MINUTES · SERVES 4 AS A MAIN OR 8 AS A STARTER
GF, IF GLUTEN FREE FLOUR IS USED

8 slices prosciutto

120 g (4¼ oz) baby spinach

500 g (1 lb 2 oz) ricotta

2 eggs

½ cup parmesan, finely grated

finely grated zest of ½ a lemon

¼ tsp freshly grated nutmeg

1 tsp salt

ground black pepper, to taste

¾ cup plain flour or gluten-free flour, plus more for dusting

2 tbsp butter

Tangy Roasted Tomato Sauce (see overleaf)

shavings of parmesan

Among the Argentine community in Búzios where I lived in 1981, the 29th of every month was the Dia de Ñoquis—the Day of Gnocchi. Bliss!

These days I like to make my gnocchi with ricotta instead of potatoes—it gives them a lovely pillowy lightness, and there's no waiting around for potatoes to bake. This dish is super-delish but very rich, so I like to serve it with a crisp, tangy salad or lots of cooked silver beet (swiss chard) to balance the meal.

Preheat oven to 200°C (400°F) fanbake. Line an oven tray with baking paper for easy clean-up.

Lay slices of prosciutto in a single layer on prepared tray without overlapping. Bake until they start to shrivel and turn golden (12–15 minutes). Allow to cool on a rack (they will crisp up).

While prosciutto is cooling, make the gnudi. Place baby spinach leaves in a colander and pour over boiling water to fully wilt the leaves. Run under cold water to cool. Squeeze tightly several times to remove all water (it's important that the spinach is dry). Finely chop spinach, then transfer to a mixing bowl with ricotta, eggs, parmesan, lemon zest, nutmeg, salt and pepper, and mix well. Stir in flour until it is just combined and the mixture forms a soft, sticky dough. Using floured hands and a floured board, divide dough into 2 portions and roll into 2 logs, each about 3 cm wide.

Dust a shallow oven tray generously with flour. Using a sharp knife dipped in flour, cut each log into 3 cm pillows and set aside on the floured tray. You should get about 24.

RECIPE CONTINUED OVERLEAF

Bring a large pot of well-salted water to a boil. With floured hands, pick up gnudi and drop into boiling water. Cook 8–10 at a time. Once they rise to the top, allow to simmer for 3 minutes—they should feel bouncy and firm, not squidgy. Transfer to a platter with a slotted spoon, shaking off excess water, and repeat to cook the rest in batches. (Gnudi can be prepared ahead to this point, chilled for up to 2 days, and brought back to room temperature before pan-frying.)

To finish, heat a little butter in a large frying pan. Cook gnudi in two or three batches if necessary, so as not to overcrowd the pan. Shake gnudi in the pan over a medium heat for 1–2 minutes each side, until lightly browned and fully heated through. Add a little more butter between batches if needed.

To serve, divide Tangy Roasted Tomato Sauce between warmed plates and top with gnudi. Garnish with prosciutto and parmesan shavings.

TANGY ROASTED TOMATO SAUCE

READY IN 1 HOUR · MAKES ABOUT 4 CUPS · DF · GF · V · VE

1.2 kg (2 lb 10 oz) tomatoes, preferably truss
¼ cup extra virgin olive oil
3 tbsp red wine vinegar
1 tsp dried oregano
2 tbsp finely chopped fresh basil or tarragon
1 tbsp sugar
¾ tsp salt
ground black pepper, to taste

Preheat oven to 200°C (400°F) fanbake.

Remove cores from tomatoes and cut larger tomatoes into quarters. Arrange in a large, shallow roasting dish, drizzle with olive oil and red wine vinegar, and sprinkle with herbs, sugar, salt and pepper. Roast until tomatoes start to caramelise on top (about 40 minutes). The mixture will be very wet.

If using truss tomatoes, lift off and discard skins (truss tomato skins are tougher than most other tomato skins). Transfer roasted tomatoes to a pot and purée with a hand wand blender. Bring to a simmer, then simmer for 5 minutes. Check seasoning and if the sauce is a little tart, add an extra pinch of sugar and more salt.

BARBECUED LEG OF LAMB
IN LEMON AND HERB MARINADE

READY IN 35 MINUTES + MARINATING + RESTING · SERVES 6–8 · DF · GF

about 1.1 kg (2 lb 7 oz) boned, butterflied and trimmed leg of lamb

LEMON AND HERB MARINADE
¼ cup lemon juice
2 tbsp extra virgin olive oil
4 cloves garlic, crushed to a paste with 1 tsp salt
2 tbsp very finely chopped preserved lemon
2 tsp chopped fresh oregano leaves
1 tsp finely chopped fresh rosemary leaves
ground black pepper, to taste
Chunky Salsa Verde Dressing (see overleaf), to serve

Ask your butcher to bone and butterfly the leg of lamb for this dish. I like to weight the lamb with a large clean stone or brick wrapped in tinfoil, or place a tray on top of it and weigh it down with a couple of heavy stones or a brick—this helps to keep the lamb flat so it cooks more evenly. Serve with rocket (arugula) leaves and crispy roast potatoes.

Mix Lemon and Herb Marinade ingredients in a large clean plastic bag or a bowl big enough to fit the lamb. Add lamb and turn to coat. Seal bag or cover bowl and chill for at least 4 hours or up to 48 hours, turning occasionally.

When ready to cook lamb, preheat barbecue grill over a medium-high heat. Remove lamb from marinade, shaking off excess, and grill for 5 minutes on each side until browned. Lower heat and cook until done to your liking (about 10–12 minutes on each side for medium-rare, depending on thickness), weighting with a stone if desired. Remove lamb from heat, cover, and allow to rest for 10 minutes before carving into thin slices across the grain.

To serve, scatter a little Chunky Salsa Verde Dressing over the lamb and serve the rest in a bowl on the side.

PICTURED OVERLEAF

CHUNKY SALSA VERDE DRESSING

READY IN 15 MINUTES · MAKES ABOUT 5 CUPS · DF · GF · V

1 cup Sicilian green olives, finely chopped

½ cup capers, finely chopped

1 small red onion, halved and very thinly sliced lengthwise

4 cloves garlic, crushed

4 tsp seed mustard

¼ cup red wine vinegar

¼ cup lemon juice

2 tsp honey

1 cup roasted almonds, coarsely chopped

¼ cup very finely chopped preserved lemon

6 tbsp extra virgin olive oil

2 cups fresh flat-leaf parsley leaves, coarsely chopped

salt and ground black pepper, to taste

I love the chunky salad-like quality of this dressing, but if you prefer you can blend it into a smoothish purée, more like a traditional salsa verde. Don't be put off by the long list of ingredients—the combination of flavours works beautifully with lamb, and is delicious with grilled chicken, beef, pork or seafood. You can also toss the dressing through pasta, quinoa or freekeh to make a simple salad.

Combine olives, capers, onion, garlic, mustard, vinegar, lemon juice and honey in a mixing bowl and leave to marinate for at least 30 minutes.

Just before serving, mix in remaining ingredients.

The dressing will keep for 4–5 days in the fridge. If possible, add almonds just before serving so they retain their crunch.

SILKY LEMON CREAMS WITH ALMOND BISCOTTI ON THE SIDE

READY IN 15 MINUTES + SETTING · SERVES 6–8
GF, IF BISCOTTI USES GLUTEN-FREE FLOUR · V

2½ cups cream
½ cup sugar
¼ cup honey
½ cup lemon juice, strained
fresh raspberries and/or blueberries, to garnish
Almond Biscotti (see overleaf), to serve

Even if you think you can't cook to save yourself, this is one of those genius recipes that will make you look like a superstar. The formula is so easy that you can carry it around in your head.

Place cream, sugar and honey in a medium pot over a medium heat. Bring to a boil, stirring, until sugar dissolves (it bubbles up a lot). Reduce heat and simmer for 3 minutes.

Remove from heat and stir in lemon juice. Strain through a sieve into 6–8 ramekins or cups and chill until set (about 4 hours). Serve topped with fresh berries and accompanied by Almond Biscotti.

ALMOND BISCOTTI

READY IN 1 HOUR + COOLING · MAKES ABOUT 36

DF · GF, IF GLUTEN-FREE FLOUR IS USED · V

2½ cups self-raising flour
   or gluten-free self-
   raising flour
1 cup caster (superfine)
   sugar
3 eggs
1¼ cups almonds

I like my biscotti light, crisp, and nice and thin, not so rusk-like they have you running to the dentist! These will keep for weeks in a sealed container.

Preheat oven to 180°C (350°F) fanbake. Line an oven tray with baking paper for easy clean-up.

Stir together all ingredients, making sure you don't over-mix the dough. (It may seem dry at first but once the sugar mixes into the eggs it will become very soft.) As soon as it comes together, pat it into 2 log shapes about 20 cm x 7 cm (8 in x 2¾ in) on the prepared tray, then flatten the top. Bake until pale golden and set (about 30 minutes).

Remove biscotti from oven and reduce oven temperature to 140°C (275°F) fanbake. When cool enough to handle, slice biscotti very thinly. Arrange slices in a single layer on the oven tray and return to oven until crisp and dry (15–20 minutes). Allow to cool on tray (they will become crisper as they cool). Biscotti will keep for several weeks in an airtight container in a cool place.

SIX

Location, location, location

Catering and food-styling days

When I returned to New Zealand in 1983, jobs were hard to come by. I spent a couple of months in Gisborne over the summer, catching up with all my old friends, but there was no work there. I headed back to my parents in Wellington, and scoured the job ads in the newspaper.

I had no idea what I wanted to do for a living, but as a fill-in job I thought I would try my hand at waitressing. I managed to convince Wellington's top restaurant, Orsini's—a chic establishment famous for its solicitous staff and the rich, creamy and butter-laced sauces that were in vogue at the time—that I was an experienced waitress, well versed in the dexterous art of silver service.

I spent days practising the finickity tonging of a fork and a spoon in one hand to transfer neat parcels of food from a serving dish to the diner's plate. Until you had figured it out, the food all fell about messily. It was like learning how to use chopsticks, but finally I got it. I figured the rest of this waitressing lark would be a piece of cake—taking people's orders and ferrying plates, maybe even getting a nice tip. I was quite excited about the whole idea, apart from the fact that each night I was required to cram my less-than-svelte figure into a tight black dress, black stockings and mile-high heels. Umberto Eco, professor of semiotics and author of such well-

OPPOSITE Promoting microwaves for Toshiba.

PREVIOUS Homeward bound—about to leave London in 1983.

known books as *The Name of the Rose* and *Foucault's Pendulum*, wrote a succinct essay in his dense and (when he talks about issues of Italian politics and semiotics) virtually impenetrable book *Travels in Hyperreality* about how tight clothing has been used to control the way women think. Try putting on a pair of high heels and a tight dress or jeans and maintaining your concentration—you'll be so busy struggling to breathe and focusing on not tripping and falling over that it'll be difficult to apply yourself to anything else.

My job on that first day was to clear tables. 'No orders. Just collect the plates after everyone at the table is finished.'

About halfway through the dinner service, a gentleman waved across the restaurant to catch my attention. He passed me his plate, complaining that his steak was too rare. I returned to the kitchen and advised the chef on duty that a customer was unhappy with his steak being too rare. Chef's fleshy complexion flushed to a hue worthy of a good burgundy. 'Too bloody rare?' Snarling, eyes bulging, his face contorted in rage, he grabbed the plate from my hands, tipped the steak on to the floor and stomped on it with both boots.

I stared, drop-jawed in disbelief. I had heard about knife-wielding, tyrannical chefs with explosive tempers, and now I had met one.

He picked up the now-flattened steak, put it into a clean frying pan with a knob of butter, and let it sizzle for about a minute. Placing his newly minted steak on a clean, hot plate, he expertly napped it with sauce and flicked a sprig of tarragon on top. He passed me the plate, glowering, then picked up his carving knife and waved it like an épée in my face and then at the door into the restaurant. His threatening gesture was clear. *Go now. Say nothing.*

Stumbling in the heels, my hands shaking, I returned the plate to the customer and put it down carefully in front of him, mumbling, 'Here you go, sir. I hope you enjoy it this time.' The man, oblivious to the fiasco that had occurred in the kitchen, downed his 'fresh' steak with relish. I went home and had a stiff gin.

On day two of my new employment, I was looking after a table of eight who were seated at the large round table in the corner of the restaurant. Seven guests had ordered the fresh crayfish in some kind of buttery brandy sauce, while one of them—the tiny old lady at the back by the wall—had chosen a light soup for her main. With seven plates of dead crayfish carefully piled up on one arm, I leaned over the back of the man sitting next to the old lady to remove her soup bowl. I felt the plates quiver and then, like a car accident, everything went into slow motion . . . The entire stack fell like a Jenga tower, the seven plates of dead crayfish crashing to the floor, leaving a trail of crayfish shells and leftover sauce down the back of the man's fancy suit. There was a collective gasp, then the entire restaurant fell silent.

'You'll be up for the dry-cleaning bill,' one of the waitresses remarked sourly.

If ever there was a 'beam me up, Scotty' moment, this was it. Amazingly, I wasn't sacked on the spot.

The next night I was a bundle of nerves.

'It's all right,' said the senior waitress. 'We've decided you can just be on the coffee service tonight, dear.'

All right?

For starters, with all the heavy silver on it—coffee pot, hot-water pot, milk jug, sugar bowl and chocolate-truffle plate—the tray weighed a bloody ton. Worse though, whoever had set it up had placed the milk jug right by the handle of the coffee pot. Another catastrophe was about to unfold. 'Coffee, sir?' I picked up the coffee pot and, as I did so, the jug and all its cold, milky contents jettisoned into his lap.

The restaurant owners, who had not been present the previous two nights, had obviously heard that the new waitress was having a few problems, and had turned up to see what was going on in their hallowed establishment. After the mess was cleaned up and all the guests had gone home, they pointed to the door. 'LEAVE. NOW.'

I didn't even ask if I was going to get paid. I simply ran, throwing off my heels the minute I got out the door.

My waitressing career had lasted a total of three dreadful nights. I was never going back to that job ever again.

Now what was I to do?

THROUGH A FRIEND OF MY MOTHER'S, I scored a salaried job as a microwave-oven consultant. The job was based up in Auckland, and would require me to work Wednesdays, Thursdays, Fridays and Saturday mornings. I needed to present cooking demonstrations and write recipes that would show that culinary success with these new-fangled machines could be achieved with simply the push of a button. I got a car, and a food allowance for recipe development. I also scored a booze account, so that I could write microwave recipes for things like hot buttered rum, whisky toddies and mulled wine. No one could believe I'd got the job, least of all me.

My sole experience with microwaves was limited to working in a pub in London. (After the failed Ibiza bikini business, I needed to save enough money to fly back home to New Zealand.) Every day a man would come in and ask for a Cornish pasty and a beer for his lunch. The pasties were kept in the freezer and our instructions were to microwave them for one minute to heat them through. I always popped the pasty in for a bit longer, hoping it might come out slightly less anaemic. It didn't. About three days into serving up my microwaved pasties to this bloke, he shoved his plate in my face and tore open the pasty so I could see the black carbonated centre. 'If you ever burn my pasty again, I'm going to report you to your manager,' he hissed, throwing the plate down on the counter and walking out.

When I landed my microwave job, I was none the wiser as to how microwaves actually worked. My new employers handed me a huge box with a shiny new microwave machine in it and sent me off. No lessons, no explanations. I had borrowed my mother's car to go to the meeting, so I drove out to my sister's house out at Scorching Bay in Wellington, unpacked the box and made a carrot cake. After 10 minutes the cake had risen but was deathly pale, so I put it on for another 10 minutes, then another, and another. I finally took it out 50 minutes later, but it still looked pale and unappetising, and I found myself wondering why people might want a machine like this. Taking the cake out of the tin, I realised that I had, in effect, constructed a new building material—the cake was as hard as concrete. As I left, my sister's partner threw my new creation under the car wheel. Mother's little Renault bumped over it as if crossing a kerb. Several months later, the cake was still intact. Even the seagulls couldn't get into it.

I MOVED UP TO AUCKLAND and into a two-bedroom flat at the bottom of Parnell with a young architect. The flat was tiny. You walked through the front door straight into the living room. To the left, against the wall, was a kitchen bench with a stove and a sink. A bank of cupboards running up the other side of the narrow galley meant there was very little prep space. The view from the living room out over the container wharf to Auckland Harbour, however, was magnificent. There were a couple of flats of young professionals on either side, and always a party happening. Several times a week I would throw impromptu dinners for 12 to 20, setting up a temporary trestle table in our living room so I had somewhere to prep the food, which we would either eat in our apartment or take to one of our neighbours' on either side.

Life was good. Twice a year, Ted (my Gisborne flatmate's lanky brother) would call in to stay en route to or from his northern hemisphere ski jobs.

The farm boy and I had connected romantically when I first got back from South America, and had been an on-and-off item ever since. I could never have imagined that the good-looking boy I spotted while hiding up a tree would one day become the guy I was dating. And the fact that he turned out to be my flatmate's brother? It seemed so far-fetched.

One day my neighbour Will, who was in the film business, came over. 'Hey, you seem like you're a really good cook,' he said. 'We're shooting a short film up north of Auckland for five days next week. Would you be able to cater for us?'

Why not? I was more than ready for something new.

I hired a generator and a couple of trestle tables, raided the office stash of demonstration microwaves, picked up a rental trailer, and finagled my way off work for a few days. I set up the trestle tables on the side of the road, where the crew were shooting, plugged the microwaves into the generator and reheated the big trays of lasagne I had made back in my tiny Parnell kitchen. Served up with a bunch of fresh salads, a couple of sweet slices, cheese and fruit and bread, my quickly assembled meal was a hit. Each night I would zoom back to Auckland and prepare a slow-cooked main course that I could reheat in my microwaves, whip up some baking and prepare some salads, then drive back up to the location the next morning to feed the crew.

That first catering job led to more, and soon I was running a business that had got busy enough for me to quit moonlighting and leave my day job. Word had got around that there was a new caterer on the block who dished up elaborate five-course lunches for a dime, and I could hardly keep up with the calls from advertising agencies and film crews.

My friend Kate came over to the flat one day to help me dream up a name for my new business. 'What about Hot on the Spot?' she said. I had a silver card made, with all the necessary details, and that was that.

The next 18 months provided a crash course in cooking, logistics and management. I worked out a bit of a formula: bulky, stodgy fare for the always-hungry crew, some fancy low-cal dips and rabbit food for the diet-obsessed talent, a vegetarian option, and something a little bit 'exotic' for the agency, who needed to feel special. Each day, I would roll out a menu of eight or nine platters that catered for everyone's tastes. It was a hit. I had never worked so hard in my life, or had so much fun doing it.

> The next 18 months provided a crash course in cooking, logistics and management. I worked out a bit of a formula: bulky, stodgy fare for the always-hungry crew, some fancy low-cal dips and rabbit food for the diet-obsessed talent, a vegetarian option, and something a little bit 'exotic' for the agency, who needed to feel special.

A FEW MONTHS AFTER I first came home from South America, my sister's partner, who was a cartoonist and writer, suggested that I write a story about my adventures. I'd written lots of letters to my family while I was away, and he thought my stories would be interesting for the *New Zealand Listener*, a prestigious weekly magazine for which he provided a weekly cartoon strip called *Bogor*.

So I wrote a story about spending Christmas in Colombia with the family of my rather dodgy then-boyfriend. My paramour's father was in attendance with not just his newest wife but also his five previous wives and all their children, and more cousins and aunts and uncles than you could imagine anyone ever being related to. At around 11 p.m. on Christmas Eve, we had dined on a big slab of dry corned beef and cassava, and then the tables were cleared for the salsa band. As there weren't enough women in our party, a bunch of broomsticks were made available for those men without partners. Around dawn on Christmas Day, somewhat the worse for wear, we all piled into the family car and headed to the local abattoir, where a bucket of fresh blood and some ox hearts were purchased. Then it was back home for a Christmas feast of boiled blood and hearts grilled over the hibachi. This was a very special treat in honour of the New Zealand guest. Oh, joy! I figured the mother of this particular boyfriend knew a thing or two about getting rid of foreign girlfriends.

I included some recipes with the story—gazpacho, a festive stollen, an egg tortilla (frittata). There was also a recipe for a ham-and-olive ring that, when I read it now, sounds totally revolting. It was a kind of economical meatloaf made with sausage meat and ham, bound together with wheatgerm, and flavoured with sherry, currants, olives and herbs, with a canned pineapple glaze. Ugh. What was I thinking?

A few weeks after sending the story in to the *Listener*, I got a letter back. Would I be interested in being a regular food columnist on a fortnightly basis? The column would be week about with Lois Daish, a well-known Wellington restaurateur. It was one of those fairy godmother moments, and heralded an exciting new era for me.

MY WORK AS A FILM CATERER naturally led to work as a food stylist, and that meant there were always places to go and adventures to be had. Food styling was a whole new world of making food look pretty for photographs or film. As well as the food, there were backgrounds, napkins, plates, cups, bowls, glasses and spoons to consider, with multiple options for each.

For one job, I flew down to the West Coast of the South Island to cater and style a yoghurt commercial for a North American film crew. The shoot had been originally planned for the Rockies, but snow had unseasonably dumped all over the verdant green grass there, so a speedy relocation was required. Fox Glacier was deemed to be the best lookalike, so a crew of maybe 20 people—including the small group from the States—descended on the area.

I was instructed to make ready for the ad's opening scene, which was to feature a rustic table laden with fruits, out in the middle of a lush green paddock. The cameras would pan through the dawn light, up into the snow-clad mountains, then back across the table of bounty as a slow drizzle of golden, sunlit honey fell onto the hero product: a large bowl of creamy, white-as-snow yoghurt.

'We want cherries. Lots of cherries,' the director clamoured. 'Money is no object.'

I rang Balducci's in New York, and Harrods in London. I contacted produce markets all over the globe, but there were no fresh cherries to be found anywhere on the planet. Cherries are an early-summer fruit. Nowhere in the world is April early summer. Early spring, yes. Summer, no. In a desperate attempt to fulfil the director's mandate, I enlisted the art department to paint small polystyrene balls with nail polish. Yes, fake cherries. One evening, the make-up department mutinied—they had discovered that we had used up all their nail-polish remover. So I popped down to the local Four Square store to buy some acetone. And there, sitting on a shelf behind the counter, was a bowl of the most perfect ornamental glass cherries. They were old and a bit dusty, but were hand-blown, probably Bavarian—and they looked just like the real thing. The shop owner was happy to lend them to me. I nearly cried with happiness.

In the catering and food-styling world, you can pretty well guarantee that there will always be a problem. Martha, the producer of the yoghurt commercial, hailed from LA and was fiscally prepared for every eventuality—she carried around an old leather doctor's bag filled with wads of cash. One time, a Western hat that had been used in the footage that had already been shot in the States got mistakenly left in Auckland, and so a private plane had to be hired to get it down. (Martha to the rescue.) No one had verified that the young boy who was masquerading as the son in this particular happy-family scene actually liked yoghurt. He didn't, and would gag each time he had to take a mouthful. The director was forking out $50 notes for each take. (Martha to the rescue again.)

We managed to sort out the problems and cover all the contingencies— except for the weather. If you've never been to the West Coast, it rains a lot there. At least every other day, and up to 11 metres a year. It rained, and it rained. The art director was a vast woman from Chicago who wore overalls, check shirts, heavy work boots, a baseball cap and no make-up. Seeking a distraction from the rain, she enlisted the services of the local schoolteacher to take her fishing. The trip was a great success, and she returned to base camp with an enormous salmon that she'd caught out off the mouth of the Windbag Creek.

It turned out, however, that the art director's interests were for a catch of a different kind. That night she turned up at the pub wearing a tightly hugging silver pantsuit and stiletto snakeskin boots. With long fake scarlet nails, batwing false eyelashes and her lips painted a gash of deep purple, she looked like an enormous, predatory spider. The schoolteacher, who was at least 10 centimetres shorter than her, and wearing sensible shorts with long socks and Roman sandals, didn't stand a chance. They didn't make it to dinner, and the school was closed the next day. I heard a few months later, through the grapevine, that true love had been declared, and the schoolteacher had headed back to the States to be with his Spiderwoman sweetheart.

FOR ANOTHER BIG-BUDGET AD, we were in Ōtorohanga, near the Waitomo glow-worm caves, with a crew of over 40, including executives from a London ad agency and animal trainers from Texas. The star of the show was butter, from a land where the grass is so green that the cows veritably dance for joy. The final ad showed the cows dancing the foxtrot out in a paddock . . . You may perhaps have seen it? The animal trainers spent three weeks training those cows in some snazzy hoofwork. (And for the close-ups of the actual dancing, fake cows' legs exactly matching the live animals' legs were manufactured and operated like puppets by humans.)

My job was to feed the crew, and also create a sumptuous picnic for the camera to feast on. Two days before the shoot, a carefully packed box containing one scone arrived on my doorstep. It was a replica scone, entirely inedible, like the waxy fake sampuru you see behind Japanese restaurant windows to display all the dishes on the menu. The fake scone was perfectly round and evenly straight-sided, golden brown, and cut in half to reveal a scattering of fake sultanas. My brief was to duplicate the sample with three-dozen equally perfect edible specimens, plus provide a variety of other suitable picnic fare, including cucumber sandwiches, apricot loaves, glazed fruit tarts, baby quiches, sausage rolls, cream sponges, cheese and fruit. Everything went off perfectly. The scones were perfect. The picnic was perfect. Everyone was happy. It was what happened afterwards, when we relocated to a hotel in Hamilton for the final night, that was less than perfect.

I had been whizzing up my nightly post-shoot cocktails for the crew in the blender, and it's possible that we had just a few too many. My two nubile young assistants decided that we needed a swim, even though it was after-hours and the pool was closed. The three of us clambered over the pool fence and were enjoying a cooling skinny-dip when suddenly the alarm went off. A loudspeaker bellowed out to the world: 'Trespassers! Trespassers in the pool area! The police have been called!'

We clambered, with speed, back over the fence. In our haste to get into my room, we slipped the sliding door off its railing. Now we had the alarm going off and the room door propped up on the wall outside. We hurtled into the hall to the elevator and pushed the button for the top floor, where we knew some of the crew were staying and would let us in. The lift arrived and we hopped in, breathing a sigh of relief. But it only made it to level one before it stopped and the doors began to open. I frantically pushed the close-door button. Outside stood a group of suited businessmen who had obviously just finished their dinner and couldn't quite believe the sight before them of three naked, dripping-wet young women.

'This lift's full, sorry,' I said, holding my arm out like a barricade, while trying to hide my frame behind the button panel just inside the door. Finally, after what was probably only about 20 seconds but seemed like forever, the door shut.

We hid upstairs for hours, before we snuck back to the pool in borrowed clothes to retrieve our stuff before anyone cottoned on.

CATERING WAS NOT THE LUCRATIVE business I had imagined it would be, and working for film crews was harder than any other kind of catering. You were always in some remote location, and nothing ever ran to schedule. Lunch at noon often turned into lunch at 4 p.m. At midnight you could find yourself out on a wild West Coast beach, dishing up a dinner that had been planned for 7 p.m.

I learnt a lot, though; mostly about what didn't work. At a tea-party shoot out in a paddock with a famous equestrian and loads of graceful, cantering horses, I sat and waited for lunch to be called while my beautiful chilled strawberry pie melted over the tablecloth and dripped down onto the grass, where it became a Mecca for every fly in the district. Note to self: gelatine melts at 25 degrees Celsius.

When I had been catering for about 18 months, my accountant called me in to his offices. 'Can you tell me, please, just why you are doing this?' he said. 'You certainly aren't making any money.'

I went home and had a think about what he'd said. But what else would I do? I was young and free. I had energy to burn. Life was fun.

I'VE FOUND IT USUALLY TAKES a disaster to catapult you into a new chapter. It's not often you choose to leave something that you like, and that you've grown comfortable doing. My swansong as a caterer was a lunch for 200 car salesmen that was held at Alexandra Park in Auckland.

The park's incumbent caterers were definitely annoyed that I had been brought in as an outsider, and insisted that I bring everything with me, including the water. Catering is a schlep at the best of times, but lugging the huge water containers up the stairs along with all the food and equipment for the lunch took a lot longer than I thought. Time was already running tight when the event manager turned up to advise that the lunch had been brought forward by half an hour. Then I discovered that my helper, who had left her head in the nappy bucket but brought along her wailing baby, had forgotten to bring the carving knives and the chopping boards. All I had was a single electric knife. I whirred my way madly through scotch fillets, chocolate cakes, bread and cheese. Meanwhile one of my waitresses had period pains and fainted in the loo.

When the 200 hungry car salesmen descended to gobble down their lunch, they didn't want my stuffed peppers or eggplant timbales. They wanted meat, and lots of it. The five beef scotches I had cooked were gone with the first 50 customers. There were mutters and complaints.

'Soon this will be over,' I kept saying to myself.

And, finally, it was. Everyone went back to their stands of Ferraris and Porsches, and I was left with the clean-up. We got everything back into the car, everyone else went home, and all that was left for me to deal with were a couple of big urns of leftover coffee. I had lugged all that water up, and I really couldn't see why I needed to lug it down again. I removed the tape closing off the kitchen we hadn't been allowed to use, and tipped a huge urn of hot coffee into the sink. It made an odd, echoey noise. I looked down and saw with dismay that the plumbing hadn't been connected. There were a couple of big bangs, and then all the lights went out.

Downstairs, coffee and grinds were dripping onto pink Lamborghinis and cream Aston Martins. I spotted three big, red-faced men in black suits racing up the stairs, smoke coming out of their ears. I did a runner, scooting out the back door, down the stairs and into my little Honda station wagon. I drove straight home and took the phone off the hook.

A FEW DAYS LATER, a magical letter arrived.

I had written to Julia Child a few months earlier to ask her advice about which direction I might take my love of food in. Julia was my queen. Her words and recipes had been my solace through the years with the dodgy boyfriend, Luke. If anyone in life could help me figure out where to take my passion for cooking, it would be Julia. I had explained that I was writing a column for a local magazine and running a small catering business, but I wanted to do something else—I just didn't know what.

The letter that came back was from Julia's husband, Paul. He said that he and Julia had talked a lot about me and my letter, and Julia thought I should come to the States. There was a food conference on in April in Seattle that she thought I might be interested in. It was being hosted by the International Association of Cooking Schools (which, a couple of years later in 1987, became the International Association of Culinary Professionals), and if I went I'd get to meet lots of people working in all sorts of interesting facets of the food business in the States.

I didn't need any convincing. I booked a one-way ticket, and within a week was winging my way to the USA.

OPPOSITE Taking orders for catering
in the days before mobile phones.

SUNSET COCKTAILS

I've always loved cocktails. They're such a great way to break the ice and loosen everyone up, especially at the start of a party.

NEGRONIS

READY IN 10 MINUTES · SERVES 4 · DF · GF · V · VE

½ cup gin
½ cup Campari
½ cup red vermouth
ice cubes
4 strips orange zest, cut
  with a vegetable peeler,
  to garnish

Negronis have a fabulous kick, but if this recipe seems too potent for your taste you can make a James Bond-style Americano cocktail by replacing the gin with a splash of soda water and a large slice of lemon. Or make a Negroni Sbagliato by swapping the gin for a good splash of chilled prosecco.

Combine gin, Campari and vermouth in a jug. Half-fill 4 lowball glasses with ice cubes. Divide cocktail between glasses and garnish each with a twist of orange zest.

PEACH DAIQUIRIS

READY IN 10 MINUTES · SERVES 4–6 · DF · GF · V · VE

flesh of 4 white peaches
  or other fruit, such
  as berries, pineapple
  or mangoes, cut into
  chunks
1 cup white rum
1 cup fresh lime juice
1 cup Simple Sugar Syrup
  (see overleaf)
3 cups ice

You can make these fabulous cocktails with all kinds of fresh fruit—strawberries are luscious. Even canned mangoes make a really good daiquiri using this formula.

Place all ingredients in a blender and purée until smooth. Divide between 4–6 cocktail glasses.

WHISKEY SOURS

READY IN 10 MINUTES · SERVES 2 · DF · GF · V

¼ cup bourbon
3 tbsp lemon juice
2 tbsp chilled Simple
  Sugar Syrup, or more to
  taste (see below)
1 egg white
4–5 ice cubes, plus extra
  to serve
a splash of Angostura
  bitters, to garnish
  (optional)

My clever American chef friend William Dissen has a deft hand with a cocktail shaker. While I was hosting William in New Zealand as part of the US Culinary Diplomacy programme, he introduced me to the pleasures of bourbon and this fabulous creamy, smooth cocktail. Choose the freshest eggs for a longer-lasting froth.

Combine all ingredients except ice and bitters in a cocktail shaker. Shake hard for about 30 seconds until frothy. Add ice cubes and shake again for another 10–15 seconds. Strain into 2 lowball glasses half-filled with ice cubes. If using bitters, shake a few drops on top.

SIMPLE SUGAR SYRUP

READY IN 15 MINUTES · MAKES 3 CUPS · DF · GF · V · VE

2 cups boiling water
2 cups sugar

This is the foundation of lots of cocktails. Make it in bulk and store in the fridge so you can have it on hand whenever you want a cocktail. It keeps for months.

Place boiling water in a heatproof bowl or pot, add sugar and stir until sugar is dissolved. Cool. Transfer to a sterilised bottle or jar and cover with a lid. Store in the fridge.

DUCK AND RED CABBAGE SPRING ROLLS

READY IN 45 MINUTES · MAKES 12 · DF · GF

4 duck breasts
salt and ground black
  pepper, to taste
1 telegraph cucumber
¼ red cabbage
4 spring onions (scallions)
1 avocado
12 round 22 cm (8½ in)
  rice paper wrappers
¼ cup chopped roasted
  cashew nuts or peanuts
2 tbsp black sesame
  seeds
36 mint leaves

DIPPING SAUCE
1 cup mayonnaise
¼ cup hoisin sauce

Regardless of how you plan to serve duck breasts, this is the best way I know to cook them to that perfect medium-rare tenderness.

Score duck skin deeply with a sharp knife in a criss-cross pattern and season both sides. Preheat a heavy-based frying pan and cook duck skin-side down over a medium heat until fat has rendered out, skin is crispy and the edges of the duck breast are just starting to change colour (10–12 minutes). Keep an eye on it and reduce heat if skin is becoming too brown. Turn duck over, turn off heat and allow to stand for 10 minutes (the heat of the fat will be enough to finish cooking). Drain on paper towels. When cool, slice thinly.

While duck is cooling, prepare spring rolls. Halve cucumber lengthwise, scrape out and discard seeds, then cut into 12 batons about 10 cm (4 in) in length. Shred cabbage and thinly slice spring onions. Slice avocado in half, then cut each half into 6 wedges.

Fill a large, shallow bowl with hot water. Wet a clean tea towel, squeeze out and spread on bench. Dunk a rice paper wrapper into the water for a couple of seconds, remove at once, shake off excess water and place on the damp tea towel. It will soften to a pliable texture.

Sprinkle each rice paper wrapper with a few nuts and sesame seeds, 3 mint leaves, a cucumber baton, slices of duck, spring onion and an avocado wedge. Fold in sides of rice paper, then roll up tightly from the bottom edge to enclose the filling.

To make Dipping Sauce, combine mayonnaise and hoisin sauce in a small serving bowl. Thin with a little water if needed.

Cut each roll crosswise into thirds or halves, and serve with dipping sauce on the side.

FUDGY CHOCOLATE BROWNIE

READY IN 1 HOUR · MAKES 20–30 PIECES
GF, IF GLUTEN-FREE FLOUR IS USED · V

2 cups chopped dates
¾ cup water
1 tsp baking soda
  (bicarbonate soda)
200 g (7 oz) butter, diced
4 eggs
2 tsp vanilla extract
2 cups caster (superfine)
  sugar
1 cup cocoa, sifted
1 cup plain flour or
  gluten-free flour
½ tsp baking powder
250 g (9 oz) dark
  chocolate chips or
  chopped dark chocolate
1 tbsp cocoa, to dust
  (optional)

Many years ago, while I was living in Toronto, I won the local newspaper's best brownie competition with this fabulous recipe. Dates are hygroscopic (meaning they tend to attract water), so they make these brownies moist and tender.

Preheat oven to 160°C (315°F) fanbake. Line a 30 cm x 20 cm (12 in x 8 in) slab tin with baking paper.

Combine dates, water and baking soda in a small pot and bring to a boil. Simmer for 1 minute, then add butter and stir until melted. Remove from heat and mash softened dates with a fork to break them up to a creamy consistency.

Stir in eggs and vanilla until well combined. Stir in sugar, then add cocoa, flour and baking powder, and stir until smooth. Stir in chocolate chips or chunks.

Smooth into prepared tin and bake until it is set in the middle and begins to come away from the sides of the tin (about 40 minutes). Cool fully before cutting into squares and dusting with cocoa (if using). Brownie will keep for up to 2 weeks in an airtight container.

SEVEN

The American dream

A culinary education

So it was that I found myself standing in the
Seattle Aquarium, marvelling at the fantastical
opening cocktail party for the 1985 International
Association of Cooking Schools (IACS) conference.

Large arrow signs marked with the names of various types of seafood
directed people to giant ice stands laid out with fancy canapés. Trays of
smoked sturgeon, salmon caviar, abalone and sides of fresh salmon cooked
over planks of cedar were arranged between tanks of live pufferfish,
seahorses and saddle wrasse. It was so over the top, and the food was
amazing. What a place to throw a party. It was genius. Why didn't we do
things like this in New Zealand? We had a great aquarium . . .

At the conference itself, I signed up for a course to scrub up my food-
styling skills. This was another league—the goal here was all about making
food look 'perfect' on the plate. We learnt to make a lookalike ice cream
that wouldn't melt (equal quantities of icing sugar, corn syrup and Crisco
shortening). For roast chicken, we were shown how to baste the bird
with a mix of water, Kitchen Bouquet sauce and detergent. After about
30 minutes in the oven, the skin would burnish to a rich, deep gold and the
chicken looked mouth-watering. Inside, they were bloody raw.

I also attended a seminar led by local forager Steve Czernetsky about

OPPOSITE Dining with Jill Roberts in her swish
uptown apartment with the tiniest kitchen.

PREVIOUS Partying in the Hamptons.

the edible wild mushrooms of the Pacific Northwest, including golden chanterelles or girolles (*Cantharellus cibarius*), the famous black morel (*Morchella angusticeps*), and a close relative of Asian matsutake called *Tricholoma murrillianum*. I also learnt about the cultivation of enoki, shiitake and oyster mushrooms.

From biochemist and culinary sleuth Shirley Corriher, I discovered the answer to many of the whys of cooking. Why, if you add too little liquid to chocolate, does it seize into clumps, as if someone has put an evil spell over your beautiful, velvety melted chocolate? (The tiniest bit of moisture, even steam, can cause flowing, shiny melted chocolate to become a solid, dull, grainy mass. Add chocolate to a lot of fluid, and it's fine.) Why, if you try to mash potatoes in a food processor, do they come out like wallpaper paste? (The blade breaks all the starch granules and all the starch runs out.) Shirley explained why, in general, things can happen in cooking that you might not expect—and what you can do to try to fix them.

Southern cook and teacher Nathalie Dupree taught me about Southern cooking: black-eyed peas, grits cakes, cornbread muffins, Mississippi caviar, and okra griddle cakes. That same year, Nathalie was inaugurated as the president of the IACS.

I took a class in Chinese cooking and learnt about velveting prawns—the method that gives that wonderful glossy, smooth texture you get from a prawn in a Chinese restaurant. It's a technique you can do well in advance of the final cooking, and one that's also used to make slices of skinned chicken breast smooth and firm.

On the thirty-fifth floor of the Sheraton hotel, a small man armed with a knife, a tray of the freshest seafood, a jar of rice vinegar, a handful of fresh vegetables, and bowls of rice, sugar and salt held us all transfixed, oblivious to the magnificent harbour views outside the windows surrounding us, as he prepared sushi. Sushi was a new food trend in the West in the eighties, and we all wanted to know how to make it. To this day, I still tip the cooked rice onto a tray and fan it to dry and cool, as I was instructed to do by master sushi chef Tak Suetsugu. Being a sushi master chef isn't like *MasterChef* on TV. Before they get to even make sushi rice, Japanese sushi chefs have to spend five years in training and apprenticeship.

A whole new world was opening up to me, and not just about North American cooking but about *all* kinds of cooking. There were so many new ingredients to try, and so many different ways to use things I was familiar with. I knew about cornmeal, but did I know about grits and collard greens? Or velveting prawns, or how to make fresh bean curd, or how to achieve the perfect sushi rice? Here at the IACS conference, I was in the ultimate melting pot, learning from foodies whose roots networked the globe. I soaked up every morsel of knowledge with the relentless hunger of a baby bird.

> A whole new world was opening up to me, and not just about North American cooking but about *all* kinds of cooking. There were so many new ingredients to try, and so many different ways to use things I was familiar with.

Most of all, I learnt about networking. I'd never done this before. 'Who are you?' 'What do you do?' And, once the people I met knew I was from New Zealand and therefore no threat, 'How can we work together?' Business cards flew through the air like confetti. It was like speed-dating, without the prospect of a happy ending. Breakfast, lunch and dinner, I was surrounded by food-obsessed people. It felt like some kind of nirvana. Here, food was the new religion. In the space of just a few days, I had a Rolodex of some of the best contacts in the food business in the USA.

During one of these mix-and-mingle events, I met a charming Frenchwoman called Danièle, who was in her late thirties, maybe early forties. In that animated manner of conversation you have when neither one of you speaks much of the other's language, I gleaned that she came from a farm in the southwest of France, was recently divorced and was in the USA to help some people establish a foie gras business in upstate New York. She kindly invited me to stay, and scribbled her New York address on a scrap of paper. 'I'll be there early in the summer,' she said. 'The apartment is waiting for you any time. I'll tell my flatmates you're coming.' I'd been to New York with my mother as a teenager, when she had taken me to Europe in an attempt to wrest me from my limpet-like attraction to then-boyfriend Billy. My memories of the city were filled with sky-high room studs, billowing curtains and amazing art collections. I couldn't wait to get back there. I squirrelled the piece of paper with Danièle's address away in my pocket.

We had the most amazing ingredients in the world, but we didn't really have a food culture that anyone knew about. I stored the thought away.

Most of the Americans I met at the conference didn't have a clue about where New Zealand was—or, if they did, they thought it was some part of Australia. But everyone loved the accent. They wanted to know all about New Zealand food. 'What's the food culture down there? What do you guys all eat?' I must have been asked a hundred times.

What *was* our food all about? I started to think about it. We had the most amazing ingredients in the world, but we didn't really have a food culture that anyone knew about. I stored the thought away.

AFTER THE CONFERENCE FINISHED, I hired a car and headed north towards Canada. En route, I stopped to forage for morels with Steve Czernetsky, whose mushroom class I had attended. It was spring—morel season—and, since I was a foreigner and therefore unlikely to appropriate his secret patch, he was happy to take me along. Well, kind of happy. For over an hour we zigzagged across the landscape in his little car, a snakes-and-ladders journey of rough tracks heading who knew where. Finally, we stopped and got out to walk.

If Steve could have blindfolded me, I think he would have. As it was, the stealth with which we entered the woods, covering our tracks with pine branches, checking no one else was about, and setting our course with a compass, made me feel like a character in a covert spy mission. Where was the film crew? Deep in the conifer forest, Steve revealed the extraordinary thing that is a true black morel. The fungi looked a little bit like a tiny pine cone stuck in the ground. Finding them is a bit like diving for pāua—you have to get your eye in, and then you can spot them easily. It's important not to confuse true morels and false ones, as there are two highly poisonous lookalikes. Cutting the stem is the easiest test: true morels are always hollow, and always attach to the stem at the base. (False morels have a spongy centre and either don't attach to the stem at the base or attach high up the stem.)

Once we had gathered a small bowl of treasure, we returned to the main road and drove to a restaurant where Steve often sold his fickle, precious bounty. The kitchen cooked up our haul with butter and garlic, and we sat out in the weak spring sunshine on the porch and ate them with a basket of fresh-baked bread and a glass of crispy, flinty, mineral Willamette Valley riesling. For a fungi so delicate and almost transparent, the morels were incredibly rich, meaty, nutty, toasty, earthy and fleetingly smoky. For the first time, I understood just why people might fork out vast wads of cash to eat them when they were in season.

ON VANCOUVER ISLAND, I DROVE north up the west coast to the Sooke Harbour House. After showing me around his kitchen garden and picking handfuls of chervil and baby rocket, my host, owner Sinclair Phillips, donned his wetsuit, gloves, flippers and snorkel and went into the icy water in search of prickly sea urchins. While I waited on the shoreline, I dipped my fingertips in the water. The sea was dead flat—not a wave breaking on the shore—but it was freezing, maybe seven or eight degrees Celsius. I hoped Sinclair wouldn't get hypothermia out there on my behalf.

Just a few minutes later, he emerged from the water triumphantly holding two enormous sea urchins above his head. They looked like iridescent balls of tumbleweed. The spines of these glorious purple urchins (*Strongylocentrotus purpuratus*) were much longer than those of New Zealand kina (*Evechinus chloroticus*), which are browny green and shaped like a bird's nest.

Back in the lodge kitchen, Sinclair scooped the five fat orange roes from each urchin into a small bowl, taking care not to prick his fingers on the needle-sharp and slightly venomous spines. In a small pot, he whipped up a beurre blanc, then in a separate pan heated a big knob of butter until it was nut-brown, and quickly pan-fried two fillets of gleamingly fresh halibut. The reserved urchin roes were folded into the beurre blanc along with a little chervil. Everything was ready. Almost ceremonially, Sinclair plated the halibut and gently spooned over the sauce. He passed me the plate, and served up another for himself.

We sat down to eat with a view over the water. The fish was impeccably cooked, the skin golden and crispy, the flesh meltingly juicy, just at the perfect point of a flake. A light anise flavour from the chervil brightened the buttery sauce, the roes flecking through and pinging a briny, fruity mango sweetness, smooth and silky.

Across the bay, late snow had fallen, forming icing-sugar lines of white between the evergreen pines. The air was fresh and incredibly clear and clean. Everything in one moment. Magical.

There was no one else there, and it was extraordinary. Sooke Harbour is now well established, with strings of awards from Condé Nast, *Travel +*

Leisure, Fodor's and *Wine Spectator*, but back then it was all just beginning. For a brief moment I thought, *Why not just stay here and rent a room in this place with Sinclair and his lovely French wife?* But I was hungry to discover more of the foodie world I had encountered back in Seattle, to learn new things, and to meet new people. Hungry for the future and to find my path in it.

IN DETROIT, I WAS THE guest of an entrepreneurial chef by the name of Yvonne Gill, a New Zealander who had emigrated to the United States in 1973. I had met Yvonne at the conference. She had owned a few restaurants and was known as 'the woman who brought quiche to Detroit'. At the time of my visit, she had just set up a gourmet takeout experiment called Yvonne's to Go, which offered quality meals prepared by toqued chefs working inside a Farmer Jack supermarket. She was way ahead of her time.

We drove over to the Polish side of town and ate pierogi in a hole-in-the-wall diner, then retreated to a bar frequented by a bunch of skinheads and purple-haired punks wearing leather jackets and Doc Martens combat boots, where a jarring heavy-metal band was playing.

Back at her large, rambling country house Yvonne taught me how to barbecue veal T-bones. She picked tarragon, thyme, oregano and rosemary from her garden, then used the herbs to marinate the steaks along with olive oil, lemon juice, salt and pepper. She lit a fire and barbecued the gigantic steaks over the embers. Out on the lawn under the flowering albizia, we ate a whole one each. They were tender and sweet and amazingly juicy.

NEW YORK WAS CALLING, and I still had the little piece of paper with Danièle's address written on it from when I met her at the conference in Seattle. So I caught a Greyhound bus from Detroit to New York, departing very early on a Sunday morning and arriving 16 hours later. For a very long time, the Greyhound, aka the Dog, was the cheapest way to travel across

North America, and the bus I rode that particular Sunday was filled with lowlifes. I didn't dare sleep for fear of being robbed.

It was just before midnight when I wearily disembarked and, after enquiring where to get a taxi, walked down to Broadway to hail a cab.

A yellow car pulled up to the kerb. 'Where ya goin, gal?'

When I replied that I'd like to go to Brooklyn, he hit the accelerator and disappeared into the night. I hailed down another cab, and the same thing happened. Next time, I shoved a $20 bill through the window and said, 'Brooklyn, please.' And off we went.

Pulling up just off the corner of Atlantic Avenue at 362 Dean Street, I thought the cab driver must have the wrong address. I checked my little piece of paper. This was it. A group of hookers was idling on the other side of the street. Outside 362 Dean Street, an assortment of bodies were passed out on the pavement. There even looked to be someone lying just inside the gate in the garden.

'Pretty rough neighbourhood you got here, gal. I'm happy to wait till you get yourself inside. Wouldn't wanna get yourself stuck outside around here this time o' night.' The driver's accent rolled out long and slow from the deep south.

I grabbed my pack from the boot, and navigated my way around the passed-out bodies to the front door. I knocked once, twice, three times. No reply. It was Sunday night and now very late. Would anyone come? Actually, was anyone there? I had just turned up—I hadn't written or called to let anyone know I was coming. I was mentally working out a plan B when the door finally opened. A short, plump guy wearing a dressing gown and slippers rubbed his eyes and yawned. 'You must be Annabel,' he said. 'We've

OPPOSITE (Clockwise from top left) My mentor and long-time friend Danièle Mazet-Delpeuch, French culinary queen; wearing my chef's whites during a week-long intensive course on nutrition; growing out my punk haircut in New York; eating out at an NYC restaurant with my Kiwi friend Jan McCartney.

been expecting you for a while now; Danièle said you might turn up one day. I'm Jay. Bedroom's upstairs. Second floor, door at the end.' He turned and headed back into the dark of the apartment.

I waved a thumbs-up at the cab driver and headed inside, navigating my way up the stairs. When I opened the door at the end, I turned on the light. It was a broom cupboard. Literally. The smallest room I'd ever seen. The single bed had a hand's width to spare down one side. But I didn't care. I don't think I even got undressed. I just collapsed, exhausted, relieved to finally be off that godawful Greyhound bus, off the scary street below and in a bed in a house with people who knew someone I sort of knew . . . well, had met . . . once. I slept like a log.

THE NEXT DAY WHEN I got up, Danièle was there waiting for me at the kitchen table. We chatted a while before she headed off to work.

A few days later, on Wednesday, we headed into the city together to the farmers' market over in Union Square. After perusing all the produce on offer, Danièle carefully chose a fat, heavy leek. Back in the squinty kitchen of the apartment, she transformed this humble vegetable into an elegant, quivering tart. I was awestruck.

For the next month, we followed this simple routine—a trip to the market two or three times a week to find the freshest, cheapest vegetables, then back to the apartment to cook. Each day we made something new, with flavours to make your heart sing. In that old-school French way, Danièle was the master of transforming the humblest ingredients into something of sublime deliciousness. Leeks were always cheap. Danièle taught me how to bake leeks and serve them with a mustardy vinaigrette and grated hard-boiled egg on top. Sometimes she would slowly braise the leeks in stock with potatoes for a soup, then chill it down and fold in a little cream for a luscious vichyssoise.

Having Mother Hubbard cupboards was no impediment to this

marvellous woman's entertaining style. Danièle gathered friends like some people collect shoes. There was a pair—or several—for every occasion. People were always coming over to the apartment to join us for lunch or dinner. No matter how simple the meal, Danièle would always set a pretty table out in the back courtyard with candles, various glasses, napkins, water and wine. Hours were spent around that table, enjoying spirited conversations with friends old and new. Often I would go with Danièle and some of her foodie friends to Chinatown to eat at big round tables with spinning lazy Susans. Usually someone in the group knew enough Chinese to navigate the menu. One day a platter arrived with lettuce cups and a fine dice of lightly sauced meat. As I rolled up my lettuce cup and popped it into my mouth, I recognised the familiar fine taste of squab. Here, in yet another guise, my favourite meat, this time tempered with ginger and garlic oyster sauce.

> No matter how simple the meal, Danièle would always set a pretty table out in the back courtyard with candles, various glasses, napkins, water and wine. Hours were spent around that table, enjoying spirited conversations with friends old and new.

From Danièle, I learnt many things, but most of all I learnt what it means to be a cook.

One day, I told her what an amazing chef she was. She got mad. Really mad. 'I'm not a chef. I'm a cook!' she yelled. She wasn't the kind of person to yell. Calming down, she explained that being a chef is a profession that requires fancy tricks and culinary gymnastics, budgets and staff. 'Cooking,' she said, 'is all about your heart, making people feel welcome, nourished and loved.' She went on, 'You need to honour what nature provides, and cook resourcefully with what's at hand. Waste nothing. Share everything.' This brilliant woman's nurturing philosophy quickly became my mantra.

Both of us were stone broke, but we ate like kings. I knew little of her past, and neither of us could then foresee her exciting future—that she would go on to become French President François Mitterrand's personal cook, that she would travel to Antarctica for a year to cook for a group of environmental scientists, and that one day a film, *Haute Cuisine*, would be made about her and her amazing life.

> 'Cooking,' she said, 'is all about your heart, making people feel welcome, nourished and loved.' She went on, 'You need to honour what nature provides, and cook resourcefully with what's at hand. Waste nothing. Share everything.'

WE WERE EIGHT PEOPLE in the apartment on Dean Street—Danièle, me and six young gay guys. I was never sure quite how Danièle had found this particular abode. I was just grateful for a roof over my head.

One of my flatmates, Dan, a tall, gloomy blond from the Midwest, was a man with a one-dish repertoire. He'd whip up his tofu and brown rice casserole at least once a week for us all, layering up cooked brown rice with a tomato, oregano and olive sauce mixed with tofu, then he'd add a layer of spinach and another of cottage cheese. The layers would be repeated before the whole thing was topped with parmesan and baked in the oven. I put this recipe of Dan's in both my *Listener* column and my first-ever cookbook. What was I thinking? I made this dish again recently for the first time in decades. It's utterly vile. The only explanation I can think of is that, back then, I was always famished. Danièle and I were living on a wish and a dream.

It was the height of the AIDS crisis and no one yet fully understood the disease. There were all sorts of unfounded fears about how it spread, and how one might catch it. Alan, the leaseholder, was incredibly promiscuous. He placed ads in the *Village Voice* worded with an implicit message, and guys would turn up at the front door looking for him almost every day. He would disappear with them up to the attic above my room.

Whenever these random liaisons turned up, I would head out to explore the neighbourhood. It was one of roughest parts of New York back then—down-and-out Brooklyn before it got gentrified, so rough that the prostitutes used to try to solicit me. Everyone spoke Spanish, and if they weren't trying to solicit me they would try to intimidate me. Fortunately, I could fire it back as good as they gave. Out on the street, filthy Spanish expletives would hurl out of my mouth at the smallest provocation. '*Que te folle un pez!*' I'd cry. '*Gilipollas, tontopollas, culo! Hijo de puta, concha tu madre!*' (If you want the translations, I'll leave you to look them up for yourself.)

It was so satisfying throwing back these juicy insults. None of my acquaintances spoke Spanish, so they had no idea what I was saying. At 92 kilos, I was still most definitely La Gordita and, having acquired a very unflattering number-two haircut, I looked a bit like a hefty punk. The vibe I gave off was definitely 'don't mess with me'. After a few weeks, the neighbours knew to leave me alone.

WHEN I HAD BEEN IN New York for a few weeks, I headed into the city to make myself known to some importers who handled New Zealand foods. It wasn't easy, as no one knew who I was, but before long I was coming home with packets of venison and cases of feijoas and kiwifruit, and a mandate to work out recipes and ideas that could be promoted to the general public in New York. At the same time, Danièle was teaching classical French techniques at Peter Kump's New York Cooking School, and she got me a job there teaching game cooking and sometimes helping out with demos. I loved it all. There was so much to learn.

One frantic day, I helped my new friend Jill Roberts prepare hors d'oeuvres for a cocktail party for the Asia Society. The apartment kitchen in her Upper East Side apartment was so tiny you could stand in the middle and touch all four walls. And, out of the world's smallest kitchen, we prepared food for 300 people: 1200 tiny spicy Himalayan pea-and-potato dumplings, 600 spicy chickpea cakes, 600 little handmade breads and pancakes, and great buckets of dips. All of it made its way down the lift of Jill's fancy uptown apartment building, past the concierge, into a cab and up to the Asia Society rooms. The food was a hit. Those recipes also featured in my very first cookbook, and they *are* delicious.

I scored some gigs doing cooking demonstrations in supermarkets, and now and then I would get a job working on-set as a food-styling assistant. I could never believe how many people were needed to photograph a simple plate of food. Back in the eighties, the food stylist's bag of tricks went way beyond the ingredients of the lookalike ice cream I'd learnt to make at the IACS conference. Real milk quickly makes cornflakes look soggy, so the stylist would use white hair cream with a consistency like sunscreen lotion as a milk substitute, or fill the bowl with vegetable shortening, pour on a very thin layer of milk, and arrange the cornflakes and any fruit carefully on top. When it came to creating steam that held for more than a few seconds, soaked and microwaved tampons were your best bet. However, if you wanted a steaming ham, then someone would have to don protective gloves and a mask, and inject the ham with a syringe of hydrochloric acid. The photographer would be poised with their finger on the shutter for the perfect moment when the 'steam' would whirl and eddy attractively over the top of the ham. Frothy coffee was made with soap foam, and a convincing chardonnay was achieved by mixing a few drops of Kitchen Bouquet into water. No stylist worth their mettle went anywhere without a little bottle of Kitchen Bouquet browning sauce in their styling kit.

In addition to the food stylist and their assistants, there would always be two or three people running around unpacking props for the 'look' of the shoot. Would there be silver trays or earthenware pottery? Was the plate going to sit on a piece of marble or a barn siding or a tablecloth? Wads of fabric would be unloaded to drape as a background. It took forever to shoot a single dish. There would be toothpicks and glue and tweezers to move peas and sprigs of herbs. If the team got four shots done in a day's shoot, it seemed everyone was happy.

My stylist's toolbox was growing, but even if these techniques were useful to make food look 'perfect', it was all totally inedible. I wanted to be able to sit down after a shoot and eat everything. It seemed so wasteful, chucking all this food in a dumpster at the end of the day.

I'M NOT SURE HOW I actually sent my dispatches for my fortnightly *Listener* column back to New Zealand, as I didn't see a fax machine in action until I was living in NYC. But every fortnight I would sit down somewhere quiet to write my little story and put together the recipes that went with it.

After the IACS conference, my columns started to feature recipes inspired by what I had learnt. Cajun-blackened fish steaks, eight-treasure dragon soup, California sushi with miso-sesame mayonnaise, Creole sausage frittata, and pecan wild rice. Hitherto unknown words like 'brunoise', 'tataki', 'jicama', 'cassoulet', 'porcini', 'carambola', 'jerked' and 'mole' made themselves comfortable in my culinary lexis.

In my column published on 24 August 1985, I wrote about how little Americans knew about New Zealand food. 'Trays of tamarillos, cape gooseberries and feijoas sit unhappily on greengrocers' shelves. They don't make it into buyers' baskets because of a lack of knowledge about what they are and how to go about preparing them. Venison too is surprisingly new and untried.' I went on to talk about the trend for excessive desserts, and the prevalence of takeout food operations, salad bars in delis and supermarkets, and the fact that, given so much choice, 60 per cent of New Yorkers ate out nightly. Recipes followed: a house salad with Belgian endive, watercress, mint, kiwifruit, red peppers and a honey mustard dressing; a venison salad with red cabbage, crispy noodles and Asian dressing; and a passionfruit sorbet.

WHILE I WAS LIVING IN NYC, Ted sent me a letter to say he was planning to come down from Connecticut, where he was working as a roofer over the summer, and wanted to know if he could come and stay for a weekend.

On the Saturday morning after he arrived, I announced that I wanted to go into Manhattan to get a lens for my camera. There was a camera shop just down from Grand Central station, so we jumped on the B-line subway on Atlantic Ave, made a change at Franklin Avenue to the Number 4 train, and exited at Grand Central about 50 minutes later. I was walking up the stairs to the street ahead of the farm boy, but when I got to the top I noticed he had stopped about halfway up the stairs. He was talking to a young woman, and their conversation looked pretty intense, but I didn't think anything of it. She was kind of mousey and short.

When Ted finally caught me up he was looking decidedly flustered. 'Hey, I n-nn-n-need to t-tt-tt-tell you ss-s-something,' he said. He always stuttered when he was nervous. 'A-a-a-actually, that woman I was talking to is the woman I've been living with.'

I stared at him blankly. This was a surprise.

The skinny farm boy had been shacked up with very wealthy Sharon in her luxe Village apartment for the past few months. In fact, her driver had brought him over to my place in her limo.

'The driver stopped about five blocks from your place and wouldn't go any further.' Now that Ted was indignant, his stutter had gone. 'He said it was too rough and dangerous. I've told her that it's all over between us now, and I'll pick up my stuff later.'

I wasn't sure how I felt about this. We had a huge row.

Ted went back to Connecticut.

I didn't know if I wanted to ever see him again.

DANIÈLE WENT BACK TO FRANCE, and my friend Mary came over from New Zealand for a few months to stay with me at the Dean Street apartment. She got the attic room, which was hotter but bigger than mine. Mary and I would head into Manhattan to catch the $2 breakfasts (fresh orange juice, eggs, toast and coffee) which finished at 11 a.m., staving off our hunger until happy hour kicked in at around 5 p.m. and we could get half-price buckets of margaritas and free finger-food. This would see us through until the next morning, when we would do it all again.

Mary and I decided to enrol in some residential courses at the Culinary Institute of America in Hyde Park, near Poughkeepsie, in upstate New York. I chose a residential course for chefs on nutrition, and although I wasn't a chef my application was accepted. Back in New Zealand, I had tried all kinds of binge diets to lose weight—consuming only liquorice and lemons was all the rage at the time. But, with almost any elimination diet that leaves you feeling deprived, you quickly put on whatever weight you lose. I needed a long-term plan that would help me to transfer my passion for food from my hips to my brain.

At my first lecture on the nutrition course, we were presented with a long table holding 100 plates, each containing a different ingredient with a value of 100 calories. Some plates were piled high with vegetables, while others held a scant handful of nuts or potato chips, or a little pat of butter or cheese. It was a revelation: not all foods are created equal. Fat has more than double the energy by weight of either protein or carbohydrates. We learnt to create meals that balanced complex carbohydrates with fat and protein. Since complex carbs are high in fibre, they digest more slowly and are also more filling, which makes them a good option for long-term weight control. I quickly came to understand that relying on butter and cream to deliver great flavour meant you'd end up inhaling too many calories. To solve the problem of low-fat food tasting bland or flat, we used foods with umami, which translates roughly from Japanese as 'savoury deliciousness'. Mushrooms, anchovies, tomato paste, parmesan, chicken stock, beef stock and fish sauce are all ingredients that contain lots of umami, so work well to boost flavours.

For my graduating dish, I flattened out a chicken breast and placed a sheet of nori on top with some roasted pepper strips and blanched ginger down the middle. This got rolled up into a log and poached in a gingery broth. Once it was cooked, I sliced it into noisettes, and served it with a brown rice pilaf and steamed ginger broccoli on a square black plate. Fiddly, but that's what they wanted. I passed with flying colours.

I enrolled in another course on regional American cookery, described by our tutor as 'a language made up of oceans, mountains and the trade routes imposed on them'. It was the first time I had really thought about how geography, climate and culture influence food, and how these contexts come to play on the plate. It became so clear that the homogenised offerings of an industrial food culture were taking so much from people's lives— their sense of place and belonging and culture.

These two courses changed everything about the way I cooked, for the better. I was on a pathway to weight loss that didn't require any diet strategies. Simply by creating food that was light, fresh and very flavoursome, the kilos fell off. I also had a framework to understand what makes up a food culture—the influences of climate, geography, religion, migration and trade, and the issues around culinary appropriation, food ethics and globalisation.

My mother had taught me that everything we eat or might want to eat starts out as a seed or a spore, and can take weeks, months, sometimes even years, before it is ready to be harvested. When you cook, she would say, even in the simple act of taking the care to wash and dry leaves for a salad, you are honouring nature. When you eat, no matter how simple the meal, it's a celebration. Set a table, light some candles, and bring a conversation to the table.

Lincoln University in Christchurch had taught me about plants and how they grow, and gave me an even greater appreciation of nature.

Danièle had taught me that being a cook rather than a chef was about home and heart and love.

> My mother had taught me that everything we eat or might want to eat starts out as a seed or a spore, and can take weeks, months, sometimes even years, before it is ready to be harvested. When you cook, she would say, even in the simple act of taking the care to wash and dry leaves for a salad, you are honouring nature.

And the courses at the Culinary Institute taught me how to make healthy food choices, and how to cook delicious, nourishing food by eating locally and by embracing and upholding culinary traditions.

A jigsaw was forming in my mind, as I started to think about how I could bring all these ideas together.

BY THIS STAGE, I HAD quite a serious Iranian boyfriend. His parents and siblings lived over in New Jersey, and Ali had an apartment in Queens. When Mary went home to New Zealand after a few months, I was on my own, either staying at the Dean Street apartment or at Ali's. He was an engineer, tall, skinny and very good-looking. Unsurpassed vanity—it took him two hours in the bathroom to get ready for work in the morning—and nasal New Jersey twang aside, Ali was a hell of a lot of fun and he adored me. He was the perfect salve for my bruised ego post the farm boy's disastrous visit.

We'd go to gallery openings, bars and parties together. Every Friday and Saturday night he'd take me out somewhere new for dinner. In 1985, New York was definitely becoming the hip and happening place to eat. Chefs were the new celebrities. Paul Prudhomme's blackened Cajun food was hot, Wolfgang Puck brought gourmet pizzas to the table, and Jean-Georges Vongerichten and Charlie Trotter had introduced a trend for reductions, infusions and essences. Composed salads, edible flowers, chilled soups, countless varieties of mushrooms, baby vegetables, and vegetable chips were all the rage. Slashes of sauces were painted onto plates as garnish, along with dustings of spice. There were herbs—lots of herbs.

> In 1985, New York was definitely becoming the hip and happening place to eat. Chefs were the new celebrities. Paul Prudhomme's blackened Cajun food was hot, Wolfgang Puck brought gourmet pizzas to the table, and Jean-Georges Vongerichten and Charlie Trotter had introduced a trend for reductions, infusions and essences.

For all his vanity, Ali could be a total clown. One night we went to a lobster bar, and he put the prickly legs up his nose and pulled funny faces. The problem came when he tried to get them out. The barbs on the legs had gone in with ease but there was no easy way to get them out. A trip to the emergency room was required, with sedation to remove the prickly legs.

One day in late November, Ali took me home to meet his parents. His mother was very beautiful, a gentle woman with long, dark hair and soft brown eyes. I could see his father didn't approve of his eldest son having a foreign girlfriend. On the table sat a nine-branched menorah with seven lit candles, and a copy of the Hebrew Bible open alongside. It was Hanukkah. Ali's family were Persian Jews, and he told me they had been friends with the Shah of Iran and his family. In 1979, they had escaped, along with an estimated 60,000 to 80,000 other Iranian Jews, to the United States. It dawned on me just what a big deal it was for Ali to bring me home to his parents. Things were getting complicated, but I knew this wasn't the forever-and-ever relationship for me. It would never work. No matter how hard I tried, I still couldn't get that farm boy out of my head.

It was time for me to leave New York and get back to New Zealand, to start building the dream. I had so many exciting ideas for how to put our little country on the map.

NIBBLES PLATTER

I always like to keep a few things on hand that I can pull together for a nibbles platter to serve with drinks. Three of my favourites appear below and on pages 206–207.

ZUCCHINI, GOAT'S CHEESE AND BASIL CROSTINI

READY IN 30 MINUTES + COOLING · SERVES 4–6 AS A STARTER · V

3 medium-large zucchini
¼ cup extra virgin olive oil
2 large cloves garlic, crushed
finely grated zest of 1 lemon
a pinch of chilli flakes
60 g (2¼ oz) goat's cheese or feta, crumbled
12–16 fresh basil leaves, finely torn, plus extra to serve
salt and ground black pepper, to taste
Croutons, to serve (see page 98)

The zucchini topping I've used in this recipe is so easy to rustle up, and tastes great when tossed through pasta or used on a tart (such as my Classic Pissaladière on page 34).

Coarsely grate the zucchini onto a clean tea towel, pull up the sides, twist, and squeeze tightly over a sink or bowl to remove liquid.

Heat oil in a large frying pan and add zucchini, garlic, lemon zest and chilli flakes. Stir-fry over a medium heat until zucchini is soft but not brown (about 5 minutes). Remove from heat and allow to cool for at least 10 minutes.

Mix in goat's cheese or feta and basil, and season to taste. To serve, spread onto Croutons and top with extra basil leaves.

MARINATED GREEN OLIVES WITH ORANGE AND FENNEL

READY IN 15 MINUTES + COOLING · MAKES 1 MEDIUM JAR · DF · GF · V · VE

2 cups green olives (not pitted)
1 tsp fennel seeds
1 tsp chopped fresh rosemary leaves
zest of ½ orange, cut with a vegetable peeler
2 cloves garlic, thinly sliced
1 cup neutral oil

These marinated olives will keep for months in the fridge, and they bring a nice pop of colour to a nibbles platter.

Place all ingredients in a pot and bring to a sizzle. Reduce heat to lowest setting and cook for 15 minutes—the oil needs to sizzle very gently so the garlic and orange won't brown. Allow to cool.

Strain, reserving oil for cooking and dressings, then transfer olives and aromatics to a serving bowl. If not serving at once, transfer olives and their oil to a sterilised jar, adding more oil as needed to fully cover.

SESAME LAVOSH CRACKERS

READY IN 35 MINUTES · MAKES ABOUT 40
DF · GF, IF GLUTEN-FREE FLOUR IS USED · V · VE

1 cup plain flour or
   gluten-free flour
4 tbsp white or black
   sesame seeds, or a
   mixture of both
1½ tsp salt
½ cup water
¼ cup extra virgin olive
   oil, plus extra to brush
2 tsp sesame oil
flaky salt, to taste

This crispy lavosh stores well in an airtight container, and can be whipped out at a moment's notice.

Preheat oven to 165°C (330°F) fanbake.

Combine flour, sesame seeds and salt in a bowl. Mix water and oils, add to the dry ingredients and stir to form a soft, pliable dough.

Divide into 4 pieces and roll each out between 2 sheets of baking paper as thinly as possible. They need to be virtually see-through. Remove top sheet of baking paper, brush dough lightly with a little extra olive oil and sprinkle with flaky salt. Slide each sheet of dough (still on its baking paper) onto an oven tray and bake until crisp and pale golden (15–18 minutes).

Allow to cool fully, then break into pieces. Store in an airtight container.

FLASH-ROASTED SALMON
WITH CHILLI LIME GLAZE

READY IN 30 MINUTES · SERVES 4 · DF · GF

4 pieces boneless,
  skinless salmon fillet,
  cut from the thick end
250 g (9 oz) cherry
  tomatoes, or 4 regular
  tomatoes, cored and
  quartered
3 tbsp water
pickled ginger, to garnish
black sesame seeds,
  to garnish

CHILLI LIME GLAZE
1 clove garlic, crushed
½ cup sweet chilli sauce
¼ cup rice vinegar
1 tbsp fish sauce
finely grated zest of
  1 lime
1 double makrut lime leaf,
  very finely shredded,
  or 3 tsp finely grated
  lemongrass

Fish is always my favourite choice for a smart dinner when you are pressed for time—it's so quick to cook and works beautifully with all kinds of different flavourways. I like to serve this salmon with cooked soba noodles and Asian greens.

Preheat oven to 240°C (475°F) fanbake. Line a large, shallow roasting dish with baking paper for easy clean-up.

To make the Chilli Lime Glaze, mix all ingredients in a bowl or small jar.

Arrange salmon pieces in a single layer in the prepared dish and divide the glaze over the top. Scatter tomatoes into the dish and drizzle water around (not on top of) the salmon. Roast until salmon is just cooked through (it should give when gently pressed) and glaze is just starting to caramelise (8–9 minutes).

Serve immediately, garnished with pickled ginger and sesame seeds.

LEMON SOUFFLÉ CAKE

READY IN 1 HOUR 20 MINUTES + COOLING · SERVES 8 · GF
V, IF VEGETARIAN SOUR CREAM OR CRÈME FRAÎCHE IS USED

5 large (size 7) eggs,
 separated
½ cup sugar
¼ cup honey
1 tsp vanilla extract
finely grated zest of
 1 lemon
¼ cup strained
 lemon juice
1 tsp orange blossom
 water (optional)
1 cup sour cream or
 crème fraîche
1 cup Greek yoghurt
⅓ cup ground almonds
⅓ cup maize cornflour
 (cornstarch) or
 rice flour

TO SERVE
1 cup Greek yoghurt
1 cup crème fraîche or
 sour cream
¼ cup Pistachio Praline
 (see page 318), chopped
 pistachios or toasted
 flaked almonds

This cake looks spectacular when it comes out of the oven, then it gradually sinks and looks rather underwhelming. But don't be deceived—you'd be hard pressed to find a more delicious dessert cake. Once it's been chilled and topped with that glorious mix of yoghurt and crème fraîche, it becomes the lightest, most moreish cake you have ever tasted, with a cheesecake-like texture.

Preheat oven to 150°C (300°F) (not fanbake). Line the base and sides of a 23 cm (9 in) diameter cake tin with baking paper, ensuring the sides extend about 4 cm (1½ in) above the rim of the tin.

Using an electric beater on high speed, whisk together egg yolks, sugar, honey, vanilla, lemon zest and juice, and orange blossom water (if using), until the mixture is creamy and pale and the sugar is dissolved (8–10 minutes).

Mix in sour cream or crème fraîche and yoghurt, beating to just combine. Stir in ground almonds and cornflour or rice flour.

Using a clean beater and bowl, whisk the egg whites until they form soft peaks when the beater is lifted from the bowl. Gently fold into the batter, about a third at a time. Pour into prepared tin and bake until golden and puffed up like a soufflé with a slight wobble (about 1 hour). It may be cracked on top.

Remove from oven (it will deflate immediately). Allow to cool in the tin, then cover and chill until ready to serve. It will keep in the fridge for up to 24 hours.

When ready to serve, mix yoghurt with crème fraîche or sour cream. Spoon on top of cake and garnish with Pistachio Praline or nuts.

EIGHT

The international man of mystery

Serendipity…fate…destiny…

When I had last spent time with the skinny farm boy in Manhattan, I hadn't been sure I ever wanted to see him again. And our very first date, several years prior to the Grand Central encounter with Sharon from the Village, had hardly been more promising. We hadn't gone out for lunch, or dinner, or even to the movies. No, the invitation turned out to be to go for a dive for pāua.

I had just recently returned from my trip to South America, and was staying in Gisborne with Debbie. Ted showed up in a wreck of a car, with 13 dogs in a trailer hitched behind. He'd made a roof-rack for his skis out of two pieces of four-by-two, drilling through the car roof and attaching the wood with wire. George Thorogood & the Destroyers blasted from two white ice-cream containers set up as speakers behind the back seat. On the way into town, we stopped outside Trend Burger bar, where Ted ordered 14 egg burgers. I stood at the counter, wondering what the hell he was going to do with all those burgers. I for one wasn't going to be eating them. We carried the stash back to the car, and Ted carefully opened up the packets, then gave one to each of the dogs in the trailer. Beth, his favourite heading bitch, got two. The dogs gulped them down, tails wagging like crazy. You could tell they'd had this treat before. Dogs love eggs.

OPPOSITE With Ted at Wainui Beach in Gisborne—
I'm wearing one of the beautiful dresses Mum made for me.
PREVIOUS Wedding bells at Old St Paul's in Wellington.

'Thh-thh-th-thhh-thought we'd go for a bbb-b-bb-biit of a ddd-ddd-dive at W-w-Wainui,' Ted said, as we got back into the car.

I'd never noticed he had such a bad stutter before then.

We drove off, and stopped at the house of one of his friends. 'Ff-ffa-fancy cc-c-ccc-coming to the bb-b-beach, mate?' Ted asked the good-looking guy who answered the door.

The front seat of the red '67 Valiant had been moved back to accommodate Ted's extraordinarily long legs, and was wedged hard up against the back seat. There was no legroom to sit in the back and, besides, the back seat was full of crates of beer. So we all crammed onto the front bench seat, the friend parked in the middle. The seat was so far back that my view was out the back window. *Strange*, I thought. *Why would you invite your best mate—a really good-looking one at that—on your first date?* Although Digby had women falling all over him, he was oblivious to his head-turning looks. But I wasn't even vaguely interested in this suave friend. It was the tall, skinny guy, the brother of my flatmate, who I couldn't stop thinking about.

The day was so rough and windy that we didn't actually make it into the water. Instead we sat in the car and drank beer. There wasn't even a picnic.

I went home wondering, *Was that an actual date?*

But there was definitely that spark.

A FEW WEEKS LATER, Ted was driving me back to town after I'd been up at the farm riding with Debbie. As we came over the crest of the hill, a pheasant ran out on to the road and the car in front of us hit it.

'Stop!' I yelled.

Ted screeched the car to a halt, thinking something must be terribly wrong.

I leapt out, dispatched the dying pheasant by wringing its neck, and shoved it in the boot. When we got back to Debbie's flat in town, I plucked and gutted my bounty, then slowly braised it with a can of guavas, orange juice and zest, onions, garlic and prunes. It was fragrant and delicious. My maybe-new-beau gobbled it down appreciatively. I'd never seen anyone eat so fast.

'Boarding school,' he said when I asked him why he ate so quickly. 'If you didn't get in quickly, there'd be nothing left to eat.'

Ted weighed in at just 65 kilos. At two metres tall, the guy was so damn skinny, he looked like a reed that would blow over in a strong wind. But, oh, could he eat! The original nose-to-tail eater, Ted would kill a sheep at the start of each week, then over the next seven days eat his way through it all by himself. Heart, liver, lungs, legs, brains. A sheep a week. Nothing wasted.

A FEW MONTHS AFTER THAT first date, Ted borrowed his dad's fancy new farm truck so we could take a trip around the East Coast. He left me in the kitchen with his mother while he went to get some gas that his dad had said was in a 44-gallon drum up in the cow paddock behind the house. I was trapped in the kitchen with Stella while she quizzed me about every aspect of my life. I just wanted to hide in the butter cupboard. I'd met her before, when Debbie had taken me up to the farm, but now that I was dating her son she was definitely wanting to suss me out.

Finally, we were off. About 300 metres down the road, the truck stalled. Ted got out, opened the bonnet, then shut it again and kicked the tyres. Like his sister, Ted knew everything you could ever know about horses and pretty much nothing about cars. I sat in the truck for a good few minutes thinking about what could be wrong. I sure as hell wasn't going back to the house. Then it twigged: the fuel line. I got out and slid myself underneath the truck, figured out where the fuel line was, and set to bleeding it. Turned out the 44-gallon drum had been filled with water.

We went down to the Patutahi Tavern to celebrate getting the truck going again. We played a few rounds of pool and had a couple of beers, then set off on our adventure. At Ruatōria, Ted suggested we call in to see the Kai Kart, which was famous for its pies. Around this time, there'd been a kind of Māori Rastafarian uprising around Ruatōria. Acts of arson and vandalism saw farmers' fences cut and stock stolen. The police station, houses, woolsheds, churches and a marae got burnt down. They even kidnapped a cop. As we were driving into town, a posse of bareback riders carrying the red, green and yellow Rasta flag pulled out in front of us. Ted slowed down, and we pulled in quietly behind them.

The group stopped at the police station, where a group of cops and kaumātua were waiting. Everyone got off their horses, except two guys who sat fixed like statues on their skewbald ponies. I figured one of them must have been a guy by the name of Joe Nepe, who was up for the murder of another local, Lance Kupenga. It had been the most bizarre ritualistic killing the country had ever seen. Nepe had decided that Kupenga was Johnny Too Bad—the local Rasta term for having the Devil in you—and his number was up. So Nepe walked Kupenga up Whakaahu, the sacred hill near Ruatōria, then chopped off his head with an axe. He kicked the head into one hole and dragged the body over to another tomo, the 'bottomless pit'—an infamous hole in the ground where bodies had apparently been thrown for centuries.

And now here we were, right as they were taking the depositions for the hearing. There definitely wasn't a good vibe. Ted and I decided it was time to hightail it out of town. Forget the Kai Kart—we were out of there. We stopped at the pub in Te Araroa, up on the cape. There was a hitching post outside for people to tie up their horses. Inside, pinned on the faded yellow

OPPOSITE Hanging out with the international man of mystery. (Clockwise from top) Ted can always make me laugh; scones on the front lawn at the farm; swimming at Mahia Beach; with our friend Mary and her daughter Belinda at Ted's family bach; and all dressed up for our first ball—I'm wearing a ball gown of my grandmother's.

wallpaper, a sign read: *The names of people smoking dope in this bar will be reported to the police. No exceptions.* A man reeking of dak pulled out a wad of cash as thick as a bible to pay for his beer. The coast has always had a feeling of the Wild West, and at this time there was a lot of dope being grown up there. The gangs were running things and operated under their own rules. There were guys with AK-47s guarding plantations, tripwires set up. Murder was in the air.

We kept on driving, all the way around the coast to Ōhiwa before we decided it felt safe to stop and stay. We collected cockles, lit a fire on the beach, and cooked them in an old tin can for dinner.

WHILE I WAS LIVING up in Auckland, Debbie was always inviting me down to Gisborne. There was a Hunt Club ball, and her brother was too shy to ask anyone. Could I come? They were hunting at Mahia. Could I come? So-and-so was having a party. Could I come? Debbie matchmade the two of us at every opportunity.

As our romance slowly bloomed, I would sometimes head down to the farm for a long weekend, and bake scones and pies and cakes in Ted's tiny kitchen. His house was a few kilometres up the road from the homestead. I'd leave Auckland around seven or eight o'clock on a Friday night, and hurtle down to Gisborne in my Honda station wagon, usually arriving well after midnight. Ted would have to be up by 3 a.m. to head off mustering, but he would be back by 11 a.m.

Often, I'd saddle up a horse and ride up the back with a picnic for our lunch. Ted said I had a great seat on a horse, but I actually didn't have a clue how to ride. He was always going on at me to be more careful. 'You're going much too fast,' he'd say. 'You'll come to trouble one day and have an accident.'

TED'S MATERNAL GRANDMOTHER, MABEL, had been dux at her high school, and was just a couple of months off graduating as New Zealand's first registered female pharmacist when she got married. Her journey to her new home on the farm involved a long drive in a service car from town up into the hills. At the end of the road, she had to jump on a horse to first cross the river, then make the 40-minute ride up through rough hill country to the homestead. It was incredibly remote.

A year into the marriage, the couple's first child was born, and then, just ten months later, Mabel delivered triplets. She had four children under one, and no home help. Can you even imagine? She went on to produce seven more healthy children. No one died on her watch, a remarkable feat at that time. The triplets, who lived into their nineties, held the Guinness World Record for being the oldest living triplets in the world.

Mabel baked bread every day and made her own soap. The family milked a house cow and ran a small dairy, grew their own vegetables, and ate meat from the farm. Fat drippings from the roast were used as the starting point for any frying, or as a spread for bread. (When I met Ted, his mother still had a big enamel cup of dripping, which she kept in the fridge and used to cook with.) The service car would deliver groceries every few months, dropping them at the end of the road by the river. Someone from the farm would ride down, pack the groceries into pīkau bags tied on to the horses' saddles, then head back over the slippery riverbed home. Mabel's grocery list consisted solely of flour, tea, dried fruit, rolled oats, salt, pepper, baking powder, baking soda, yeast, cayenne pepper, and rice for rice pudding. That was it. Healthy but basic. They were Irish-born Presbyterians, these grandparents. Practical and incredibly hard-working.

Things hadn't changed much a generation later, when her grandson Ted was born. He rode his horse bareback over full wire fences to school. The grocery list now included jelly crystals and canned herrings in tomato sauce. After school, Ted and Debbie would steal the jelly crystals, pull the blankets off their beds and race their horses up to the back paddock. There, they would set up the blankets like tents, play cowboys and Indians, and eat the crystals.

Ted's mother was more interested in cattle than in cooking. A good fruit cake and vaguely edible mince on toast were the sum of her culinary prowess. I had grown up on a diet of gourmet meals from my mother's kitchen, so Ted's mother's cooking was a rude shock to my taste buds. What's more, in my family Christmas was a really big deal. My parents were very social and had a wide group of friends, both in New Zealand and abroad. My mother would spend weeks baking treats for friends and neighbours, making the tree pretty, and filling the house with Christmas decorations. Every year the folded strips of crêpe paper would come out of the Christmas box, and get hung in long lines from the picture rails around the walls. By the time we got to Christmas, there would be hundreds of cards floating down the walls on colourful crêpe ribbons. All cards received were carefully marked off in the Christmas notebook. If a card didn't come in from someone my parents were expecting one from, there would be a debate—people didn't tend to get divorced much in those days, so if they didn't write it usually meant they had carked it. The name was gently crossed out of the book with the date written alongside. Christmas Day was one long feast, starting with a full cooked breakfast, moving on to neighbourly elevenses with fruit-mince pies, and then a long, late, excessive lunch—the whole stuffed turkey, gravy and every vegetable known to humankind hoopla. Pudding came in layers—berries and pavs and meringues and puddings and chocolates and cherries and nuts. At the end we would stumble, catatonic, from the table to sleep until the next round of eating later in the evening.

My beau's family could not have been more different. Christmas was the day you got a half-day off. The first time I spent Christmas with them, I turned up full of excitement, laden with treats and gifts. There was no sign of anything Christmassy—no tree, no decorations, no sign of any presents.

'Lasagne's nearly ready,' Ted's older sister, Anne, called from the kitchen. I sat sobbing in the bathroom for a long time. I'd never been so homesick.

Many years later, in the very sad year of my own lovely mother's death, Mum insisted we have Christmas dinner at home with her.

'I'd love to cook,' I said.

'No,' she mumbled. (She could hardly talk at this stage.) 'No.' I had to lean forward to understand. 'No, I've got a lasagne in the freezer.'

And so it was: lasagne for Christmas dinner. Ted could not have been happier—I had been banging on about that Christmas lasagne with his family for a couple of decades by then.

I HAD BEEN BACK IN New Zealand for a few months post New York and was living in Auckland when Ted arrived back; his dad had dropped dead from a heart attack.

It was 1986, and Ted had been in Portugal, working as a tennis coach. I hadn't seen him since that shambolic weekend in New York when I had found out he was shacked up with rich Sharon. Debbie invited me to come down to Gisborne for her neighbour's big party, and Ted was there. He was hilariously drunk. He got up on the stage and did air guitar with those longest of long legs. Man, could he dance.

The two of us laughed and danced into the dawn. Ted might have only weighed 65 kilos, but he picked me up like I was a feather pillow, and carried me across the paddocks in his arms to his little house on the farm. It was a good two kilometres.

We've been together ever since.

ON THE STRENGTH OF MY bacon and egg pie, Ted proposed to me on one of my weekend visits from Auckland. It wasn't a drop-on-your-knees kind of proposal. More like a 'Hell, this pie is good! Will you marry me, honey?' situation.

I was in my late twenties, and I wasn't ready to be married. I'd only ever had one marriage proposal before, during my South American sojourn. I had gone to the festival of the Virgen de la Candelaria, on the shores of Lake Titicaca, and the procession of hundreds of people wearing grotesque masks, whistling and whooping as they danced through the town, was like nothing I had ever seen. I climbed up onto a truck to get a better view, and was busy clicking away with my camera when a man called up to me, 'Tu fui robado.' I thought, *How odd. He's telling me he's going to rob me . . .* But no, it was: 'You have been robbed.' I looked down. In a flash, my life fell apart. My shoulder bag was empty—my passport was gone, all my money, everything. The bag had nothing left in it. I started to cry. The man, who had seen it happen, called the military. I was escorted to the general's tent, and a squadron of soldiers were dispatched to find the offender. The general offered me a glass of Krug champagne from a stack of cases stashed among the hay-bale seats set up around the tent, and reassured me not to worry, all would be found.

After a few hours, my passport and belongings—less US$100 that I wasn't about to argue over—were returned. By this stage, a great deal of champagne had been consumed, and the general and I had danced a kind of hip-hop in the town square. Things were getting very jolly. '*Deliciosa*,' I simpered politely, munching on some sweet, indecipherable joint of meat that was being passed around, and slurping down more Krug. '*Es muy deliciosa. ¿Algo regional?*' I asked, wanting to know if it was something local.

His eyes lit up. 'Ahh!' he exclaimed. '*Sí, es muy especial. Cuy!*'

I gulped, faltering at the idea of eating a kid's favourite pet.

And then out it came: I was, the general told me, a woman of great taste and great beauty, a woman who could bear his heir, he who would be the next *presidente*. In the midst of this streaming torrent, he dropped to his knees and proposed, imploring that I accept him as my husband for evermore. The prospect of being married to a Bolivian general, especially one who considered firearms part of his wardrobe, was not something I felt my mother, or the children I hoped I would one day have, would be very happy about. Especially when they came to discover Daddy's penchant for eating guinea pigs.

In these parts of the world, one is not usually inclined to disagree with the military. And so, with a racing heart, on the pretext of a bathroom visit, I grabbed my handbag with its restored contents, and climbed onto the toilet seat to reach the window and remove the top louvres. Once out of the window, I made a run for a moving bus back to La Paz.

In the morning I reset my compass and left Bolivia.

FAST-FORWARD A FEW YEARS TO 1988, and I found myself back in South America, this time as a media guest for *Cuisine* magazine. It was my first trip back since my big adventure. Air New Zealand had just started flying direct from Auckland to Buenos Aires, and they wanted to promote the route so they'd sent me to write about it. Ted paid his own way and came along too.

We were picked up by a chauffeured limousine and taken to a fancy suite in a big hotel. The next morning, we went down to the local tourism office to get our itinerary. 'You must meet our most famous chef, El Gato,' said the director. El Gato? There weren't too many people with that kind of name. The same name as my neighbour and good friend from Búzios, the man with whom I'd played backgammon every day. But he wasn't famous. Well, not as far as I knew . . .

Our driver was given directions to a fancy country club just out of the city, and we were told to be there at noon. We arrived at this beautiful estate with glorious formal gardens. And there, waiting to greet us was my old friend. 'La Gordita!' He rushed to embrace me. 'I had no idea. It's actually you. You're here. How wonderful. And this must be . . . your husband?'

'Ahh, my boyfriend, actually.'

El Gato shooed the driver away. 'I will get these good people home safely,' he said. 'Go, take the afternoon off.'

Over lunch, Ted proposed again.

I wasn't sure why we needed to get married. I told him, finally, about poaching on his farm all those years earlier, thinking that might dissuade him. It didn't. Two bottles of champagne later, he proposed again. I was a little slower with my refusal this time. Around 5 p.m., when we had practically emptied El Gato's cellar, Ted went down on his knee for a third time. This time I didn't refuse.

'Ahhh, we must celebrate,' said El Gato when he heard the news. He had been in the kitchen, quietly cooking away for us, all afternoon, plying us (and himself) with booze. We jumped in his white two-door Mercedes, Ted and I squeezed into the back seat together. It was a manual, but El Gato treated it like an automatic, scrunching the gearbox to shreds as we hurtled into the city. 'I have twelve famous restaurants in Buenos Aires,' he said proudly. 'I must show you them all.'

> I wasn't sure why we needed to get married. I told him, finally, about poaching on his farm all those years earlier, thinking that might dissuade him. It didn't. Two bottles of champagne later, he proposed again.

We bunny-hopped from restaurant to restaurant. At around midnight, we arrived at the most exclusive of El Gato's establishments, down in the Recoleta, drunk to beat the band. Miss Argentina turned up with her friend, an even more beautiful brunette with legs up to her armpits and the most spectacular curves. I started to feel like a shrinking wallflower. These women were outrageously good-looking. El Gato made them stand up and do pirouettes to show off their figures. I could feel my feminist hackles rising. The old power games, where women ply their charms and men fork out money, were still alive and well here. Footballer Diego Maradona's manager joined us, and before we left he gave me a big watch with Maradona's name inscribed on it, insisting I take it as a gift.

We got back into the Mercedes and bunny-hopped to a nightclub. Hundreds of people snaked down the pavement, lining up to get in. El Gato drove at the cordon, literally jumping the kerb. He opened the door and half fell out onto the pavement. A security detail rushed to the rescue. It was like being with royalty. They carefully picked him up, helped me and Ted out of the car, and escorted us all inside to a private room to wait while a huge area of the dance floor in the main club area was cleared and set up with sofas for us to sit on. Every time you scratched your head, another bottle of champagne would arrive.

ON THE DAY OF OUR departure, someone sent a 12-bottle case of fancy champagne to our suite. Ted and I drank and drank and drank, but there was no way we could drink it all. In the car driving to the airport, we were handing bottles out of the window. We arrived at check-in just 40 minutes before our flight back to Auckland was due to depart. There was only one flight a week. What a kerfuffle—there were literally minutes to spare as we were rushed through security and on to the plane.

Somewhere in the very south of Argentina the plane landed, and we had to all pile off in the freezing cold and sit on plastic chairs in a concrete bunker while they refuelled. Ted and I were practically comatose. A hellish hangover was just starting to kick in, but I had the most beautiful emerald engagement ring on my finger, and I couldn't stop looking at it.

IT TOOK ANOTHER THREE YEARS before, in 1991, Ted and I actually got married. I did the catering for our wedding, preparing a delicious lunch for the small group of friends and family we invited to my parents' home in

Wellington. Over the next three years, we had two beautiful children, first Sean and then Rose.

Ted always was a big-picture thinker, and naturally business-minded—much more so than me. And, having spent eight years of his life skiing around the globe, working on the farm in between, he had developed a deep love for the mountains. Every winter, we would head to Wānaka to take the kids skiing. We were staying with some friends in their new holiday home in Queenstown on a cold spring day in 1996 when Ted suggested, out of the blue, that we take a drive over to Wānaka. He had something he wanted to show me and, even though he was playing it all very low-key, I could tell he was excited.

We packed a picnic and made the hour's drive over the hill from Queenstown to Wānaka. After a coffee stop and some map-checking, Ted drove us another 10 minutes out of town, and down a gravel road to the shores of the lake. He parked the truck on a rough track near the water, and we bushwhacked through a dense wall of thorny rosehips, blackberry and bracken, stopping at a rickety fence at the base of a hill.

'It's somewhere about here,' he said, waving his arms expansively into the wilderness.

I felt mud, cold and claggy, seeping up over the top of my gumboots. '*What* is here?' My response was less than enthusiastic.

'Our land!' he replied excitedly. 'We've just bought this piece of land.'

A bog on the side of a hill covered in prickles and bracken in the middle of nowhere? Well, this had never figured anywhere in my imagination of holiday-home locations. 'Well, *un*-buy it.'

My suggestion was met with some chin-scratching and a gaze out to

OPPOSITE Wedding-day fun. (Top) All smiles with my lovely sister, Prue, my new husband and his mum, Stella. Patrick Steel made my suit—shoulder pads and all—and the jacket featured handmade lace I had brought back from Spain. (Centre right) We turned my parents' house into a series of dining rooms for the wedding feast.

the furthest horizon. The deal had been done. Signed, sealed, delivered. The bog on the hill was ours, and ours alone.

I was furious. For months, I was in a stand-off with my husband. I couldn't believe he could have done this. All our friends were buying fancy houses in Queenstown, and we had bought this shitty bog on the side of the hill. Sure, it was 25 acres on the edge of the lake, but what the hell was the man thinking? Today it might seem that buying land in Wānaka is a no-brainer, but in 1996 it was a backwater. Most people didn't know it even existed.

> I was furious. For months, I was in a stand-off with my husband. I couldn't believe he could have done this. All our friends were buying fancy houses in Queenstown, and we had bought this shitty bog on the side of the hill. Sure, it was 25 acres on the edge of the lake, but what the hell was the man thinking?

And then, on one of our visits down to Wānaka, everything changed. It was one of those lightning-bolt epiphanies. Our neighbour along the bay had invited us for dinner to meet some of the locals. As we were enjoying pre-dinner drinks, a framed newspaper clipping on the living-room wall caught my eye. It was from back in the 1960s, in one of those big English papers, the *Times* or the *Guardian*. There was a picture of a very beautiful garden, and the headline 'The Five Most Beautiful Gardens in the World'.

'Where is this garden?' I asked our host, Bindy.

'It's here,' she said. 'My mother, Marsy, created that incredible garden right here. She used to carry all the water up from the lake in buckets.'

A shiver went through me as I thought about our boggy piece of land. It had a bounty of natural spring water, so no bucket-lugging was going to be needed. We had peat in the hillside, plateaus of rich loess soils wind-blown from the glaciers, and a climate that so many wonderful plants would thrive in. Here, right under my nose, was everything we needed to create the garden of our dreams.

Never for an instant had I imagined that the vision Ted and I shared could be realised in such a seemingly inhospitable block on the side of a rough bit of hill. It still gives me goosebumps to think about it.

AND SO OUR WĀNAKA ADVENTURE BEGAN. In 2000, four years after Ted first bought the land, he designed a tiny cabin that gave us a home base. Every holiday, we'd jump on a plane and make the journey south. Summers were all about the lake—sailing, swimming, fishing and picnicking. We'd often make expeditions up into the wilderness to places with names like Siberia or Paradise, or don our packs and take on one of New Zealand's famous Great Walks. These adventures were often exhausting, but always ended with a sense of accomplishment once we were safely back to the comforts of the cabin. Sometimes we'd head over to the West Coast to fish for crayfish and cod in the wild sea, explore the huge rivers and walk in the rainforest.

Ted had a big idea about farming the high country and creating lifestyle-farm experiences that city families could enjoy and afford. He was always ahead of his time. We became partners in two 10,000-acre farms: one near Wānaka, and one more remotely on the shores of Lake Benmore in Canterbury. The Benmore farm was a fantastic place in the summer. It was so wild and isolated. There was no cellphone coverage, no electricity and very little in the way of home comforts, but everyone loved being there. There was a great feeling of freedom that came with being so far off the beaten track and away from the trappings of daily life.

Accessing this wilderness experience involved a harrowing drive on a rough farm track that ran all the way down the side of the lake. The landscape was pure rock, not a skerrick of green. You felt like you could be in Afghanistan. Precipitous cliffs lurked on the edges of hairpin bends. One small misjudgement at the wheel could see you jettisoned into the deep blue lake below. Getting in and out was such a drama that if for any reason you left anything behind, you just had to do without it.

> There was a great feeling of freedom that came with being so far off the beaten track and away from the trappings of daily life.

One summer, I forgot the salt. You can cook without a lot of things, but salt is not one of them. I had 16 people to feed and three wild turkeys to barbecue, and brining was the only means I knew to render the birds tender and juicy. Without any salt, my dinner plans—and, actually, our whole holiday—were scuppered. My husband, seeing my distress, disappeared with the look of a man on a mission. Half an hour later, he reappeared with an axe under one arm and a big hunk of pink crystal in the other hand. 'Salt lick,' he said, handing it over. It looked exactly the same as the tiny crystal of expensive Himalayan salt I had purchased in Paris a few months earlier. In fact, it was the same. I'd forked out €7 for fewer than 50 grams of this pretty pink salt crystal, and it turned out that we were buying it for the farm for $180 a ton including delivery!

I got a hammer and started breaking down my giant crystal. It took a while, but finally I had a jar of rock salt that I could use. The turkeys came out beautifully and, with salt in hand, the rest of our holiday dining was also rendered delicious.

WHEN I STARTED TO MAKE TV, I asked Ted if he would come and work with me. I needed someone clever who could look after the business side of things so that I could focus on production and being creative. Our friends thought it was a crazy idea. We were famous for having a very volatile relationship, and they were sure that working together would split us up. Actually, it made us stronger.

Ted is the ultimate international man of mystery. You never see him, but he's always there, behind the scenes, masterminding the plan, making sure everything is OK, and everyone is safe and happy. That doesn't mean he can't drive me mad—or me him, for that matter! But having someone in your life who has your back, who makes you laugh, who believes in you and your dreams, who helps you make them happen, and who also enjoys thinking about the things that make your eyes glaze over? Well, that's a spot of luck.

BACON AND EGG PIE

READY IN 1½ HOURS · SERVES 6–8

3 sheets ready-rolled
  flaky puff pastry
250 g (9 oz) streaky
  bacon, diced
2 potatoes, peeled,
  cooked and thinly sliced
3 tbsp chopped soft fresh
  herbs, such as parsley,
  basil, chives or spring
  onion (scallion) tops
14 eggs
¾ cup milk
1 tsp salt
ground black pepper,
  to taste

My husband proposed to me on the strength of this legendary pie. It's good for both lunch and supper, and robust enough for a picnic. Serve warm or at room temperature with a salad and pickles or chutney.

Preheat oven to 200°C (400°F) fanbake. Place a pizza stone or flat oven tray in the oven to heat (the pie will sit on this and the heat will help it to crisp).

Cut a piece of baking paper to cover the base and reach about 4 cm (1½ in) up the sides of a 40 cm x 30 cm (16 in x 12 in) baking dish. Remove baking paper and lay it flat on a bench. Dust it with a little flour and lay 2 pastry sheets on top. Join the pastry sheets by pressing them together firmly with a small overlap. Roll out pastry to cover the paper. Lift the paper with the pastry still on it and lay it into the baking dish (it will reach 4 cm (1½ in) up the sides).

Sprinkle bacon over pastry. Top with sliced potato and sprinkle with herbs. Break 8 whole eggs over the top. Lightly whisk the remaining 6 eggs with milk, salt and pepper. Pour evenly over the whole eggs.

Roll out the remaining sheet of pastry very thinly and cut it into narrow strips. Arrange strips in a lattice pattern on top of pie, trimming off any excess.

Place pie on heated pizza stone or oven tray and bake until pastry is starting to puff and turn golden (12–15 minutes). Reduce oven temperature to 180°C (350°F) fanbake and bake until pastry is golden and cooked through on the base (a further 35–40 minutes). Bacon and Egg Pie will keep for 2–3 days in a covered container in the fridge.

SLOW-ROASTED TAMARIND LAMB SHOULDER

READY IN 4½ HOURS + DRAINING + MARINATING · SERVES 6–8

about 2.2 kg (4 lb 14 oz)
  bone-in lamb shoulder
2 cups couscous, to serve

LABNE
2 cups natural Greek
  yoghurt
1 tsp salt

TAMARIND MARINADE
6 cloves garlic, roughly
  chopped
3 tbsp tamarind paste
¼ cup red wine vinegar
¼ cup honey
1 cup white wine
finely grated zest and
  juice of 1 orange
1 stick cinnamon, broken
  into pieces
2 star anise
1 tsp salt, or more to taste
ground black pepper,
  to taste

Lamb shoulder is one of those cuts that requires very little love—just long, slow cooking. It emerges from the oven meltingly tender, with a heady fragrance and burnished skin. Just perfect when paired with Cucumber Salad, Labne and couscous.

To make the Labne, line a large sieve with a paper towel and place over a bowl. Pour yoghurt into lined sieve and allow to drain overnight in the fridge. Discard liquid or reserve to use as a replacement for buttermilk in baking. Stir salt into yoghurt, transfer to a serving bowl and chill until ready to serve. It will keep for 2–3 days in a covered container in the fridge.

To make Tamarind Marinade, combine all ingredients. Add lamb and turn to coat. Cover and marinate in the fridge for 4 hours or up to 24 hours.

When ready to cook, preheat oven to 150°C (300°F) fanbake. Place lamb skin-side down in a deep-sided roasting dish and pour over the remaining marinade. Cover dish tightly with a lid or a double layer of tinfoil (it needs to be very tightly covered so the lamb steams and the liquid doesn't evaporate). Cook for 1½ hours.

Carefully turn lamb over so it is skin-side up. Re-cover tightly and cook for a further 2½ hours, checking now and then and adding a little water if it seems to be drying out.

While lamb is in the last hour of cooking, make the Cucumber Salad.

INGREDIENTS AND RECIPE CONTINUED OVERLEAF

CUCUMBER SALAD

2 tbsp sugar

3 tbsp rice vinegar

1 tsp salt

1 tsp fine white pepper

2 Lebanese cucumbers, sliced

4 radishes, very thinly sliced

1 cup fresh mint leaves, torn

2 tbsp pickled ginger, chopped

seeds of 1 pomegranate (optional)

Mix sugar, vinegar, salt and fine white pepper in a medium, non-corrosive bowl, stirring until sugar and salt are dissolved. Add cucumber and radishes, toss to coat, then allow to stand until needed. Just before serving, mix in mint, pickled ginger and pomegranate seeds (if using), reserving a little of each to garnish the lamb.

Prepare couscous to packet directions.

Remove lamb from oven and increase oven temperature to 200°C (400°F). Remove tinfoil or lid from dish and baste lamb with pan juices. Return to oven, uncovered, until lamb is golden (a further 10–15 minutes).

Transfer lamb to a serving platter, cover with tinfoil and a clean tea towel and allow to stand for 15–20 minutes before serving.

Drain pan juices into a wide bowl, allow to stand for 5 minutes to cool, then add a handful of ice cubes. Once the fat has solidified, remove and discard it. Transfer pan juices to a pot and simmer until reduced to about 1 cup.

To serve, fluff couscous and place on a serving platter. Arrange lamb on top, shredding into chunky pieces with two forks. Spoon reduced pan juices over the top. Scatter with reserved mint, pickled ginger and pomegranate seeds (if using), and serve Cucumber Salad and Labne on the side.

STICKY BUNS

READY IN 1 HOUR + RISING · MAKES 10 · V

STICKY BUN DOUGH

1 cup milk

1½ tsp dry yeast

¼ cup sugar

60 g (2¼ oz) butter, melted but not hot

3 cups high-grade (bread) flour, plus extra for dusting

½ tsp salt

CINNAMON FILLING

½ cup sugar

1 tbsp ground cinnamon

90 g (3¼ oz) butter, softened but not melted

SYRUP GLAZE

¼ cup sugar

3 tbsp water

When our kids were small, we were lucky enough to have the help of some wonderful Swedish au pairs, who gave me this best-ever bun recipe.

To make the Sticky Bun Dough, gently heat milk in a small pot until lukewarm. (It should feel neutral to the touch when you dip your finger into it, not hot.) Remove from heat, sprinkle yeast over the top and whisk lightly to disperse. Whisk in sugar, then allow to stand for 3 minutes. Add butter and stir to combine.

Mix flour and salt in a large bowl and make a well in the centre. Add milk mixture and stir until just combined. Tip dough onto a lightly floured surface and knead until smooth and silky (60–100 kneading strokes) or knead in a mixer with a dough hook for 5 minutes. Place in a large, lightly oiled container, cover with a clean tea towel and leave in a warm place until almost doubled in size (about 1 hour 20 minutes).

When risen, roll out to a 40 cm x 25 cm (16 in x 10 in) rectangle on a lightly floured board.

To make Cinnamon Filling, mix sugar and cinnamon. Brush dough with butter, then sprinkle with cinnamon mixture. Starting at the longest edge, roll up dough tightly into a cylinder and cut into slices about 4 cm (1½ in) wide. You should have about 10 scrolls.

Line a 23 cm (9 in) round cake tin with baking paper. Arrange scrolls in tin, allowing 1–2 cm (½–¾ in) between them. Cover with a clean tea towel and leave to rise in a warm (not too hot) place for 20–30 minutes.

Preheat oven to 200°C (400°F) fanbake. Bake scrolls until golden and cooked through (about 20 minutes).

While scrolls are baking, make Syrup Glaze by heating sugar and water in a small pot, stirring, until sugar is dissolved. Boil for 3–5 minutes. Brush scrolls with hot syrup as they emerge from the oven.

NINE

Money, money, money

Life in the fast lane

New Zealand in 1986, when I returned from
New York, was pumping. Everyone, even my
hairdresser, was investing in the stock market.
As soon as I was back in Auckland, I registered
a new company called The Culinary Institute
of New Zealand. It was time for business.

I worked up a concept for the country's then-biggest supermarket chain, Woolworths, which I called 'Fresh'. It was an umbrella campaign that was all about providing variety to consumers through recipes and menu plans that focused on fresh seasonal produce available at the supermarket. I took 'Fresh' to the Woolworths head office and explained the logic behind the concept. People weren't just shopping for toilet paper and mince anymore. They needed ideas, recipes and inspiration to suit their various lifestyles, budgets and tastes. Big families needed to stretch their dollars. Empty-nesters had spare cash and time on their hands. Single people and busy working couples had no time but maybe some spare cash. The health-and-fitness fanatics wanted to count their calories. Some people liked new tastes, others were traditionalists.

It was one of those right-place, right-time moments. I signed a deal that included using my face to promote the campaign, and we set to creating a

OPPOSITE Launching *Fresh* magazine for Woolworths—
check out the hair and the orange pantsuit!

PREVIOUS A mock-up for a Woolworths promo.

bunch of recipe cards, menus, shopping lists, posters and mini magazines. That contract went on to run successfully for the next seven years.

After signing the Woolworths contract, I started developing ideas about creating umbrella campaigns, this time to support smaller producers and niche exporters, and took them to the New Zealand government. I also visited various food producers with ideas about how they could promote their products to different market segments. More and more clients came on board. And, all the while, I kept my hand in some high-end catering, with a fun young team to help me.

Two or three times a week I would throw big dinners, and there were always weekend parties with drinking and dancing. People would bring along a bottle or two of wine to contribute, in the way we do here in New Zealand, but it was all cheap and cheerful. Anything we didn't drink, I'd put away in the ugly old sideboard in the flat. One cold May day a few months before Ted had moved in with me, I was on deadline for my *Listener* column and struggling to think what to write about. I went to the sideboard and rummaged through the wines and found a bottle with a French label that looked interesting. I opened it and took a sip. It was like velvet—elegant, silky and sensuous, its red hue clinging rich and weighty to the inside of the glass. I'd never tasted anything like it.

I'd always scoffed at the over-the-top descriptions of wine writers. That wines could be 'brooding' or 'racy' or 'tight', or taste like gasoline or pencil lead, or smell like a wet Labrador was one thing, but a wine with 'a saline clam broth savour that milks the salivary glands . . .' It was impossibly pretentious. And yet, here it was. I could smell truffles and leather and blackcurrants and the faintest hint of violets. I had no idea that a wine could taste like this. Over the course of the afternoon and the evening, I drank the entire bottle. I don't even recall what I ate with it. The only thing I can remember is that extraordinary wine. And that I managed to write a fabulous column.

The next morning, I couldn't wait to stock up my little booze cupboard. I headed over to the wine shop on Broadway in Newmarket, and plonked the empty bottle on the counter. 'I'd like a case of this please.'

The sales lady laughed. 'Ha,' she said. 'Are you kidding? Come with me.'

She took me to a small glass cupboard where, behind lock and key, some bottles of vintage champagne and a few other bottles with French labels were held. She reached inside and pulled out a bottle of the Château Margaux, and handed it to me carefully.

'Well, forty dollars. That's not bad,' I said.

'It's four *hundred* dollars,' she said icily.

I handed the bottle back to her, a queasy feeling in my tummy. My head was rushing. Someone had brought me this wine, and not only had I not opened it (rule number one, when someone brings over a fancy bottle of wine), but worst of all I had no idea who it could have been. I felt terrible.

To this day I still don't know—so thank you, whoever it was!

IT WAS A CRAZY BUSY TIME, running multiple projects in a million different directions, but in less than a year I was bringing in a seven-figure income.

About 10 months into my new business, the Culinary Institute, Ted came up to stay after a nasty accident with a chainsaw. He had been cutting wood and the chainsaw had slipped and gone through his gumboot and right through the bone in the top of his foot. It had happened some way from his house, and he was lucky not to have bled to death. He had to spend weeks in hospital after the marrow became infected, and almost had to have his foot amputated. On discharge he was told he had to be on bed rest, so he came up to Auckland, lay on the sofa, chatted up all my pretty young staff, and looked over my accounts.

'You don't have any idea how much money you're making, do you?' he said.

He was right: I didn't. But every morning I got up excited about the day ahead and thinking about how to make these ideas work.

But working wasn't the only thing I did. I partied. Ohh, how I did party. Before the stock-market crash, I joined the revellers who played like there was no tomorrow. It was always in the lead-up to Christmas when things really went crazy. From party to party to party, the food and booze flowed in rivers—a stream of silver trays, laden with smoked salmon bagels, crisp-fried Cajun shrimp, baby leek and smoked bacon quiches, spicy venison sausage rolls, crispy duck wontons, chicken tandoori kebabs, and beef carpaccio crostini, partnered with a swill of Bolli, martinis, peach mojitos and sludgy margaritas. By the time Christmas actually arrived, we were all feeling decidedly ropey, our digestive systems struggling to deal with the contents of a dozen or more caterers' fridges and way too much booze.

> But working wasn't the only thing I did. I partied. Ohh, how I did party. Before the stock-market crash, I joined the revellers who played like there was no tomorrow.

Competitions abounded at that time—challenges to see which restaurant could produce the best plate of venison or lamb—and I was often asked to be on the judging panel. A lot of dodgy restaurants entered these contests, hoping to get some visibility, so as a judge you might find yourself in a back-of-beyond hole-in-the-wall establishment having to wade through a plate of something truly dire.

One evening, I arrived for my assignment only to discover that the

opposite New York, New York. (Clockwise from top left) Taking time for a coffee at French bakery Once Upon a Tart, which has since closed; strolling the city streets near Brooklyn Bridge; selecting produce at a city farmers' market; chatting with Emilio Vitolo at his Italian restaurant Emilio's Ballato; and checking out Katz's Deli.

restaurant's owner was the son of a good friend of my mother's. A plate of venison steak arrived covered with a vomit-looking sauce. I checked the menu. Ahhh, so we had a banana beurre blanc tonight. I couldn't just leave the plate untouched, but there was no way I could bring even a forkful of that revolting food to my mouth. Not only did it look nauseating, but it smelt disgusting.

Feigning a cold, I asked for a stack of paper napkins and then, when no one was looking, lined my expensive new handbag with them. I shovelled most of the food on my plate into the bag, popped it under my chair and called for the bill. I couldn't wait to get out of there, and get that food out of my nice handbag and into the bin. Never again.

AND THEN, AS IS THE way of life, *kerboom*. Everything changed.

In 1987, I went to Te Anau for a Woolworths conference. When I arrived, I'd seen a sign advertising horse treks, so in the morning before the conference got under way, I gathered a dozen or so people to join me for a few hours' trekking. I chose the first horse—a magnificent, shiny black 16-hander. He looked like a racehorse.

At the end of the trek, our guide suggested we might like to go for a canter. We had come out on to an old riverbed and I was about sixth in line. I settled into my saddle, gave the horse a light kick and—wooooah—we were off. I had never been on a horse going so fast, and right away I knew I was in trouble. Soon, we were way out in front.

My horse had a mouth like a gutter—harder than hard. There was no chance of reigning him in to slow him down. Then, out of nowhere, he stumbled, dropping his left shoulder out from under me.

Time suddenly slowed down, everything unfolding before me frame by frame, like a movie reel. Without me even realising, my instincts kicked in. As I jettisoned off the front of the horse, I formed myself into a judo roll—and then it all went black.

I REMEMBER COMING TO with people standing all around me. A woman was holding me down. She later told me I had tried to get up, but there was blood pouring out of my mouth.

It took forever for the ambulance to get into the paddock where I had fallen, by which stage I wasn't in any great shape. The ambulance then drove me to Invercargill Hospital, almost two hours away, where the new CT scanner revealed that I had badly crushed my T4 vertebrae along with eight ribs. The fracture was unstable, and there were bits of bone looking like they could easily sever my spinal cord. The whole area was like a bag of broken bones.

They dosed me up with morphine, and for the next few days I floated down the most beautiful river canyon. The water was forest-green, smooth, with a gentle, warm current. I looked up to high cliffs coated in lush green bush on either side. Apparently, I was addicted to morphine within a few days and frothed at the mouth when they took me off it.

Mum was by my side when I finally woke up. She would sit with me for hours and read to me. The doctors told me I had a maybe 5 per cent chance of walking again. Meanwhile, behind the scenes, Ted had arranged a conference call just after the accident happened, with several of the country's top spinal specialists, to work out what the best strategy would be for my safe recovery. It was deemed too dangerous to operate, so they wrapped a four-by-two block of wood in a towel, put it just below my shoulders under the break, and draped me on top of it. It sounds archaic, like something out of medieval times, but the experts believed this was the only safe way to ensure the bones would heal without shifting and cutting through my spinal cord. I lay there over that block of wood for months. Every day eight nurses would assemble to ever-so-carefully lift me, without moving anything, so they could change my sheets and wash me.

Ted flew down to take turns on shifts with my parents. He perked up when they offered him accommodation in the old nurses' home, until he realised he was the only person there. The nurses had all moved out years earlier. The hospital food was inedible, but every day Ted would talk his way into the hospital kitchen and make me delicious scrambled eggs. He also found out that my horse *had* actually once been a racehorse. He was furious. 'A racehorse trekking. Should never be allowed. Just not safe,' he ranted and raved.

> The hospital food was inedible, but every day Ted would talk his way into the hospital kitchen and make me delicious scrambled eggs.

Occasionally friends would fly down to visit, but there was not a lot I could do except read and think. I had to learn to walk again before I could leave the hospital, and I was discharged several months later, 10 kilos lighter and wearing a heavy brace. I was very frail, but I could walk by myself with a stick. On the day of my departure, the house surgeon called me into his office to tell me he had researched cases like mine from all over the world, and the news wasn't good. With such an acute angle of spinal crush, no one had ever made a full recovery. It was important for me to know that, at some stage in the future, my spine would collapse. Wow. Bedside manner 101: MAJOR FAIL.

I flew on my own back to Auckland, and was teary all through the flight. Ted wasn't there to meet me, because he was running late. By the time he finally arrived, I was completely hysterical.

A FEW YEARS LATER, I went back to visit the kind nurses who had looked after me.

'What happened to that dreadful house surgeon?' I asked.

'Oh, you mean Dr John. The one who was so up himself,' said Rowena, a sparkly redhead with one of those impressive South Island chests that comes out like a bench seat.' We got our own back on him. You remember you were in the orthopaedic ward with all those senile old ladies who'd broken their hips and their legs? Well, I don't know if you know this, but when old people get doddery they are awfully prone to self-pleasuring in public. Old Myra was always doing it, so we taught her to call out John's name. He would come hurtling down the hall when he heard, only to be greeted by the gruesome sight of Myra enjoying herself.'

YOU MIGHT IMAGINE THAT an accident like this would have made me stop and reflect. Reflect, yes. Stop, no.

With my second chance, I didn't want to waste a minute. Instead of slowing life down, I sped it up. Something inside said 'GO!' More clients for the Culinary Institute, fancy new premises down in Parnell in the Axis building with lots of offices, a big boardroom and about 12 full-time staff. We had a cooking school, a consultancy and a small ad agency. There was so much work we could hardly keep up.

Christmas was always my favourite time of year. Each October we would start the elaborate preparations for client gifts—hand-painting boxes and filling them with hundreds of delicious chocolate truffles we'd made, preparing and decorating hundreds of exquisite Christmas cakes, and hand-printing cards. There was no limit to the extravagance of this endeavour. It took months, cost a fortune and had Ted scratching his head in disbelief. It all came to an end one year, however, when we made about a hundred kilos of panforte and someone used salt instead of sugar. The whole lot had to be biffed. Secretly, I was certain Ted had set it up.

In 1991 the Child Health Foundation came to me with a campaign to promote better eating for children. We joined forces, and I managed to get Woolworths on board, along with a few other sponsors to help cover costs. We produced a series of weekly menu-planners showing how to 'Feed a Family of Four for $100 a Week', and created recipes and shopping lists that we then ran past the Department of Health to ensure they met the nutritional needs of children. Each week, we would send the following week's menu plan and recipes, along with all the ingredients, to two random families, who would check that everything worked and was easily achievable. Sometimes we would get a call to say an extra loaf of bread was needed or some more milk, and we would adjust the shopping list accordingly. The uptake was incredible. Over about 18 months, we printed 700,000 free booklets, which were distributed in Woolworths supermarkets all over New Zealand.

In the end, however, the print costs became too much for the supermarket to bear, so they had to stop the promotion. But the campaign showed me there was huge demand for skills and knowledge around healthy eating on a budget. The divide in New Zealand had really started to open up—the poor were really poor, and the middle class were sliding further and further back, just trying to make ends meet. After hearing an argument on the radio one day between a couple of politicians about parents not being able to afford a decent lunch for their kids, I decided to take myself to Wellington to meet with the Community Funding Agency. I wanted to see if they would support a project I had started in South Auckland, where I spent a day a week teaching a small group of mothers from a Flat Bush school the basic premise behind the 'Feed a Family of Four' campaign. I was happy to donate my time to these classes, with the idea being that each mother I taught then went on to teach her own small group, and so on. I was excited about where this idea could lead. These women were so knowledgeable and resourceful, and so skilled at stretching their dollars to feed their often very large families. If anyone should be paid, it was them. The power of creating change in their communities lay so obviously in their capable hands.

But I came out of my meeting in Wellington shattered. While I'd been told my idea was to be applauded, I'd also been asked if I knew what the primary issue was for between 12 and 15 per cent of New Zealand's population. I shook my head. 'Personal safety' came the reply. It was such a shocking and frightening answer, something I could never have anticipated. But, of course, when you are worried about domestic violence, there's no way you can think about what you might be eating today, let alone next week. When I had grown up, New Zealand had the third-highest standard of living in the world.

New Zealand was in trouble, and I wanted to try to do something about it. I thought that maybe if I focused on the ways that, throughout my life, food and cooking had helped and nourished me—not just physically, but also emotionally, and when I was broke as well as when I had money— then maybe I could use this to help others feel empowered and nourished in their own lives.

I didn't quite know yet *how* I would do it, but I knew the world was a better place when people cooked and shared food together around the table. So that's where I started.

SASHIMI PLATTER WITH GINGER CORIANDER DRESSING

READY IN 30 MINUTES · SERVES 6–8 AS A STARTER · DF · GF

600 g (1 lb 5 oz) boneless, skinless trevally, kingfish or other white fish fillets

finely grated zest of 1 lime

2 medium radishes, very thinly sliced then cut into tiny batons

a handful of fresh chives, finely chopped

a handful of fresh coriander (cilantro) microgreens

2 tsp sesame seeds, toasted

flaky salt and ground black pepper, to taste

GINGER CORIANDER DRESSING

½ cup sushi seasoning

¼ cup lemon juice

2 tbsp mirin

2 tsp rice vinegar

2 tsp sugar

1 tsp finely chopped long red chilli

100 g (3½ oz) fresh ginger, finely grated or blitzed to a purée in a food processor

½ cup fresh coriander (cilantro) leaves

You need the freshest fish for this simple recipe, which is like a cross between ceviche and sashimi. The fish can be sliced in advance and stored covered in the fridge for a few hours prior to serving, and the zingy light dressing will keep for several days in the fridge.

To make Ginger Coriander Dressing, place all ingredients except ginger and coriander in a jug or clean jar. Using your hands, squeeze the juice of the ginger into the dressing, discarding pulp. Stir to combine. The flavours will develop over the next 15–20 minutes (the dressing will also keep in the fridge for several days).

Use a very sharp knife to cut the fish across the grain into paper-thin slices, and place in a bowl. Mix in half the dressing and leave to marinate for 3–5 minutes. Drain well before serving, discarding liquids.

Add coriander to the remaining dressing and stir to combine. Divide fish between individual serving plates or arrange on a serving platter. Spoon a little dressing over the fish. Sprinkle with lime zest, radish slices, chives, coriander microgreens and sesame seeds. Season with salt and pepper and serve immediately, with the remaining dressing in a small jug or bowl on the side.

TRAY-BAKE CHICKEN CAESAR SALAD

READY IN 1 HOUR · SERVES 4

4 boneless chicken
  thighs, ideally skin-on
8 rashers streaky bacon
4 trusses cherry or truss
  tomatoes
finely grated zest of
  ½ a lemon
3 tbsp extra virgin
  olive oil
salt and ground black
  pepper, to taste
about ⅓ loaf ciabatta or
  sourdough bread, torn
  into coarse chunks
1 large or 2 baby cos
  (romaine) lettuces
a handful of fresh basil or
  flat-leaf parsley leaves,
  to garnish
grated parmesan,
  to garnish

CAESAR DRESSING
1 tbsp extra virgin olive oil
2 cloves garlic, crushed
5 canned anchovies, with
  a little of their oil
1 cup cream
½ cup grated parmesan
  (about 40 g)
finely grated zest of
  ½ a lemon
ground black pepper,
  to taste

Caesar Salad is one of those timeless recipes that everyone loves. Throwing everything into the oven to cook makes fast work of this fabulous recipe, and the dressing can also be made ahead of time.

Preheat oven to 200°C (400°F) fanbake. Line 2 shallow roasting dishes with baking paper for easy clean-up.

Arrange chicken, bacon and truss tomatoes on one tray. Sprinkle chicken with lemon zest, drizzle everything with oil and season with salt and pepper. Arrange bread chunks on second tray, drizzle with oil and season with salt and pepper to make croutons. Bake until chicken is fully cooked through (20–25 minutes). Allow to cool for 10–15 minutes.

While chicken bakes, make Caesar Dressing. Heat oil and sizzle garlic and anchovies over a medium heat for about 30 seconds, mashing up anchovies to a paste. Add all remaining ingredients to pan and boil hard until thick enough to coat the back of a spoon (about 2 minutes). Cool before use. The dressing will keep for a few days in a jar in the fridge. It thickens on cooling, so warm gently to loosen, or thin with a little water as desired.

To prepare the salad, cut lettuce into wedges or cut leaves in half and pile onto a serving platter. Drizzle with ¼ cup Caesar Dressing and toss to coat.

Cut each chicken thigh into 3–4 pieces and each bacon rasher into 4 pieces. Arrange evenly over salad with tomatoes and croutons. Drizzle with more dressing, then serve the remainder in a small jug or bowl on the side. Garnish salad with basil or parsley and grated parmesan to serve.

THE ULTIMATE CHOCOLATE CAKE WITH CHOCOLATE GANACHE

READY IN 1¼ HOURS + COOLING · SERVES 16

CF, IF GLUTEN FREE FLOUR IS USED · V

3 cups self-raising flour or gluten-free self-raising flour
2 cups caster (superfine) sugar
¾ cup Dutch cocoa, sifted
2 tsp baking soda (bicarbonate soda), sifted
3 large (size 7) eggs
200 g (7 oz) butter, at room temperature
1 cup natural yoghurt or milk
1 cup boiling hot coffee
1½ tsp vanilla extract
fresh raspberries, to garnish (optional)

CHOCOLATE GANACHE
500 ml (1 pint) cream
500 g (1 lb 2 oz) good-quality dark chocolate (at least 50% cocoa solids), coarsely chopped

This is probably the most popular recipe I have ever written. My kids used to win prizes with this in school competitions—it's ridiculously simple to make, and the recipe produces a giant perfectly risen cake with a lovely, tender chocolatey crumb.

Preheat oven to 160°C (315°F) fanbake. Grease the sides of a 30 cm (12 in) diameter springform cake tin (or 2 x 20 cm [8 in] tins) and line the base with baking paper.

Place all ingredients except raspberries in a large bowl, electric mixer or food processor and mix or whizz until fully incorporated. Pour into prepared tin and smooth top. Bake until a skewer inserted into the centre comes out clean (1 hour for large cake, 45 minutes for small cakes). Allow to cool in the tin. If not using at once, store in an airtight container in the fridge for up to a week.

While cake is cooling, make Chocolate Ganache. Heat cream in a medium pot until not quite boiling (you'll know it's ready when bubbles start to form around the sides of the pot). Remove from heat and add chocolate. Allow to stand for 2 minutes, then stir until chocolate is fully melted into cream. Whisk until smooth and glossy (you'll think it won't come together, but it will). Once cool, but not chilled, whip ganache to a light, fluffy consistency with an electric beater. Slather the cooled cake with Chocolate Ganache and top with fresh raspberries (if using).

If not using ganache immediately, store in a jar in the fridge for up to 2 weeks. It will solidify as it cools, so if you want a runnier consistency gently warm in a pot or microwave before use.

TEN

Writing and publishing

Finding a voice

My mother always said (figuratively, of course) that I'd come out of the womb with a wooden spoon. She knew I was a cook long before I did. I had my first dinner party when I was 14, but I remember it more for the fact that Dad rushed in as we were about to sit down, his face and throat all puffed up. He'd been stung badly by his precious bees, and it was obvious that it was getting hard for him to breathe. We had to drop everything and rush to the hospital.

As I became a more confident cook in my early twenties and branched out into trying recipes from my mother's vast selection of cookbooks, then later the library, I realised that sometimes—actually quite often—the recipes in books didn't work. You'd be halfway through, and then suddenly you'd be lost, with no idea what had gone wrong or how to get back on track. It took me years to figure out that the recipe could be wrong, and not me. If the writer had missed out a step or got the ratios wrong, it was never going to work, no matter what you did.

Mutiny at the dinner table is one of life's greatest humiliations. Trust me—I've been there! The failed eggplant frittata (truly disgusting), the baby-poo apple and pumpkin soup (sickly sweet and claggy), the aforementioned microwave carrot-cake fiasco. When people don't like the

OPPOSITE Cooking for a photoshoot in *NZ Life & Leisure* magazine.
PREVIOUS Figuring out the jigsaw of the layout is my favourite part of making a book.

food we make, the sense of failure is crushing. Awful, disgusting, inedible—these are not the words we're looking for when people eat our food. We want plates scraped clean, gushing compliments and positive affirmations. So much of cooking is about confidence. When a recipe goes wrong, you feel like a failure.

So I made it my mission to write recipes that eliminated, as much as possible, any risk of disappointment for the home cook. Essentially, a recipe is like a road map—it should get you safely and expeditiously from a set of ingredients to a dish you can put on the table with confidence and pride. Maybe it's a rogue engineering gene from my dad's side, but I can quite clearly see if something is missing from a recipe or when the dots don't join up. Once, when I was giving a cooking demonstration in Noosa, a man in the audience put his hand up and asked, 'How did you learn to engineer such a good recipe?' *Yes!* I thought, fondly remembering my dad, the clever engineer.

> We want plates scraped clean, gushing compliments and positive affirmations. So much of cooking is about confidence.

For three years I was a judge on the Julia Child Cookbook Awards. Each summer I would have to load boxes of books into our car to take away on our summer holidays. There were literally hundreds of books I had to read and cook from. Sometimes you could see right away that things weren't ever going to work, or that a recipe was so complicated no one would understand it or bother to engage.

Looking back, I can see my cooking has become a lot simpler over the years. I guess it's like mastering anything. After you've written as many recipes as I have, you know the subject deeply, and even when you are trying new ideas there's an instinctiveness about the ratios, quantities, processes and timings. I'm not talking about any tricky cheffy stuff—no spherification or foam or how to use alginate or liquid nitrogen or any of those other fancy chemistry techniques that famous restaurants like El Bulli used to employ. That kind of stuff is the domain of a chef, not a cook. I actually got to attend a cooking demo by Ferran Adrià, the chef and innovator behind El Bulli, in Adelaide in the early 2000s. He made 'pasta' by heating carrageenan (an ingredient made from red seaweed that has thickening and setting properties like gelatine) and water. He set the mixture in a shallow tray lined with plastic wrap, then cut it into fettuccini-like strips. We could, he explained, flavour it with something like porcini stock or miso to create a flavoured noodle. He then combined the same carrageenan-and-water mixture with raspberry purée, put it into a gas canister and heated it, and out came raspberry foam. It was brilliantly clever, but it wasn't the kind of cooking I was interested in.

EVEN THOUGH IT DIDN'T PAY very well (writing copy, like cooking, has never been a highly paid job) my fortnightly *Listener* column was always one of my favourite things to work on. In one of my columns, I advised people how to ascertain the degree of doneness in a piece of meat. There is a simple little trick you can do, just by pressing the flesh at the base of your palm, which compares to the degree of doneness of meat protein.

You start with an open hand and press the squidgy, fleshy part at the base of your thumb—or the Mount of Venus, as this part of the palm is called. The texture when your hand is fully relaxed is about the same as raw meat. When you touch your thumb and first finger together, you get a fractional tightening in the same spot—this is equivalent to rare (blue) meat. Middle finger to thumb, it's bouncy with a little give, like medium-rare meat. Ring finger and it's quite firm—your meat is cooked to medium. Baby finger, there's an almost rigid tension in the muscle —you've completely overcooked the meat and you probably need to go and open another bottle of wine so people won't remember your disaster.

Regrettably, my sub-editor failed to notice that, in the column, I was urging my readers to gently palpate the Mound of Venus (in your crotch) rather than the Mount of Venus (at the base of your thumb). A letter was sent to the editor. I've dined out on it ever since. 'Dear Sir/Madam, I was testing out Annabel Langbein's method for determining the doneness of meat the other day. My husband walked in the door. "What on earth are you doing?" he said, horrified. "I'm just testing the meat, dear, like Annabel Langbein said to see if it's the right degree of rareness!"'

IN 1986, A LOCAL PUBLISHER approached me wanting to publish a book containing my *Listener* columns. Fabulous illustrations by Barbara Henderson accompanied my fortnightly column, and the book was envisaged as a collection of my published recipes with her charming artwork. We started planning things, and then, in a truly horrifying turn of events, my wonderful illustrator was brutally murdered at her home in Tākaka. I abandoned the project and said goodbye to the publishers.

A few months later, once the awful shock had softened, I thought, *Hey, I could do this myself.* So I hired a locally based Japanese photographer, Masono Kawana, and we set up food shots all around my Auckland flat. After each shoot, we would have a party to eat all the food—I wasn't having any of that fake NYC styling. I brought clever art director Sally Hollis-McLeod on board to design the book, do the illustrations and work on the layouts. We laid everything out on my living-room floor. Hours and days would pass while we moved double-page spreads around and checked for mistakes. In those days it was all done with scissors and glue—no computer technology. If you made a mistake, you had to painstakingly cut out the type and replace it. The whole process was incredibly time-consuming, but I was hooked. I loved the jigsaw puzzle of making a book—the way it had to feel whole through and through, the way each recipe had to have its own story and place within a bigger theme. It was like a fashion collection, but with food.

My then brother-in-law (the one who had first encouraged me to submit a story to the *Listener* back in 1984) suggested I use a printer in Hong Kong, so once the final files were ready I flew up there to check the pages as they came off the printer's press. I'd never been to Hong Kong before, and it was all so exciting. The hustle of life on the street, new smells, new tastes. The printer was located in the non-Western part of the city, and no one there spoke any English. It was all such a foreign culture to me. You'd stop for lunch at a casual, cheap Formica-table restaurant in a shopping mall, and there would be duck tongues, marinated jellyfish and salads of rubbery black fungus on the menu. The texture of some of the Chinese food was anathema to my Western palate—I found that slippery, slithery stuff impossible to stomach.

> I loved the jigsaw puzzle of making a book—
> the way it had to feel whole through and
> through, the way each recipe had to have its
> own story and place within a bigger theme. It
> was like a fashion collection, but with food.

One day the printer took me to a restaurant near the factory. A huge bowl of fish-head soup arrived at our table. I wasn't sure how to deal with all the bones. Everyone else seemed to be able to manoeuvre them around in their mouths, then neatly spit them out. That certainly wasn't happening for me. Before I knew it, I'd swallowed a fish bone. *Bread*, I thought. *That's what we do. Eat bread to loosen the bone and get it down my throat.*

'Bread! Bread!' I called out to the waiter. It was obvious I was in some trouble, but bread is not a standard menu item in this part of the world and, as no one besides the printer spoke any English—and his was very limited—they had no idea what I was talking about.

'Bed,' said the printer. 'Bed.' He leapt out of his chair in a panic. 'Hospital.' And off he rushed to find the phone.

The last thing I wanted was to be taken off to some foreign hospital. I pointed at the bones in my soup bowl, and motioned a stranglehold around my throat to the waiter.

'Ahhhh.' He gave me a thumbs-up and raced out to the kitchen, returning quickly with a small glass filled to the brim with a thin black liquid. He motioned for me to trust him. Down the hatch in one gulp. Black vinegar. An entire glass. It was impossibly sour, but like magic the acidity softened the bone and down it slipped. Problem solved.

A FEW MONTHS LATER, 10,000 copies of my first cookbook, a 146-page paperback called *Annabel Langbein's Cookbook: Featuring recipes from the New Zealand Listener*, arrived. Pallet after pallet of the book with its bright-pink cover and image of a plate of mussels in front of a blown-out view of Auckland Harbour, plus an inset photo of me with a perm, had to be stored in the garage. It was one of those 'Oh no, what the hell do I do now?' moments. Making the book was one thing, but selling it? I hadn't even thought about that.

Ted decided to take things in hand, putting on his sales hat (who knew?) and visiting various bookshops. He made a few small sales, but no one was particularly interested in a book by a relatively unknown author, especially one who had self-published. 'Who is Annabel Langbein?' people said. 'No one self-publishes.'

Not to be deterred, Ted made an appointment to see the head buyer at Whitcoulls, then the biggest bookshop chain in the country. He came home in a state of great excitement. 'I've met someone who knows more about books than everyone in New Zealand put together.' The woman was

Doris Mousdale, and she had liked the book. She also gave Ted lots of ideas about what he needed to do. He hung on her every word.

We filled the car with books and visited bookshops all around the country. No one would ever buy more than five copies. It was so disheartening. In the end, we had to remainder thousands of copies at cost. This wasn't a business model with any kind of future but, while this first publishing exercise was a financial disaster, the feedback from people who had purchased the book was great. They loved my recipes and were hungry for more.

A COUPLE OF YEARS HAD passed when Doris got in touch to ask whether I might be interested in producing a new cookbook exclusively for Whitcoulls. That seemed like a great idea. It took out the whole palaver of warehousing and distribution and selling door-to-door. Everything under one roof in one deal.

Whitcoulls quickly sold the first print run of 10,000 copies of my book *Smart Food for Busy People*, and went on to reprint and sell another 15,000 copies. For the next few years Whitcoulls commissioned me to produce a new book for them each year. It was a great little sideline to my consultancy work through the Culinary Institute and, while not the most profitable part, writing recipes and making books was actually the thing I enjoyed doing the most.

IT WOULD HAVE BEEN THE END of 1986 or early 1987 when Julie Dalzell got in touch to talk about a new magazine she wanted to publish. We sat on her sofa and talked for hours about her vision. It was so exciting. The first issue of *Cuisine* magazine was published in 1987. I wrote 63 of the 89 recipes, covering the gamut from easy to fancy, indulgent to slimming— home-made red pepper pasta with pāua, mussels with Pernod and fennel, chilled tangelo soufflé, crêpes with smoked salmon and asparagus, home-made sushi. It was such a buzz to be part of this new magazine, which made us all feel proud about the exciting cooking and wine culture that was emerging in New Zealand.

The greatest benefit to being a food writer in the late eighties came in the form of press junkets, like the one that took me to Buenos Aires when Ted proposed. There was no internet, no Facebook, no Instagram. People got their information from magazines, newspapers and TV. Travel companies and tourism bodies would bend over backwards to bring journalists to their countries, and there was no holding back on the extravagance with which they would entertain a humble food writer.

It was such a buzz to be part of this new magazine, which made us all feel proud about the exciting cooking and wine culture that was emerging in New Zealand.

My first junket was to Hong Kong in June 1988. I was put up in the Regent and ate from jade bowls in restaurants where a single serving of Japanese abalone cost NZ$3000—more than the price of a return airfare. At a fancy dinner with local dignitaries and international food writers, I found myself seated next to the general manager of the Hilton hotel chain. 'We are opening a new hotel in Shanghai,' he said. 'I would love to invite you to be our guest for the opening.'

'Wow, that sounds amazing,' I replied.

'Fly up there, and you can stay as long as you like. Everything's on us. You just need to get yourself there.'

It was too good an offer not to take up—and that's how I found myself at the opening of Huashan Lu's Hilton Hotel in Shanghai. This was the first Hilton to open in mainland China, and back then a one-night stay would have cost the average worker the equivalent of 20 months' salary.

I arrived to a red-carpet welcome—literally. A metre-wide red carpet was rolled out as I exited the cab, and I had to pace myself not to walk faster than they were laying it out. As I checked in, I was welcomed and advised that all my charges would be covered: 'Food, wine. As much as you like. You'll just need to cover any phone calls you make.'

The public relations manager, Rosa, escorted me to a suite with a stunning view out over the newly forming city below. The Shanghai Hilton was the city's first wholly foreign-owned commercial building. The 43-storey triangular hotel lifted the city's skyline to a new height of 143 metres, by far the tallest building on the landscape. A bottle of Cristal champagne sat chilling in a flashy ice bucket, and a five-layered black lacquer tray set with intricately sliced meats and vegetables formed into collages of various animals awaited my enjoyment. (These really were the halcyon days in which to be writing about food.)

I couldn't wait to tell Ted. For the next 20 minutes, I lay on the bed drinking champagne and eating tiny morsels from my lacquer trays while I regaled him about my trip—firstly Hong Kong and all the tastes and colours and smells there, and then here, wow, Shanghai from the sky. I was so excited to be right there, right then.

'Ted, it's amazing. You can almost see the world changing in front of your eyes.'

ON THE SECOND NIGHT OF my visit, the hotel threw a spectacular cocktail party to announce its opening. Around 700 people were packed into a glamorous state room, including Zhu Rongji, who was then the mayor of Shanghai but would later become premier of China. Artists staged Chinese folk dances and traditional opera outside the hotel, while the Shanghai Symphony Orchestra performed Western music inside. A tray of food stacked high with some kind of small, crisp golden offering appeared. Everyone else rushed at it greedily. I popped a handful into my mouth, and a millisecond after the initial crunch it disintegrated into a lipid slime in my mouth.

Rosa beamed. 'Roasted silkworms,' she said. 'Such a delicacy.'

I returned her look blankly, a ball of worms rolling around in my mouth. Every ounce of my being went into rebellion. There was no chance to run; the room was packed tight. Grabbing a neatly pressed linen napkin from the hand of a passing waitress, I emptied the contents of my mouth before they could make any further headway into or out of my body.

The memory is so potent, it almost makes me gag just to recall it.

A FRIEND FROM GISBORNE WAS working in Shanghai at the time as a translator for a big Swedish tool company. He'd been to Beijing to study Mandarin and spoke better Chinese than many of the locals.

Peter took me under his wing and we explored Shanghai. In those days, you could go into a shop and ask for something in the window, but you wouldn't actually be able to buy it—it was there just for display. Time after time, I'd see something wonderful that I wanted. 'Coming soon,' Peter translated the shopkeepers' repeated responses. The shops' offerings of things which you could actually purchase were very humble and utilitarian—bowls, plates, woks and lots of cheap, garish polyester clothing.

All the big shops had pneumatic cash systems. The sales assistant would put your money into a canister, then it would get sucked up through a tube that went along the ceiling to the cashier in the office. A few minutes later the tube would arrive back at the till with the right amount of change.

In 1988, Shanghai was an intriguing city, still retaining some of the mystique of its powerful, often corrupt past. Many parts felt decidedly

OPPOSITE (Clockwise from top) Exploring Shanghai; welcoming our firstborn, Sean, to the world; cuddles with Rose; and boating on Auckland harbour (I picked up those mother-of-pearl sunnies on a trip to Italy).

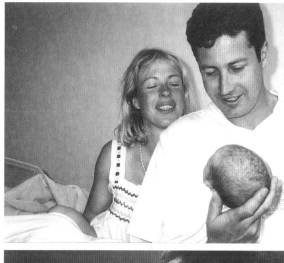

European, with curving, tree-lined streets, but the luxurious family mansions were now stacked ten to the dozen with multiple families living in them. The nightlife for which Shanghai had once been so famous consisted of about three demure nightclubs. There were almost no restaurants, but everywhere on the street there were dumplings. Stacks and stacks of dumplings cooking in giant bamboo steamers. There were supposedly no flies in China, which seemed an incentive for the storekeepers to leave food out well past its use-by date. At the Stateside Market, plucked grey ducks oozed on the bench, while lacklustre fish with sunken eyes and slabs of grey fat-encrusted meat lay among piles of limp, semi-rotten vegetables.

The new five-star Hilton was a beacon of light in this otherwise bleakest of culinary landscapes. I made friends with the executive chef, and spent several days in the hotel kitchens, which were set up to feed 3000 people a day. There were no centralised distribution systems or warehouses back then, and Chef told me that, when he wanted frozen food, he had to jump in an enormous truck and drive up to Mongolia. Every few months he and a driver would make the long journey north, literally driving the truck into a mountain where everything was frozen solid purely by virtue of the climate. The deal would be finalised with roasted scorpions and a double toddy of two small cups of *baijiu* (pronounced 'be-joe'), a fiery liquor of 130 per cent proof strength, clear as a pristine spring. Drunk as skunks, they would then have to make the long drive back to the hotel.

While I was considerably better educated about the purges of the Cultural Revolution than I had been when I lived up the Whanganui River as an idealistic Maoist teenager, I had no idea that China had also lost most of its food culture through that era. To be a cook, a butcher or a baker was a highly elevated position with considerable status. Legend has it that the founder of the Shang dynasty in the second millennium BC appointed his cook Yi Yin to be prime minister. Chef told me that, in the Cultural Revolution, cookbooks and food reference books, along with much of the knowledge and history of Chinese cooking, were lost. This was Chef's real interest. He had old photographs and stacks of handwritten manuscripts, and he wanted to bring all this knowledge back.

One night, I was invited for a special degustation dinner at the Hilton's new premium restaurant, so I asked if I could bring my friend Peter along as my guest. 'Of course,' said Chef, adding that there would be no charge for the meal or the wines. Like my stay, this was all on the house. The restaurant would have seated about 300 people, but Peter and I were the only guests, aside from an elderly man and a very attractive young woman who could only have been his concubine. We ate and drank, and ate and drank, making our way through an extraordinary 12-course menu of delicate, thoughtfully prepared food paired with a selection of beautiful French wines. It was astonishingly good. Chinese food like I had never tasted it before.

MANY OF PETER'S FRIENDS WERE working in new manufacturing businesses and having nervous breakdowns. Two thousand designer dresses all with the zip on the wrong side. No printers to print labels. A hundred thousand pairs of shoes with the wrong buckles. Trying to get things made was a nightmare.

Trying to get around the city was also hell. Cars were relatively new and not many people knew how to drive. People on bicycles were constantly getting mowed down. The sound in the city was one long, bawling siren. You would knock on the window of a taxi and the driver would just carry on reading their book. Why take someone for a ride and risk having an accident and getting fined when you get paid the same for just sitting in your car?

After about five days I decided it was time to head back to Hong Kong. I asked the concierge if he could please organise a flight back for me. 'Of course, madam,' came the politest of replies.

The next day and the day following I asked the same question and got the same encouraging response: 'Ahh, yes. The ticket is coming, madam.'

But there was no ticket.

In the end I went to Rosa. 'How do I get out of here?' I asked.

'No worries. I'll organise it for you now.'

A few hours later Rosa called my room. 'I really hate to tell you this, but you're going to need to buy a flight on the black market.'

When I went to check out, the front desk printed out a bill for my room. It was for US$800. 'What's this for?' I asked, completely taken aback.

'Ahh, madam, that is the bill for the telephone call you made the day you arrived.'

In the scheme of things it was cheap, but for a single phone call—wow. Thank heavens I hadn't rung Ted every day.

BY 2010, I HAD 12 COOKBOOKS under my belt, 10 of which I had published myself, plus editions of *The Best of Annabel Langbein* in nine languages. My cookbooks had won numerous national and international awards. With the profile I had gained, and *The Free Range Cook* airing on TV One, New Zealand's largest channel, the thinking was that we would get great presales of an accompanying cookbook. But it was not to be.

The Global Financial Crisis of 2007 and 2008 was still taking its toll. Bookshops were cautious, and no one wanted to carry excess stock. We printed 20,000 copies of the first edition of *The Free Range Cook*. When the TV series launched, I hit the road to tour the country, with book-signing events and cooking demonstrations. By the time episode four had aired, queues were starting to form outside bookshops. Something was definitely happening. I began tracking the book's sales, and could see the sharp lift

OPPOSITE The cover photo for *The Best of Annabel Langbein: Great food for busy lives.*

week on week. I called the printer and ordered another 20,000 copies, and then a week later another 20,000 copies.

There was a huge time lag between ordering the books and getting them delivered, as they not only had to be printed but also had to come from China. I started to look at the curve. Sales were rising exponentially, and we were coming up to Christmas. There was still time to get another print run in. What a gamble. I went to Doris, who now had her own bookshop in Newmarket, and asked her what actually happened to sales in the weeks leading up to Christmas. Armed with the information she shared, I made the call to print another 50,000 copies. And so it went. I just kept printing books, and they mostly made the market before stock ran out.

> Within a year we had broken every sales record in New Zealand, selling a staggering 160,000 copies of *The Free Range Cook*. Probably the thing that excited me more than anything was the fact that *everyone* was buying the book, not just the usual foodies.

Within a year we had broken every sales record in New Zealand, selling a staggering 160,000 copies of *The Free Range Cook*. Probably the thing that excited me more than anything was the fact that *everyone* was buying the book, not just the usual foodies. The TV series had touched people old and young, rich and poor, and the message I had wanted to convey had struck a chord: this simple idea that good food was easily within everyone's reach. It didn't have to be expensive or time-consuming, and with fresh, seasonal ingredients and the simplest of kitchens (in my case, often a gas burner on the back of my old Jeep J20 pickup) you could feel connected and useful, live more healthily and sustainably, and have a hell of a lot of fun.

In Hastings at a signing one day, a down-and-out couple with bare feet and dreadlocks waited patiently in line to meet me. 'We just wanted to say thank you,' they said. 'We live in a caravan with our four kids, and last night we made your caramelised onions to go with our sausages and we all sat up together to eat it. You know, you have changed our lives.'

I felt so humbled. This was what I had set out to achieve.

I went on to write and publish two more TV-series cookbooks, six soft-cover magazine-style cookbooks and, most recently, my two opus editions: *Essential Volume One: Best-ever meals for busy lives* and *Essential Volume Two: Sweet treats for every occasion*. The tally comes to 32 cookbooks. In my database there are 10,000 recipes that I have written. In my head there's always a new one brewing. I guess you could call it an obsession.

The thing is, when it comes to food, there's always something new to discover and learn.

MARGHERITA PIZZA WITH PROSCIUTTO, MOZZARELLA AND ROCKET

READY IN 30 MINUTES · SERVES 4–6

1 recipe Perfect Pizza Dough (see overleaf)

50 g (1¾ oz) finely grated parmesan or pecorino, plus extra to serve

250 g (9 oz) fresh mozzarella or bocconcini, torn into small pieces

12–16 slices prosciutto

120 g (4¼ oz) rocket (arugula)

a drizzle of extra virgin olive oil or lemon-infused oil

flaky salt and ground black pepper, to taste

TOMATO SAUCE

1 cup tomato passata

2 tbsp extra virgin olive oil

1 tsp dried oregano

½ tsp sugar

½ tsp salt

ground black pepper, to taste

When the kids were aged about six and eight, we lived for a few months in a tiny village in the northwest of Sicily. Every week we would head down to the port city of Trapani for pizza from a hole-in-the-wall joint that always had queues of people waiting outside. What made it so good? It wasn't just the amazing location—the pizza was beautifully simple. It wasn't laden with loads of fillings. These days I love my pizza cooked with just a simple tomato topping and layered up with a fresh salad.

Preheat oven to 240°C (475°F) fanbake. Sprinkle pizza stones or oven trays with polenta or semolina and place in the oven to preheat. (If you don't have polenta or semolina, use baking paper in the next step.)

Press or roll out each ball of Perfect Pizza Dough on a floured surface or a sheet of baking paper. Roll dough out to ½ cm (¼ in) thickness. If making 4 large pizzas they will be about 30 cm (12 in) in diameter.

To make the Tomato Sauce, combine passata with oil, oregano, sugar, salt and pepper.

Spread each pizza base with 2 tablespoons sauce, leaving a 2 cm (¾ in) border around the edge. Scatter with finely grated parmesan or pecorino.

Slide pizzas onto hot pizza stones or oven trays (if not using polenta or semolina, keep pizzas on their baking paper when you transfer them). Bake until crust is puffed and charred in spots, cheese is melted, and underside of crust is golden brown (8–12 minutes in a normal oven or even quicker in a pizza oven).

Top hot pizzas with torn mozzarella or bocconcini, prosciutto and rocket, then drizzle with oil and season. Sprinkle with extra parmesan or pecorino and serve.

PERFECT PIZZA DOUGH

READY IN 30 MINUTES + RISING · MAKES 4 LARGE PIZZA BASES OR
6–8 SMALL PIZZA BASES · DF · V · VE

2 cups warm (not hot)
　water
2 tsp sugar
2 tsp dry yeast
4 cups high-grade
　(bread) flour, plus extra
　to knead
1 cup semolina or an
　extra cup of high-grade
　(bread) flour
3 tbsp extra virgin
　olive oil
1 tsp salt

**Start making this yeast dough at least 2 hours
before you want to eat, or make it the day before
and allow it to rise overnight in the fridge.**

Place water and sugar in a large bowl or electric mixer
and stir until sugar is dissolved. Sprinkle with yeast and
allow to stand in a warm place for 10 minutes.

Add flour, semolina (if using), oil and salt, and
mix to form a soft, sticky dough. If it's too firm add
a splash more water. Throw the dough onto a bench
several times to get the gluten working, then knead
for about 5 minutes by hand (use a little oil to prevent
sticking) or in a mixer or breadmaker until smooth.
Transfer to a lightly oiled bowl, cover with a clean tea
towel and leave in a warm place until doubled in size
(30–40 minutes).

Turn risen dough out onto a lightly floured board,
form into a log and cut into 4 even pieces if making
large pizzas, or 6–8 pieces if making smaller pizzas.
Shape into balls, cover with a clean tea towel and leave
to rise in a warm place for 15 minutes. Perfect Pizza
Dough will keep for 2–3 days in the fridge and can
be frozen.

PASTA CARBONARA

READY IN 30 MINUTES · SERVES 4

3 eggs
2 egg yolks
80 g (2¾ oz) finely grated
   parmesan, plus extra
   to serve
½ cup coarsely chopped
   fresh flat-leaf parsley
   leaves
½ tsp salt
ground black pepper,
   to taste
500 g (1 lb 2 oz) dried
   linguine or fettuccine
2 bunches broccolini, cut
   into thirds, thick stems
   halved lengthwise
2 tbsp extra virgin
   olive oil
6 rashers bacon, finely
   chopped
2 large cloves garlic,
   crushed

When life has you constantly on the run, carbonara is a great recipe to have up your sleeve. The key is to avoid overcooking and scrambling the eggs—and my method for putting it together ensures this doesn't happen.

Whisk eggs and egg yolks in a serving bowl big enough to hold all the cooked pasta and broccolini. Mix in parmesan, parsley, salt and pepper.

Bring a large, heavy-based pot of well-salted water to a boil. Add pasta and cook for 1 minute less than packet instructions, adding broccolini in the last 2 minutes of cooking time. Scoop out about a cup of pasta cooking water and set aside. Drain pasta and broccolini into a colander.

Add oil to pasta pot and fry bacon until crispy and starting to brown. Reduce heat, add garlic and cook for 30–40 seconds without browning. Add ½ cup reserved pasta water and stir to lift the bacon brownings. Add pasta and broccolini and stir to combine. Cover and heat through until very hot (1–2 minutes).

Tip hot pasta into egg bowl and toss to combine, adding more reserved pasta water if the mixture looks at all dry. It should nicely coat the pasta. Adjust seasonings to taste and serve immediately, garnished with extra parmesan.

CARROT SLAB CAKE

READY IN 1 HOUR + COOLING · MAKES 24 PIECES
DF, IF UN-ICED · GF, IF GLUTEN-FREE FLOUR IS USED · V

4 eggs
2 cups raw or white sugar
1 cup neutral oil
1 cup wholemeal flour or
   gluten-free wholemeal
   flour
1 cup plain flour or
   gluten-free flour
¼ tsp salt
2 tsp cinnamon
1 tsp mixed spice
1 tsp ground ginger
1½ tsp baking soda
   (bicarbonate soda)
1 tbsp orange juice
3 cups grated carrot
1 cup raisins and/or
   chopped walnuts

CITRUS CREAM CHEESE ICING

150 g (5½ oz) cream
   cheese
100 g (3½ oz) butter, at
   room temperature
finely grated zest of
   1 small orange
2 tbsp orange juice
3 cups icing
   (confectioners') sugar
a pinch of salt
3 tbsp thread coconut,
   lightly toasted, to
   garnish (optional)

One of the joys of oil-based cakes is that they are so quick to make, and the results are nice and tender. Everything just goes into the bowl and the cake always comes out perfectly. Cooking the cake in a slab tin means it goes a lot further. You can also cook it in a regular cake tin or in muffin pans—you'll just need to adjust the cooking time (a little shorter for muffin pans and a little longer for a deeper traditional cake).

Preheat oven to 160°C (315°F) fanbake. Line a 20 cm x 30 cm (8 in x 12 in) slab tin with baking paper for easy clean-up.

Place eggs, sugar and oil in a large bowl and whisk to combine. Add flours, salt, cinnamon, mixed spice and ginger, and stir with a large spoon until evenly combined.

Dissolve baking soda in orange juice, add to mixture with carrots and raisins and/or walnuts and stir until evenly combined. Pour into prepared dish and bake until cake is risen and set and springs back when gently pressed in the centre (about 55 minutes).

Allow to cool before turning out onto a rack.

To make Citrus Cream Cheese Icing, blend cream cheese, butter, orange zest and juice in a bowl or food processor until smooth. Beat in icing sugar and salt, adding a little more icing sugar or water if necessary to achieve a spreadable consistency. Spread over cooled cake and top with coconut (if using). Carrot Slab Cake will keep for a week in an airtight container in a cool place.

ELEVEN

Going global

Taking on the world

When Sean was four and Rose was two, I hit a wall. No one had ever told me that if you live on adrenaline for too long you'll get sick.

After 80 days your body starts to produce lots of cortisol, which unlike adrenaline makes you feel like shit. My chronic burnout expressed itself first as anxiety, and then as depression. It was like being in a storm at sea, with these huge waves of anxiety threatening to drown me. In the end I had to stop working and just walk away from it all.

I was one of that generation of second-wave feminist women who thought we could have it all: great jobs, wonderful marriages, fabulous sex lives, perfect children. Superwomen? Yes, that was us. But actually, in my experience, I found it doesn't work like that. Something has to give, whether it's you, or your marriage, or your kids. There just isn't enough to go around. In my case, it was me. I had a fantastically supportive husband who adored me and was a wonderful father, I had au pairs to help with looking after the children, but even with all the support in the world my life was just way too busy. Ten days after Sean was born, I was back working full-time at the Culinary Institute. We had the launch of a new supermarket chain, and I remember taking this tiny baby in his car seat into a fancy frock shop. I bought myself a cute cream crêpe suit with a pleated

OPPOSITE Tramping with my babies—we're heading to the Rob Roy Glacier Track in Mount Aspiring National Park.

PREVIOUS Sampling negronis in the rooftop bar of SIXTY SoHo hotel in NYC.

skirt to wear to the launch. When I got home, the baby threw up all over it.

I had this idea of someone I should be, and it was about being good at everything. No matter what part of my life I was in, what I was doing was never enough. I felt like a failure. I started having panic attacks, and they got worse and worse. Things got to a point where I couldn't drive over the Auckland Harbour Bridge for this crippling feeling of panic and fear. Every horizon started to look black. I couldn't sell the business. It was all so much about me and my ideas that it wasn't really a business anyone else could buy.

> I had this idea of someone I should be, and it was about being good at everything. No matter what part of my life I was in, what I was doing was never enough. I felt like a failure.

Later, after a lot of therapy, I came to understand that I had never processed my brother's death, and that grief has a way of catching up with you if you don't work through it fully. Grief is universal, but, in my experience, it's not a linear process. Everyone has different ways of getting to some point of acceptance. That doesn't make things less sad; it just helps you to live with what happened and be more resilient. As a teenager, I was numb. I wasn't ready or equipped to go through the process of grieving. I pushed my emotions aside and challenged myself to the extreme so as not to feel this terrible pain. But it still caught up with me, eventually.

I took myself home to Auckland and didn't work for pretty much a whole year. At the time, Ted had this big business employing nearly 2000 people and he was working really hard. He was quite happy to carry the

OPPOSITE Family times. (Clockwise from top left) Kayaking the Raukokere River; fishing adventures in the Bay of Islands; Christmas in Auckland; hanging out with a friend's pet goat in Mahunga; a weekend escape in Rotoiti; and enjoying a Wānaka snowstorm.

load financially, and in fact always had been happy to be the breadwinner if needed. I had worked through having both of our children not because I had to financially, but because I had been afraid of losing my place in the world. I thought that if I got off the bus and stopped working I'd never get back on again.

But, with time, my mind started to clear. Thinking about it, I realised I wasn't alone in what I was going through. Life was busy and frantic for everyone. And I knew people wanted ideas and solutions. I had all these great recipes that I used when my life was mad crazy busy, and I knew that cooking was a simple way to feel useful and successful when everything else might be going to custard. So I started to work on a new book—a big book that would help people to get interesting, delicious, healthy meals on the table in a flash. I flew over to Sydney with some layouts in my bag to meet with Murdoch, a big food publisher there. 'This is great. We can take it to the Frankfurt Book Fair. It's perfect timing.' The Murdoch publisher was very enthusiastic.

'Do you mind if I take it to Frankfurt?' I asked.

'God, no! Go for it. Take it. You'll do really well.'

It was 1997. Ted and I worked out that we needed to play tag team, and we couldn't both be away at the same time. It was too tough on our kids, so Ted agreed to take some time off from his business to stay home with them while I went to Frankfurt. I asked Doris Mousdale if she would come with me. She often went to the fair as a buyer, and knew the ropes. She'd been my 'Go, girl! You can do this!' cheerleader for some time, endlessly supportive and nourishing of my ideas, and we had become great friends. I booked us an el cheapo hotel near the railway station for what was to become the first of many hilarious adventures to Frankfurt together.

The Messe Frankfurt exhibition space is one of the biggest in the world, with more than one-third of a kilometre of stands. For five days each October, it's dedicated to selling books. There are even buses to take you from one pavilion to another. I had booked the smallest possible panel—a single metre wide—on the New Zealand publishers group stand. As I was setting up, an awful panic started to overwhelm me. There were just so many exhibitors, so many stands, so many books. Who would want mine?

I hadn't had an anxiety attack in months. This one hit like a steam roller. I locked myself in the toilet for two hours, with all these negative thoughts racing around my head. *What on earth do you think you are doing here? This is nuts. It's never going to work. How could you be so stupid to think this was going to work?* My mind was like a stuck record.

And then the chat in my head started to take on a more optimistic and motivating tone. *Well, what have you got to lose? You're here now. You can do this. It's cost all this money to get here. Just get on with it.* For the next hour, I gave myself the pep talk of all time.

I came out of the ladies' room with my head up. I was on a mission.

DAY ONE OF THE FAIR, I wandered around trying to meet with English and North American publishers. No one wanted to see me. I didn't have a single meeting. The girls who worked on the big publishers' front desks were in charge of the diaries with everyone's appointments. People made meetings months in advance, I was told. They had agents. No one ever represented themselves.

It seemed that, if you hadn't pre-arranged a meeting, you had to have slept with the managing director, or the MD's cousin's brother, or an influential someone who knew someone else influential. I hadn't. This was not going to be as straightforward as I had thought.

I tried to hold on to the words of the Murdoch publisher: 'This is great. You'll do really well.' I had an instinct that this book was going to work. I just had to figure out how. I went to the bar at the fair and eavesdropped on people's conversations. There was definitely something happening. People were talking about this German publisher who was doing big deals—really big deals.

That night I phoned our old au pairs. We had kept in touch with all of them, and I had their phone numbers in Sweden and Norway and Denmark and Germany. I asked each of them if they could do me a really big favour: in the morning, could they pop down to their local bookshop, check out the cookbook section, and tell me the name of the publisher on the biggest and most beautiful books, especially the ones written by English-speaking authors?

The next morning I went shopping and bought myself a pair of very expensive Versace pants. Gianni Versace had died only a few months earlier. I loved his clothes, and had a whole wardrobe of them back at home from my black-belt shopping days. The pants were very flattering, bright green satin with big black-and-white spots. There was no chance of not being noticed. Then I called the au pairs back. They all had one name for me: Koenemann. I checked the fair catalogue, and there it was.

'I'm off to the German stand,' I announced to everyone at the New Zealand stand.

'You've gotta be nuts,' they said. 'It's hard enough to sell books in the English-language market, let alone foreign rights.'

Doris stayed to look after the stand and ply anyone who came by with the delicious cheese and wine I had brought over from New Zealand.

It wasn't hard to find the Koenemann stand over in the German Hall. It was a huge, beautiful designer space with people milling about everywhere. Soft, elegant lighting, a bar, and Scandi wood-panelling behind shelf after shelf of beautiful books. At 11 a.m. the place was already buzzing with people sipping champagne. All the guys were smoking cigars.

'Do you have an appointment?' asked the pretty girl on the desk.

'No,' I said. 'But I have an idea that I think will make Mr Koenemann a lot of money.'

The secretary went over to a tall blond man in a crisp suit who was smoking a cigar and drinking champagne, and whispered something in his ear. He turned and came over to me. 'What have you got, then?' he said, holding out his hand.

The book I held was still in what's known as the 'galley' stage—all the pages were there, loosely bound in their chapters, but the whole book was not yet held together. He took them from me and did a quick flick-through, then called over two other guys. They gave a cursory run through the pages, and both nodded. The tall blond man looked directly at me. There was nothing friendly in his gaze. This was business. 'I'll take half a million copies. World rights.'

I was completely thrown. 'Ahhhh, I don't actually want to sell world rights. I . . .'

He raised an eyebrow, and handed me back my galleys. 'That's the deal.' Turning on his heel, he returned to the conversation I had interrupted.

The whole thing had taken less than two minutes.

I stood there, stunned. I had just turned down a deal for half a million books. But, if I gave Koenemann world rights, that would mean forfeiting the right to publish the book myself in New Zealand. At home, people knew me. I had been selling from bookshop to bookshop—and I was selling an awful lot of books. Kiwi booksellers wouldn't know who this Koenemann publisher was. My book wouldn't work at home with a big German brand on it.

So now what?

THAT NIGHT, I BARELY SLEPT. I tossed and turned, and got up early the next morning to get to the fair before it opened. Being an exhibitor meant I could get in early. I made a beeline for the German stand and yes, there was my man, Mr Koenemann himself, with no one else around.

'Excuse me, Mr Koenemann,' I said, clutching my now rather limp galleys. 'I just wondered if I could talk to you about my book.'

He gestured to a chair. I took a big breath and sat down. 'I come from New Zealand. It's a tiny country down in the bottom of the Pacific, but everyone knows me there and I sell direct to all the bookshops. If I could just keep the New Zealand rights, and maybe Australia . . .'

He held my gaze. 'You can have the English-language rights,' he said. 'I'll take 300,000 copies, foreign rights.'

'OK, that sounds great,' I said, trying not to show my excitement.

We shook hands on the deal.

'Come to my party on Friday night,' he said. 'Here's the address. Everyone will be there.' He handed me a card with the name of an Italian restaurant on it.

I went back to my tiny New Zealand stand, lay down on the floor and drank four mini bottles of vodka. No one actually believed me when I said I'd done a big deal.

AT THE KOENEMANN PARTY ON Friday night, hundreds of people from every country in the world were packed into a smallish Italian restaurant on the outskirts of the city. When I arrived, Koenemann was in the cellar playing Rachmaninoff on the piano. Upstairs, people were dancing on the tables and, on the tables that weren't topped with swaying, gyrating bodies, there were huge platters of food. Rivers of booze flowed all night.

Koenemann had been the financial controller for the huge Taschen publishing empire before he went out on his own. The man was whip-smart. I met the translator from Zagreb who would translate my books into nine languages, the designer from Germany, the print binder, the paper broker, and lots of other people like me who made books. Koenemann's catalogue was huge, and covered every category of non-fiction.

I got back to the hotel at 5 a.m., asked the taxi driver to wait for me while I packed my bag, and managed to make my early flight to Paris. I got there just in time for my favourite market over on the Avenue de Saxe in the 7th arrondissement. Doris woke up after I left and later told me the hotel room looked like a hurricane had gone through it. When I arrived at my friend Georgie's apartment in Paris, she pointed out that my shirt was on inside-out. I made it to the market, but then had to retire to bed for the rest of the day, nailed by the hangover to beat all hangovers.

Once I was back in New Zealand, all the paperwork started to arrive. I needed a really good lawyer. I called Wendy Pye, one of New Zealand's biggest publishers at the time, and she kindly gave me the name of the lawyer she used for all her international deals.

I was away, and soon the money was in the bank.

My confidence soared. I could do this.

AT THE FRANKFURT BOOK FAIR the next year I went back to Koenemann's stand. Six months earlier, I'd gone to the London Book Fair, and been unsuccessful at selling any rights for my title *Best of Annabel Langbein*.

'I'll take 200,000, English language,' Koenemann said. 'You can keep New Zealand.'

There were always incredible parties during the fair, and Doris got loads of invites from big publishing houses. For the launch of Paulo Coelho's *Eleven Minutes*, there were hand-painted invitations, a samba band was flown in from Rio, and Coelho himself took to the stage to sing, astonishing us with his gloriously smooth voice. We got back to the hotel as they were serving breakfast. We were always the last to arrive, and the last to leave. Each year, Edouard Cointreau, who owned and ran the Gourmand World Cookbook Awards, threw elaborate parties—buffets sagging with Madagascar prawns, sides of salmon in aspic and giant standing rib roasts, which we swilled down with Gosset champagne.

All the publishers hung out at the Frankfurter Hof—you'd find the Dutch in one corner, the Norwegians in another, the French always out front smoking. It was a great place to do business. At the start, Doris and I would stay in some flea-pit hotel on Kaiserstrasse, but as business got better we upgraded. By the end I'd made the Frankfurter Hof my home for the week.

IN 1999 I STARTED TO put together an idea for a new series of books. I wanted people to know more about the remote Pacific Islands, places where people lived successfully with very few of the trappings of Western civilisation. Living solely from the sea and the land requires a keen intelligence and immense resourcefulness. I wanted my next book to dispel the assumption that stuff and consumerism equals success and progress.

So I travelled to the Pacific with photographer Kieran Scott, and took my chillybin off the beaten track. We went far from the tourist droves, to remote places in the outer islands of Rarotonga, Fiji and Vanuatu, where a traditional way of life was still being practised. I had lots of fun creating some exciting new dishes, drawing on my faithful chillybin, which was filled with flavourings and fresh ingredients. Meanwhile, Kieran shot beautiful images of the landscapes and people.

Back at home, I worked up some layouts with a designer and, as October rolled around, headed off to Frankfurt yet again. If Koenemann's stand had been big the previous year, it was even bigger and flashier this year. The serious young woman with an attractive face and long dark hair who always followed Koenemann around, taking down the details of all his deals, was looking a tad harried. I presented my sample page spreads—about eight gorgeous visual layouts, with recipes and locations from our Pacific shoot.

'I want to make a cookbook series. It's going to be about Old World and New World ways of cooking, and the influences that go into making each food culture unique.'

'What's the next one going to be about?' Koenemann asked, turning over my spreads without looking up.

'Italy,' I replied. 'It's the mother of Western cooking.'

My new backer spent the next 10 minutes saying nothing, just flicking back and forth through the pages. Finally he looked up. 'I'll take 1.2 million copies, world rights.'

I couldn't believe my ears. We shook hands on the deal on the spot. I wasn't about to quibble about New Zealand rights on this one. The pretty notator wiped a bead of sweat from her brow.

I HAD RECEIVED TWO OF the six payments due, and taken our kids on a fabulous sabbatical to Italy for four months in 2000 to write the next book in the series, when Koenemann went spectacularly broke. He was now bankrupt.

His demise caused huge ructions in the publishing world. Printers, paper makers, banks . . . The entire European publishing world and all the businesses surrounding it were thrown into disarray. It took more than two years for things to get back on their feet.

Luckily, my clever lawyer had written a contract that ensured I would get all my rights back. But few publishers want old titles. They want new titles, new ideas. The Dutch and the Germans bought small print runs of my next book after the Italy book, *Cooking to Impress Without Stress*. But it was slim pickings—lunch money compared to the Koenemann deals.

Now what to do?

IN APRIL 2006, ABOUT A YEAR after it was launched, I discovered YouTube. The night is etched into my mind for the disaster that unfolded. I remember being in one of those funks when I couldn't think of what to make for dinner. I wondered if there was any food on this new YouTube thing. Once I found out that there was, I started hunting out recipes to deal with the buckets of eggplants I had to hand from the Sunday market over in Takapuna.

The video that caught my eye was called 'Victoria's Secret Eggplant

Frittata', and the billing read: 'Made without eggs—just 675 calories. You will not find this recipe in any cookbook. A true secret.' The Victoria in question could never have been confused with a lingerie model. She was ancient and rounded, with a heavy Brooklyn drawl. Once I got past the cringe-worthy start of the clip to the bit where this old woman was nimbly slicing up the eggplant, I figured Victoria knew her stuff. I watched for the full six and a half minutes, then headed into the kitchen infused with confidence and excitement about the dinner I was going to make.

An hour later, the kitchen looked like a bomb had hit it. Around 9 p.m., I dished up quite possibly the most vile thing I have ever made. No one ate it, and there were hisses and murmurs, mutiny and disappointment all round. I felt such a failure. I had never had such a disastrous cooking experience before. It was humiliating.

I woke up the next morning thinking, *I can do this much, much better.*

I decided that my next book would be interactive, with QR codes directing people to videos of me cooking the recipes. I hired a director and found a couple of sponsors to underwrite the production, and away we went. The final product, *Eat Fresh*, had codes for eight little video clips that we put on YouTube. As far as I know, we were the first publishers in the world to do this.

At the 2007 Frankfurt Book Fair, people were still feeling the fallout of the Koenemann empire collapse. But a prestigious French publisher, a Norwegian publisher, the Dutch and the Germans all came on board to buy *Eat Fresh*. Businesswise, the numbers were still tiny—5000 copies here, 3000 copies there. It hardly covered the stand costs.

OPPOSITE Our Italian sabbatical. (Clockwise from top) Climbing the hill behind our house in Macari, Sicily; eating at Trattoria Bruno Bruni in San Vito lo Capo; visiting a pastry shop in Trapani with Rose and my schoolfriend Alice; and making gnocchi at one of the agri-tourism farms we stayed on.

ONE DAY IN MARCH 2008, I was in my Auckland office when the phone rang.

'Hello,' a posh English voice bellowed down the line. 'This is Bernard Macleod from FremantleMedia. We've been looking at your video clips on YouTube, and we'd like to meet you. Can you come to Cannes for the MIP fair?'

'Great,' I said. 'Yes, that would be great.'

I hung up, wondering who Fremantle was. And what was MIP? I had just said I'd be there.

The next month I flew to France and dragged my Paris-based friend Georgie down to Cannes with me. Our meeting was lunch at the Majestic Hotel, down on the waterfront. It was stuffy and formal, and the French waiters were bored and arrogant. You could have taken a cricket bat to the *sole meunière* and made a hole in the wall.

There were two other Fremantle execs there with Bernard. 'We like your clips,' they said.

'Thank you.' I was right out of my league here. I figured that these guys were interested in my two-minute clips because they were high-quality filler content that cable channels could use. So I started to talk about the idea I had for this.

Bernard, a very tall man with a powerful presence, leaned over the table. 'No no no,' he interrupted. 'We want you to be a star.'

'Me?' I said.

'Yes.'

'Does that mean you're going to give me some money?' I was thinking about the costs of my airfare and just getting here.

'Well, we could give you some money for a pilot for a TV cooking series, and if that works then we can do a joint venture for the production—so, we would pool our resources and share the profits.'

I'd been around the traps long enough to know you don't just say yes when it comes to your intellectual property. I said I was very flattered, and asked if I could come back to them. Actually, I didn't really think any kind of deal would happen.

WE PUT A BUDGET TOGETHER for a pilot for a series, and Fremantle agreed to pay half. I hadn't quite formed the idea, but I knew Ted wanted to call it *The Free Range Cook*.

My little export publishing business entitled me to apply for a 'one for one' grant that the government was offering to explore new export opportunities. You spent a dollar and you got a dollar, so the cost of development and research was halved. I used the money to hire a woman who had been the chief executive of the Food Network in the USA to help me nut out the strategy, and I headed over to New York. Erica was eye-wateringly expensive, and gave me all sorts of depressing stats on why my brand wouldn't work in the States, but she did help me to figure out what I needed in order to do a licensing deal and not a joint venture.

For the pilot, Ted and I had some fun. He marked out all the cuts on a side of lamb and told me what they were good for. I chose the best one, then cooked it up. I always thought Ted should have been the talent, but he said he was better suited to being an international man of mystery.

And soon we were making TV. We had come from the land of 'no'. TVNZ had said no to all my ideas. No, I was too old. No, it wouldn't work. No, people wouldn't watch it. But, now that I had Fremantle behind me as our funding partners for the series, TVNZ decided to sit up and pay attention. They agreed to give us a prime-time slot on a Saturday night.

I had no idea how hard this TV business would be. Creating, presenting and co-producing that first series was a challenge like no other. No one told me before we started shooting that you needed multiple takes in order to get different angles. When the director asked me to do the same thing over and over, I thought it was because I was doing something wrong. Likewise,

I had no idea that if the light changes in the middle of a shot you have to start all over again. Or that a skydiving plane will probably decide that it is going to whine its way high up into the sky in the background where you are filming, having never done anything of the sort before, simply because you are filming.

Creating *The Free Range Cook* series felt a bit like climbing a really big mountain. You head off full of energy and excitement, armed with everything you think you might need. About halfway up, when things are starting to hurt, there's a blizzard. You're freezing to the bones, and all your socks are wet. You think, *Maybe this wasn't such a good idea.* Three-quarters of the way up, you think you might actually die. You swear you will never, ever do this again. Finally, almost impossibly, you arrive at the top, and there is an incredible sense of achievement and exhilaration and joy.

I remember Ted and I sitting around the table with our kids over dinner one night before we had pushed the go button to commit to the production. We told our then-teenagers that we needed to put a lot of dosh into the pot, but we had no idea if what we were trying to do would actually work. If it didn't, there would be lean pickings for a very long time.

'Go, Mum!' was their response.

IN 2010 TED, ROSE AND I headed to Cannes for the sales launch. Sean had gone off to uni in Melbourne, and Rose was supposed to be studying for exams. However, Bernard and his wife, Louise, had a suite at the Majestic Hotel, and said Rose could spend the days there studying while we worked at the fair. Luckily, the weather was freezing, otherwise Rose would have spent the entire time on the suite's expansive balcony, sunbathing in the world's smallest bikini. As it was, she couldn't wait to tell us what the rack rate was for the suite: 'Thousands, Mum. It's thousands of euros a night.' Maybe *this* was the business to be in . . .

It was pretty amazing to arrive at the MIP festival and see an enormous photo of myself up on one side of the entrance, and a photo the same size of Jamie Oliver on the other. I had brought a suitcase filled with pretty packages of home-made cookies and, after each meeting, would hand the ribboned bags out to our prospective licensing partners. No other talent ever attended meetings, let alone brought home baking, but everyone seemed to like it.

After all the hard work, we were rewarded with the series going on to sell into more than 90 territories. We became the number-two property for our distributors, FremantleMedia, after Jamie Oliver.

ALMOST RIGHT AS WE LAUNCHED, the business model changed. Food had become like children's television: an increasingly cluttered market offering cheap product no one wanted to pay for.

We ploughed on, making season two, and then season three, all the while achieving increasing sales and increasing ratings. In New Zealand, by the end of season three, we had achieved the highest ratings ever—number three over all channels and time slots for three weeks, with over 600,000 people watching the show each week. TVNZ had made lots of money out of advertising during our show, but that didn't mean they were going to pay us any more for our NZ-based series than they would for what they could buy in from offshore. I had an incredible team helping to make the series and the accompanying books, and everyone had worked so hard, but we just couldn't make it work. I felt so frustrated and angry.

At our last meeting it all got too hard. We had got these incredible ratings, we had achieved international recognition, we had sold our series into 90-plus territories, and I had won Best Home Chef in the People's Choice Awards in the USA, but we couldn't get the funding to make a new series here in New Zealand.

It was time to move on to new ideas.

BUTTER COOKIES

READY IN 45 MINUTES + CHILLING · MAKES ABOUT 75

GF, IF GLUTEN-FREE FLOUR IS USED · V

550 g (1 lb 4 oz) butter
1 cup sugar
4½ cups plain flour or
  gluten-free flour
4 tsp baking powder
1 tsp vanilla extract
6 tbsp sweetened
  condensed milk
flavourings of your choice
  (see overleaf)

When I was a kid all my friends wanted to come home with me for afternoon tea, because my mother always had a stash of tins and jars in the pantry full of delicious home baking. This is her Butter Cookie recipe, and I have added three different flavour combinations to the base recipe to make a Cookie Sampler. You can also freeze portions of raw dough, whip them out of the freezer in the evening and bake them before school or morning tea.

Beat butter and sugar together until pale and creamy. Stir in flour, baking powder, vanilla and sweetened condensed milk until the mixture comes together in a ball. (The raw dough can be prepared ahead to this stage, frozen until needed and then defrosted before baking.)

To make a Cookie Sampler divide dough into 3 portions and mix different flavourings into each portion (see overleaf).

When ready to cook, preheat oven to 170°C (325°F) fanbake. Line 3 or 4 oven trays with baking paper for easy clean-up. Shape cookies according to instructions for different flavourings and arrange on prepared trays. Bake until lightly golden and set (about 15–20 minutes).

Allow to cool on the tray for 10 minutes then transfer to a rack to cool completely. Butter Cookies will keep for several weeks in an airtight container or jar. If they become a little stale, refresh for 5 minutes in an oven preheated to 190°C (375°F) fanbake.

CHOCOLATE CHIP COOKIES

Mix 200 g (7 oz) chopped dark chocolate into 1 portion of cookie dough. Chill for 15 minutes then roll into walnut-sized balls, place on prepared baking trays and flatten slightly.

PISTACHIO AND CRANBERRY COOKIES

Combine ½ cup chopped pistachios and ½ cup dried cranberries. Mix half of this into 1 portion of cookie dough. Chill for 15 minutes, then roll into walnut-sized balls, place on prepared baking trays, and flatten slightly. Press remaining pistachios and cranberries on top.

JAM DROP COOKIES

Roll dough into walnut-sized balls, place on prepared baking trays and press a small indent in the middle of each ball with your thumb. Drop ½ teaspoon strawberry or raspberry jam into each hole.

THAI BEEF SALAD

READY IN 1 HOUR + MARINATING · SERVES 6–8 · DF · GF

2 tbsp sweet soy sauce

2 tbsp fish sauce

1 large clove garlic, crushed

about 1.3 kg (3 lb) whole beef fillet, trimmed

salt and ground black pepper, to taste

400 g (14 oz) cherry tomatoes, halved

about 150 g (5½ oz) baby spinach leaves

3 Lebanese cucumbers or 1 telegraph cucumber, sliced

3 radishes, thinly sliced

1 small red onion, halved and thinly sliced

½ cup fresh coriander (cilantro) leaves, stalks removed

½ cup Thai basil leaves or Vietnamese mint

1 packed cup fresh mint leaves, torn coarsely

Sweet Chilli Dressing (see overleaf)

TO SERVE

½–1 long red chilli, finely sliced

crispy shallots

chopped roasted peanuts

lime cheeks

You can make this sensational salad using a cheaper cut of meat such as hanger steak (onglet), flat-iron steak or skirt steak. Just be sure to cook until rare or medium-rare—no more. To prepare this salad ahead of time, cut up the vegetables and herbs, cover, and chill. If you like, you can cook the meat up to about an hour before serving and set aside, then combine all the ingredients just before you dish up.

To prepare beef, place sweet soy sauce, fish sauce and garlic in a shallow roasting dish big enough to hold beef. Add beef and turn to coat in marinade. Cover and marinate in the fridge for at least 1 hour or up to 12 hours.

Preheat oven to 240°C (475°F) fanbake.

Season beef with salt and pepper, tucking thin end of fillet under so it doesn't overcook. Roast beef to rare or medium-rare (about 25 minutes for a fillet this size). Test for doneness by using a meat thermometer to check that it is 60–65°C (140–150°F) or by squeezing it in the thickest part—it should still have some give. If it feels firm, it's overdone.

Remove from oven, cover with tinfoil and a clean tea towel, and allow to stand for at least 15 minutes.

While beef is resting, make salad by combining all remaining ingredients except Sweet Chilli Dressing in a serving bowl. Just before serving, add ½ cup Sweet Chilli Dressing and toss to combine.

When ready to serve, carve beef and arrange on a serving platter. Pile salad on the side and scatter with chilli, crispy shallots and peanuts. Serve with the remaining Sweet Chilli Dressing and lime cheeks on the side.

PICTURED OVERLEAF

SWEET CHILLI DRESSING

READY IN 5 MINUTES · MAKES ABOUT ¾ CUP · DF · GF

½ cup sweet chilli sauce
2 tbsp rice vinegar
2 tbsp fish sauce
finely grated zest of
  1 lemon or lime
1 tbsp lime juice or
  lemon juice
2 single makrut lime
  leaves, central rib
  removed and leaves very
  finely shredded

This is such a useful dressing whenever you want a bright, clean, fragrant Asian finish. I often make It in bulk and keep it in the fridge ready to marinate, glaze or dress any kind of protein or toss through a salad. You can't go past it drizzled over a bowl of fried rice with a fried egg on top. All the aromatics and umami round out the palate, so it tastes rich but there's no fat or oil involved.

Place all the ingredients in a small jar and shake to combine.

The dressing will keep in a covered container in the fridge for at least a week.

STRAWBERRY PARFAIT
WITH PISTACHIO PRALINE

READY IN 30 MINUTES + CHILLING · SERVES 8 · GF · V

750 g (1 lb 10 oz)
strawberries, hulled and
coarsely chopped

¾ cup sugar

1½ tbsp lemon juice

2 tsp orange blossom
water (optional)

3 cups cream, chilled

½ cup crumbed Pistachio
Praline (see overleaf) or
crumbed sweet biscuits,
to serve

This is my go-to dessert when strawberries are in season (and I even freeze the purée so I can enjoy it when they're out of season). Orange blossom water adds that elusive exotic flavour, but don't overdo it—a little goes a long way. A small bottle will keep in the pantry for years, and it's not expensive to buy.

Heat berries in a medium pot with sugar, lemon juice and orange blossom water (if using), stirring to dissolve sugar. Once mixture simmers (about 5 minutes), remove from heat, whizz to a purée in a food processor or with a hand wand blender, cover and chill for at least 30 minutes. (The purée can be prepared ahead to this stage, chilled for up to a week or frozen until needed.)

To serve, whip cream to soft peaks, then fold in half the chilled strawberry purée. Divide a third of this mixture between 8 small jars or glasses, then divide half the remaining purée over the top. Divide another third of the cream mixture between the jars or glasses, then the last of the purée, followed by the last of the cream mixture. Sprinkle each parfait with a tablespoon of crumbed Pistachio Praline or crumbed sweet biscuits and serve immediately.

PISTACHIO PRALINE

READY IN 30 MINUTES + COOLING · MAKES 1 CUP · DF · GF · V · VE

½ cup shelled pistachios
¾ cup sugar
2 tbsp water

Often, it's the little garnishes and finishing touches that transform an everyday dish into something special. Praline is one such thing: a fine crumb of caramel and nuts that's easy to make and will keep in a sealed container in a cool place for weeks—even months if you store it in the fridge. Don't make it on a humid day; like any kind of toffee it will get sticky.

Preheat oven to 180°C (350°F) fanbake. Line an oven tray or shallow oven dish with baking paper for easy clean-up.

Place pistachios on prepared tray and roast for 5 minutes.

Heat sugar and water in a small, heavy-based pot over a medium heat, swirling pot gently from time to time (do not stir as this can make it crystallise). When syrup is a clear, deep golden brown, add pistachios, then immediately tip onto prepared tray. Tilt tray to spread pistachios in a single layer. Allow to cool.

When set hard, transfer to a clean plastic bag and smash into small pieces with a rolling pin. Praline will keep for months in an airtight container.

TWELVE

Back to basics

Closer to nature

I would have been about 25, cooking a gig for the Deer Farmers Association at the Nelson Agricultural & Pastoral Show, when I got the overwhelming urge to go bush. After three long, hot days cooking hundreds of kilos of venison over a gas barbecue, and spreading the word of its virtues (there are many), I was well and truly cooked.

I knew I just needed to get out of town, away from people and back to nature. After my earlier years in the bush, I knew it would get me back on an even keel again. I met an exhibitor at the show who was touting the beauty of Abel Tasman National Park, and how amazing the track through it was, and that was all it took.

I grabbed a paella pan (yes, a really heavy cast-iron one), my cooking knife, some rice and a bag of seasonings, and headed over to Golden Bay in my little rental car. I spent the first night at the old Telegraph Hotel in Tākaka, and managed to persuade the girl at the front desk to lend me a sleeping bag and a rucksack. (We're talking a long time ago, when Tākaka was even more of a hippy enclave than it is now, so borrowing gear was an easy ask.) Into the rucksack went a warm jumper, my toothbrush and toothpaste, some insect repellent, a box of matches, a torch, a few bits of fruit, my bag of rice and the bag of seasonings. On the outside, the

OPPOSITE Nipping across Lake Wānaka in the old Sunstreaker jetboat.

PREVIOUS In my happy place: our Wānaka vegie garden.

deadweight of the paella pan. I'd been told there were huts along the track that you could sleep in, so off I headed, leaving the car at the start of the track. There were mussels and sea lettuce aplenty, so it was easy enough to put together a kind of rough, tasty paella to eat for each of the two nights I stayed in the huts along the trail.

I could feel myself slowly letting go, winding down and chilling out. The chattering babble of a stream, the lulling whisper of the waves, the earthy smell of the bush, cooking over a fire, washing in a stream and feeling the crisp cold hit my face.

A hike in the wilderness is a great analogy for life. You never know what's around the corner. You might be walking in a glorious open grassy field one minute, and next thing there's a dirty big bog to navigate, a tricky river to cross or you're scrambling for a foothold on a cliff. Random, unpredictable, often out of your control. Good bits and bad bits. You just have to keep putting one foot in front of the other. A walk, like life, is also something you have to do for yourself. You can't live the expectations of others, or step in the exact same prints as your forebears. Secondhand dreams don't work. You have to make your own road, and go through the trials yourself. That's how you figure out what matters to you. That's how you build resilience. Experience it all. Feel it all, good and bad. Fight for the things that matter.

I hadn't realised how much I needed that nature fix on the Abel Tasman track until I actually got it. I could feel myself slowly letting go, winding down and chilling out. The chattering babble of a stream, the lulling whisper of the waves, the earthy smell of the bush, cooking over a fire, washing in a stream and feeling the crisp cold hit my face. Days that started with the sunrise and ended with darkness falling. These simple things were just what I needed.

IT WAS MANY YEARS LATER that I worked out precisely why being out in nature makes me feel so good.

Following the 2009 swine-flu epidemic, tourism in Mexico experienced a major slump, which meant there were some amazing deals on hotels. At the time, I had been working like a mad thing in New York—as well as trying to get *The Free Range Cook* into the States, I had also been working on a big internet deal with Time Inc. I was totally exhausted. I didn't even think about potentially getting sick. All I could think was, *Wow, I can get an incredible holiday for next to nothing.* And so I did, booking into a remote luxury eco-resort called Verana, on the coast south of Puerto Vallarta.

Getting to Verana is an adventure in itself. First you take a 45-minute taxi from Puerto Vallarta down to Boca de Tomatlan, then you jump into a speedboat and blitz about 20 minutes down the coast through the waters of Bahía de Banderas. As you come into view of the bay of Yelapa, the driver cuts the engine, and you drift in towards the coast. There are mules standing on the rocks, and your luggage is strapped to their backs, then you hike up the hill into the jungle. It's dreamy and lush and beautiful.

It didn't take me long to discover that I was the only person at the resort who was not on honeymoon. And so I headed to the kitchens. The chef was local to the nearby village of Yelapa, just a 20-minute walk away, but his fame had extended to North America and Europe—and with good reason. Each day, as part of his mise en place, he would prepare 16 fresh salsas, each offering differing degrees of fieriness and flavour. I could always find him working outside the kitchen over a fire, where he brewed rich slow-cooked pork braises in big terracotta dishes that he set on a thick piece of steel over the embers. The locals would bring fresh cheeses that he would crumble over eggs and sauces, and tortillas that he would grill and fill, or fry for corn chips. Everything was sourced and made locally, either in the resort or in the village nearby. It was all so fresh and incredibly delicious.

The driving principle behind Verana is biophilia, or the idea that humans have an innate and genetically determined affinity with the natural world. Biophilia and biophobia sit at opposite ends of the spectrum when it comes to human responses—while snakes and spiders are common phobias, the beauty of a natural view and the iridescent colours of a butterfly's wings or a tropical fish's scales touch us in a positive and uplifting way. Aristotle talked about biophilia as a love of life, with 'philia' denoting the ways we feel good about something, but it was Harvard entomologist Edward O. Wilson who first proposed the hypothesis of biophilia in 1986. In its essence, the theory is that we humans possess an innate tendency to seek connections with nature and other forms of life for the very reason that we are part of nature, a species that evolved among other species. The natural world is in our DNA.

Verana resort was full of references to biophilia and to Wilson's work. One of his quotes stuck in my mind: 'Humanity is a biological species, living in a biological environment, because like all species, we are exquisitely adapted in everything: from our behaviour, to our genetics, to our physiology, to that particular environment in which we live. The earth is our home. Unless we preserve the rest of life, as a sacred duty, we will be endangering ourselves by destroying the home in which we evolved, and on which we completely depend.'

The seed was planted.

BEYOND OUR PRACTICAL DEPENDENCE ON things like clean water, soil, air, bees and fresh food, there is also a deep happiness and satisfaction that comes from our direct interactions with nature. Establishing or re-establishing this connection isn't just a feel-good thing. It's critical if we are to in any way reverse the habitat destruction and rapid species extinction that is now under way in our world. If your life is spent in front of a screen or in worlds of virtual reality, you have no opportunity to marvel at the diversity and splendours of the natural world. But failing to appreciate nature and to treat it with respect and care fails all living things. It fails our very existence as humans.

Sustainability is an overused buzzword these days, but at its heart it's about creating and defending a path that will enable future generations to survive and thrive. It's about ensuring that those who come after us get to experience wild, healthy nature, and the resources and biodiversity of this amazing planet.

> Sustainability is an overused buzzword these days, but at its heart it's about creating and defending a path that will enable future generations to survive and thrive.

I've become increasingly aware in recent years of how precious and vital diversity is to the resilience of our food systems. As a consequence of mass production, farmers all over the globe are using fewer and fewer breeds and varieties. They find themselves needing to produce certain-sized animals to fit on assembly lines for processing and transportation, or having to get crops to ripen all at the same time, or needing crops to grow as quickly as possible. Since the 1900s, farmers worldwide have turned to high-yield uniform crops, which can withstand global transportation and supermarket shelf-life, instead of growing multiple local varieties. We can grow two or three times as much now as we could 50 or 60 years ago but, according to a 2009 article published in the *Journal of HortScience*, some varieties of vegetables and fruits have lost up to 40 per cent of their nutrient content. Today, 75 per cent of the world's food is generated from only

12 plants and five animal species. University studies point to modern hybrid species that have been developed for higher yields, easier handling, better appearance and marketability, often at the expense of nutritional content.

But there is some light in all of this. The popularity of heirloom and heritage fruits and vegetables is on the rise, not just because they taste better but because they're better for you. As well as being more nutrient-dense, they also help to ensure genetic diversity in our food chain. When you support growers who produce heritage varieties, you are helping to preserve the rich diversity of the food crops that our forebears created. You are helping to carry that diversity into the future.

FAST-FORWARD TO 2017, AND MY calendar for the year was full of jobs offshore to promote New Zealand food and issues around sustainability.

Just before the America's Cup, I travelled to Bermuda to help raise awareness about lionfish, a species that poses a serious threat to marine habitats in the area and, increasingly, around the world. It was great to represent New Zealand as one of six celebrity chefs from the host nations of each America's Cup team. I had an idea to make these bony little fish into fishcakes, which could then be manufactured as a way to create employment on this cash-strapped island, but when I saw all the fancy equipment my fellow chefs were carrying in I realised I needed to up the ante. I ended up preparing a delicious lionfish ceviche with herbs and greens foraged from the island, and I topped it with my crispy fishcakes and a fresh ginger-coriander sauce. I wanted to show people that everything on the plate

OPPOSITE (Clockwise from top left) Representing New Zealand at the Lionfish Chefs' Throwdown in Bermuda; out on the harbour watching the America's Cup pre-races with Captain Mike Jones; prepping for a pop-up restaurant event during New Zealand Week in China; taking time out to be a tourist and visit the Great Wall; and learning about climate change as a guest of Antarctica New Zealand.

could be locally sourced, but it wasn't easy, as this idyllic island isn't in any way self-sufficient.

Later that same year, I went to China to take up an assignment as ambassador for New Zealand Week. This involved developing menus and recipes for a series of pop-up restaurant events in Shanghai and Beijing, doing interviews and filming, and hosting meet-and-greets. While I was in Beijing, the e-commerce giant Alibaba held its annual sales event, the 11.11 Global Shopping Festival, which, over a 24-hour period, generated a staggering US$25.3 billion in sales. The next day, it was pretty much impossible to walk down the footpath, there were so many delivery boxes piled sky-high. Billions and billions of dollars' worth of *stuff*. I felt physically sick.

Less than a month after getting back from China, just before Christmas 2017, I found myself in Antarctica. I had been invited as a guest of Antarctica New Zealand to learn about some of the important scientific research being undertaken around climate change. Out there on the ice, in the vast, empty white spaces, a deep silence reigned. My thoughts turned inwards, and I started to think about all that stuff going into everyone's apartments in China. It would most likely be thrown out when the next giant Alibaba sale rolled around. How did we get so obsessed with stuff? It might seem cheap—that amazing gadget with all those moving parts that's only $4, or those shoes that are only $10—but, actually, it's not cheap. There's a price, whether environmental or social. We just aren't paying it in ways that we can see now—or, if we can see, we choose not to look.

Once upon a time, millions and millions of years ago, when volcanic activity created a very high CO_2 atmosphere on Earth, Antarctica was covered with rich forests, and no snow or ice. You might be surprised to know that fossils of both plant and animal life, including dinosaurs, abound on the icy continent. Over dinner one night, I met a scientist who had that day found some fossilised remains of *Nothofagus* (southern beech) way up high in the dry valleys.

Being in Antarctica made me realise the fragility and vulnerability of our planet. It made me understand how things can so easily and so quickly change. We are seeing it now, as climate change renders vast tracts of the world inhospitable, as crops fail, as seas rise. For so many millennia, the Earth has maintained an environment where humanity can prosper, but it could—and may—become a hostile environment. It has all happened before.

Realising this was a powerful moment. The fierce yet frail power of nature in Antarctica down at the bottom of the world could not have sat in starker contrast to the rampant, resource-gobbling consumerism I'd witnessed after that Alibaba sale in China.

Having seen first-hand, from Bermuda to China to Antarctica, some of the pressures at play in our world, I was starting to realise how pivotal it was for us to make changes to the way we shop and cook and live. We need to do it not just for our own health, but for the health of our planet. And it seemed to me that, of all the places in the world, New Zealand is in the best position to lead the planet in terms of environmental stewardship.

I returned home with a resolve to use less, waste less and tread more lightly.

OUR DAUGHTER, ROSE, CAME HOME that Christmas. She'd been a cash-strapped student for many years and, like many of her millennial generation, her approach was and still is vested in the well-being of our planet. Her actions are tempered by a commitment to ethical food production, sustainability and health.

I had started working on a new cookbook, and Rose and I were talking about how it could empower people to use less and waste less. We discussed how it might encourage positive habits that are kinder on our wallets and on the environment, and more nurturing for our bodies and minds.

The day before she was due to fly back to Melbourne, Rose had a really nasty waterskiing accident and fractured three vertebrae. Luckily, her fractures were stable, and she didn't have to go to hospital, but she was in a lot of pain. For a couple of months, she had to spend most of her time lying down in Wānaka. And that's when it came to me: why not make this Rose's project? She had a wonderful vision, and so many exciting new ideas to share. It seemed like the perfect time to combine our different skills and knowledge. So, while Rose lay in bed and wrote recipes and copy, I got into the kitchen and put all her recipes through their paces. When it came to the photography shoot, Rose art-directed the whole project from the daybed. It was a silver lining to what was an otherwise very stressful situation. I loved working with my talented daughter. Our cookbook, *Together*, went on to win Best Book at the 2019 NZ Food Media Awards.

> Rose and I have ended up in the same place in the way we each approach cooking. We both love flavours that are fresh and vibrant, and food that makes you feel vital and strong.

Even though we come from different generations and different directions, Rose and I have ended up in the same place in the way we each approach cooking. We both love flavours that are fresh and vibrant, and food that makes you feel vital and strong. More than anything, we love to bring people together around the table in simple celebrations that empower us to feel connected.

OPPOSITE In the vegie garden with Rose,
shooting our cookbook, *Together*.

THESE ISSUES OF HOW WE LIVE and what we buy have become closer and closer to my heart the older I get. The New Zealand we live in today is very different in terms of standards of living from the country that I grew up in. Like everyone, I want to see our country build a strong and successful future, so that our children and our grandchildren can enjoy this extraordinary place. I don't think that's a naïve idea.

Since my late twenties, my philosophy around food and cooking has been based on an idea of healthy eating that's not dogmatic or restrictive. I want to feel healthy and strong, but I'm interested in doing this in a way that celebrates variety and tastes delicious. I'm not really interested in fads, but I do love learning new things and discovering how to use new ingredients. Michael Pollan, author of *The Omnivore's Dilemma*, famously said to 'eat food, not too much, mostly plants', and I reckon that's a useful mantra to live by. As is the advice about not eating anything your grandmother wouldn't recognise as food. Or, as Ted often says, 'Eat fresh food, not barcodes.'

Roll back a hundred years and everything people ate was a natural ingredient, everyone was a locavore, there were no processed foods, and few foods existed with more than one ingredient. Everything came into the home as individual ingredients, to be combined and cooked to order. There were no numbers or additives or preservatives, apart from salt and sun and air.

IN 2014 TED MOVED A BARN that we'd built in the early 2000s down next to the Wānaka cabin and converted it into a studio, so that we could shoot season three of *The Free Range Cook: Through the seasons*. It was such a lovely space. Within a year, he and I decided to move down to live in Wānaka full-time. Both the kids had left home and were at university in Melbourne, so we didn't need to stay in the city.

We started here from nothing—a blank canvas and a dream. Every day I climb the hill to the vegetable garden that is located, somewhat inconveniently, a good 300 metres up the hill, and I find something to pick for our lunch. In the autumn, I squirrel the season's harvests into jars of preserves that will carry us through the winter. People often say, 'Oh, it's so much work. Why would you bother?' But I love the rhythm of my life here, the simplicity and honesty of it. In the words of Leonardo da Vinci, 'Simplicity is the ultimate sophistication.'

When I want to think about dinner, I wander up to the garden again and see what's ready to harvest. I can't believe the pleasure that growing my own food provides. Sure, it's hard work, but otherwise I'd be buying a gym membership. This way, I get fit and at the same time feed myself with fresh, nutrient-dense, spray-free food. It feels honest and real.

> When I want to think about dinner, I wander up to the garden again and see what's ready to harvest. I can't believe the pleasure that growing my own food provides.

I feel so lucky to have lived the life I have, and that it's brought me here to this amazing place, where I can be with Ted by the lake, so close to nature. Seeing the weather come in with a storm, the play of light on the hills and the lake, watching the seasons roll over, you feel part of the cycle of life. In the little eyrie bedroom of our studio, there are four skylights that look up to the heavens. Two face east and two incline to the west. Each provides a different framed view of the stars, and through the year the parade of constellations across the night sky travels through these frames, an ever-turning cycle east to west, as the Earth makes its annual revolutions around the sun. Over the years I have come to know the months, on a clear night, when the light of the full moon will fall on my pillow, first from the eastern skylight and later, as the night rolls on, through the northwestern window. Away from the lights of the city, the stars are so bright here, and the moonlight of a full moon can easily waken you.

It's also the greatest privilege to be part of a community like Wānaka, where people respect each other, go out of their way to help when help is needed, and are thoughtful and caring. At the end of the day, all we really have is our respect, love and care for one another. Ultimately our humanity is the deciding predictor of who we are and how we live our lives. We are so fortunate to be born in this country, and I feel so lucky that I don't have to struggle just to survive. My mother used to say, 'We have a duty to be happy and to make the most of whatever we have, as we are the lucky ones.'

I can't think of a better place to express care and kindness than at home, around the kitchen table. Here at the table with family and friends, both old and new, we are nourished—by the gifts of the Earth, the support of friends, the curiosity of ideas, and the conviviality of conversation. The cook is the bridge, in whose hands the bounty of nature is transformed creatively and resourcefully into the meal on the plate. It is the cook who brings us together to the table, to this place where we can freely share ideas and be ourselves.

One, and together, we will always belong and find our place at the table.

ROASTED VEGIE BUDDHA BOWL WITH MISO MAPLE DRESSING

READY IN 1 HOUR · SERVES 2 · DF · GF, IF TAMARI IS USED
V · VE, IF MAPLE SYRUP IS USED

1 kūmara (sweet potato), peeled and diced
1 large beetroot, peeled and diced
1 small red onion, cut into thin wedges
8–10 button mushrooms, halved
400 g (14 oz) can chickpeas (garbanzo beans)
2 tbsp neutral oil
salt and ground black pepper, to taste
a little sugar
1 head broccoli
2 handfuls spinach
flesh of ½ an avocado
2 tbsp tamari sunflower seeds or chopped tamari almonds, to garnish

RICE
1 cup white rice
1½ cups water
pinch salt

MISO MAPLE DRESSING
1 tbsp white miso
1 tbsp maple syrup or honey
1 tbsp soy sauce or tamari
1 tbsp rice vinegar
1 tsp sesame oil

You can put these Buddha bowls together with any combination of vegetables you fancy. The super-simple Miso Maple Dressing adds the ooh-ahh factor to the dish.

Preheat oven to 180°C (350°F) fanbake. Line a roasting dish with baking paper for easy clean-up.

Arrange kūmara, beetroot, onion and mushrooms in a single layer at one end of tray. Rinse and drain chickpeas and spread out at other end of baking tray. Drizzle with oil, season with salt and pepper, and sprinkle sugar over kūmara, beetroot and onion. Roast until vegies are tender and starting to caramelise and chickpeas are getting crunchy (about 40 minutes).

While vegies roast, cook rice. Place rice in a pot with water and salt. Bring to a simmer, stir, cover tightly, and cook for 12 minutes. Remove from heat and allow to stand another 10–15 minutes without uncovering.

Boil a jug of water. Cut broccoli into small florets and coarsely chop spinach. Place in a heatproof bowl, add a little salt and cover with boiling water. Allow to stand for 2 minutes, then drain well.

To make Miso Maple Dressing, place all ingredients in a small jar and shake to combine.

To serve, fluff rice with a fork and divide between two bowls. Top with roasted vegies, chickpeas and green vegies. Cut avocado into wedges and dip in chopped seeds or nuts to coat cut surfaces. Divide avocado between bowls and drizzle with dressing. Garnish the salad with remaining tamari sunflower seeds or tamari almonds.

POTATO FOCACCIA WITH ROASTED GARLIC, OLIVES AND TRUSS TOMATOES

READY IN 1 HOUR + RISING · MAKES 2 LARGE LOAVES · DF IF MASHED
POTATO IS DAIRY-FREE · V · VE IF MASHED POTATO IS DAIRY-FREE

1½ cups warm (not hot) water

1½ tsp dry yeast granules

1 packed cup cooked mashed potato

¼ cup extra virgin olive oil

about 4½ cups high-grade (bread) flour, plus extra for shaping

2 tsp salt

½ cup pitted Kalamata olives

1 head Roasted Garlic, cloves peeled (see overleaf)

400 g (14 oz) truss tomatoes

2 tbsp extra virgin olive oil

2 tsp fresh rosemary leaves

a little flaky salt

Adding some cooked mashed potato to this dough makes the yeast rise faster and ensures that the finished bread will be nice and moist. I find this dough is even better when made a day in advance and allowed to rise overnight in the fridge. You can also store the dough in the fridge for up to 48 hours or freeze it to cook a fresh loaf another day.

Place warm water in large mixing bowl, bread machine or electric mixer with a dough blade, and sprinkle yeast on top. Allow to stand for 2 minutes.

Mix in potato and oil, then add flour and salt, and mix until the dough just starts to come away from the sides of the bowl (it will be very sticky).

Knead dough about 30 times with lightly oiled hands, or knead for 3–4 minutes in a mixer or breadmaker. It should be soft, and so sticky that it coats your hands. If kneading by hand, pick up the dough and throw it onto the bench a few times to get the gluten working. Press kneaded dough out flat, scatter with olives and roasted garlic, roll up dough into a log and knead to combine evenly.

Transfer dough to a lightly oiled bowl, cover with a tea towel and leave in a warm place until doubled in size (3–4 hours). Alternatively, allow to rise overnight in the fridge.

When ready to cook, preheat oven to 220°C (425°F) fanbake and place 2 pizza stones or flat oven trays on the centre shelf. Line 2 oven trays with baking paper.

RECIPE CONTINUED OVERLEAF

Turn risen dough out onto a lightly floured board and divide in half. Shape into 2 balls, place one on each lined tray and flatten to about the size of an oval dinner plate.

Divide tomatoes between loaves, pressing them into the dough. Use your fingertips to create dimples between tomatoes. Drizzle with oil and sprinkle with rosemary and flaky salt.

Slide each loaf of bread (still on its baking paper) off its tray and onto a hot pizza stone or flat oven tray. Bake until the loaves are golden and sound hollow when tapped (about 20 minutes). Transfer to a rack to cool.

ROASTED GARLIC

READY IN 1 HOUR · MAKES 1 SMALL JAR · GF · DF · V · VE

3 heads garlic
extra virgin olive oil

I like to make extra roasted garlic and store it in its cooking oil in the fridge for later use. It keeps for weeks, and the garlic and its cooking oil can be used in dressings, sauces and risotto.

Preheat oven to 150°C (300°F) fanbake.

Separate garlic into individual cloves, trim the base of each clove where it attaches to the root and place them in a small, shallow roasting dish. Cover with olive oil and roast until soft (40–45 minutes). Allow to cool before fishing out garlic and removing skins. If not using at once, transfer garlic and oil to a jar and chill until needed. It will keep for several weeks in the fridge.

TOFFEE APPLE TART

READY IN 1 HOUR · SERVES 6 · V

200 g (7 oz) flaky
  puff pastry
50 g (1¾ oz) butter,
  melted
¼ cup vanilla sugar or
  plain sugar
3 apples, peeled,
  quartered, cored
  and very thinly sliced
  lengthwise
3 tbsp apricot jam,
  thinned with a little
  water
No-Churn Vanilla Ice
  Cream (see overleaf), or
  store-bought vanilla ice
  cream, to serve

This is such a simple idea that transforms a sheet of pastry and some apples into something quite magical.

Preheat oven to 170°C (325°F) fanbake. Line an oven tray with baking paper for easy clean-up.

Roll out pastry on a lightly floured bench to create a 30 cm x 24 cm (12 in x 9½ in) rectangle. Place on prepared tray. Brush with half the melted butter and sprinkle with half the sugar. Lift pastry, shaking excess sugar back onto tray, and flip to place the buttered and sugared side down.

Arrange apple slices in an overlapping pattern on pastry. Brush all over with remaining butter and sprinkle with remaining sugar. Bake until golden and crisp (about 50–55 minutes).

While tart is baking, warm apricot jam with a splash of water then strain through a sieve. Remove cooked tart from oven and brush with apricot glaze while it is still hot. Serve with generous scoops of vanilla ice cream.

NO-CHURN VANILLA ICE CREAM

READY IN 15 MINUTES + FREEZING · MAKES ABOUT 2½ LITRES · GF · V

2 egg whites

¼ cup caster (superfine) sugar

2½ cups cream, chilled

380 g (13½ oz) can condensed milk

2 tsp vanilla extract or vanilla paste

Home-made ice cream doesn't come much simpler than this. It's so smooth and easy to scoop. Once you've mastered the base recipe, have fun playing around with flavourings—see below for some ideas.

Using an electric beater with a clean whisk, beat egg whites and sugar until they form a thick meringue and sugar is dissolved (about 5 minutes). Transfer meringue to another bowl and set aside.

Add cream, condensed milk and vanilla to the mixing bowl used for the egg whites (you don't need to clean it) and beat until mixture is very thick and soft peaks form when the beater is lifted from the bowl.

Gently fold the reserved meringue into the cream mixture until evenly combined.

Transfer to a freezer-proof container and freeze until set (at least 6 hours). No-Churn Vanilla Ice Cream will keep in the freezer for several weeks if tightly covered. Remove from the freezer 10 minutes before serving to allow it to soften slightly.

MACADAMIA ORANGE ICE CREAM

Add ¾ cup coarsely chopped roasted macadamias, the finely grated zest of 1 orange and ½ cup marmalade.

SALTED CARAMEL AND WALNUT ICE CREAM

Use a 380 g (13½ oz) can of caramel condensed milk instead of ordinary condensed milk, and add ¾ cup chopped toasted walnuts and a good pinch of flaky salt.

RECIPE INDEX

ACKNOWLEDGEMENTS

THERE ARE MANY PEOPLE I would like to thank whose encouragement, support, hard work and care have helped me along the journey. My parents aren't around anymore but I still want to acknowledge them for their unequivocal love and support, and for letting me be me. My sister, Prue, who has always been so kind and loving. Ted, who from day one believed in me and has supported and helped me to realise my vision and dreams. Our amazing kids, Sean and Rose, who nourish me as a person as well as loving me as their mother.

In my business: Des Flynn, thanks for supporting my ideas right from the early days; Doris Mousdale, thanks for being my 'go girl' mascot and giving me the confidence to take my projects out into the world; John Wallace, thank you for your ongoing publishing support and helpful business advice; and Bernard Macleod, thanks for being a fabulous advocate and helping me to navigate the world of international television.

Over the years in my office, there have been some very talented and hard-working people in my team who have gone above and beyond; without their energies, talents, support and skills we would not have been able to achieve the wonderful things we did. Thank you especially to Natalie Keys, Harriet Booth, Melissa Bulkeley, Christine Arden, Jane Binsley, Angela Gough and Kate Battersby.

I feel incredibly lucky to have wonderful friends who enrich and support my life in so many ways. You know who you are: thank you for always being there, for lashings of kindness and lots of fun.

To the team at Allen & Unwin, a huge thank you—I've had the dream team to work with. Publisher Michelle Hurley, thanks for encouraging me to embark on this project and for your unflagging support along the way. Thanks also to publishing director Jenny Hellen, project editor Leanne McGregor and publicity manager Abba Renshaw.

Kate Barraclough, thank you for the inspired design—easy to navigate and a pleasure to browse; Kimberley Davis, thanks for your thoughtful edits on the copy; and Jane Binsley, thanks as always for your keen eye for detail on the recipes. Thanks also to proofreaders Claire Davis and Kate Stone, and to Tessa King for the index.

William and Hannah Meppem, thank you for the gorgeous food photos; and Aliscia Young, thanks for the cover photo and the lovely portraits inside.

Finally, thank you to all the wonderful New Zealanders who share my love of food and cooking and are such fabulous fans. I feel very lucky to be part of your community and live in this amazing country.

IMAGE CREDITS

Aliscia Young: front cover & pp. 153, 239, 285, 337, 343 & 347; **William Meppem**: pp. 35, 37, 41, 63, 65, 69, 95, 99, 101, 121, 125, 127, 145, 149, 151, 173, 177, 179, 205, 209, 211, 235, 237, 241, 257, 259, 261, 283, 287, 289, 311, 315, 317, 339, 341 & 345; **Emily Hlaváč Green**: pp. 103, 175, 249 (all) & 290; **Kate Battersby**: pp. 320 & 333; **Ted Hewetson**: pp. 319 & 322; **11th Hour Racing/Alexander Masters**: p. 329 (top left); **Gwyne Bright**: p. 10; **Alix Carere**: pp. 6–7; **Eleni Hogg**: p. 329 (bottom left); **Kerry Lim**: p. 329 (centre right); **Aaron McLean**: p. 264; **Nick Tresidder**: p. 279; **Courtesy Michele Hine**: pp. 49 (top), 72 & 77 (all); **Courtesy Richard Thompson**: p. 49 (centre & bottom right); map on p. 4 by **Megan van Staden**. All other images are from Annabel's private collection.

First published in 2020

Text © Annabel Langbein, 2020
Images as credited on page 351

Allen & Unwin
Level 2, 10 College Hill, Freemans Bay
Auckland 1011, New Zealand
Phone: (64 9) 377 3800
Email: auckland@allenandunwin.com
Web: www.allenandunwin.co.nz

83 Alexander Street
Crows Nest NSW 2065, Australia
Phone: (61 2) 8425 0100

A catalogue record for this book is available from the National Library of New Zealand.

ISBN 978 1 98854 761 9

Design by Kate Barraclough
Set in Adobe Jenson Pro and Brandon Text
Printed in China by C & C Offset Printing Co., Ltd.

3 5 7 9 10 8 6 4 2

MIX
Paper from
responsible sources
FSC
www.fsc.org
FSC® C008047